Family, Faith and Love
Beyond Immigration

PARKE | PRESS

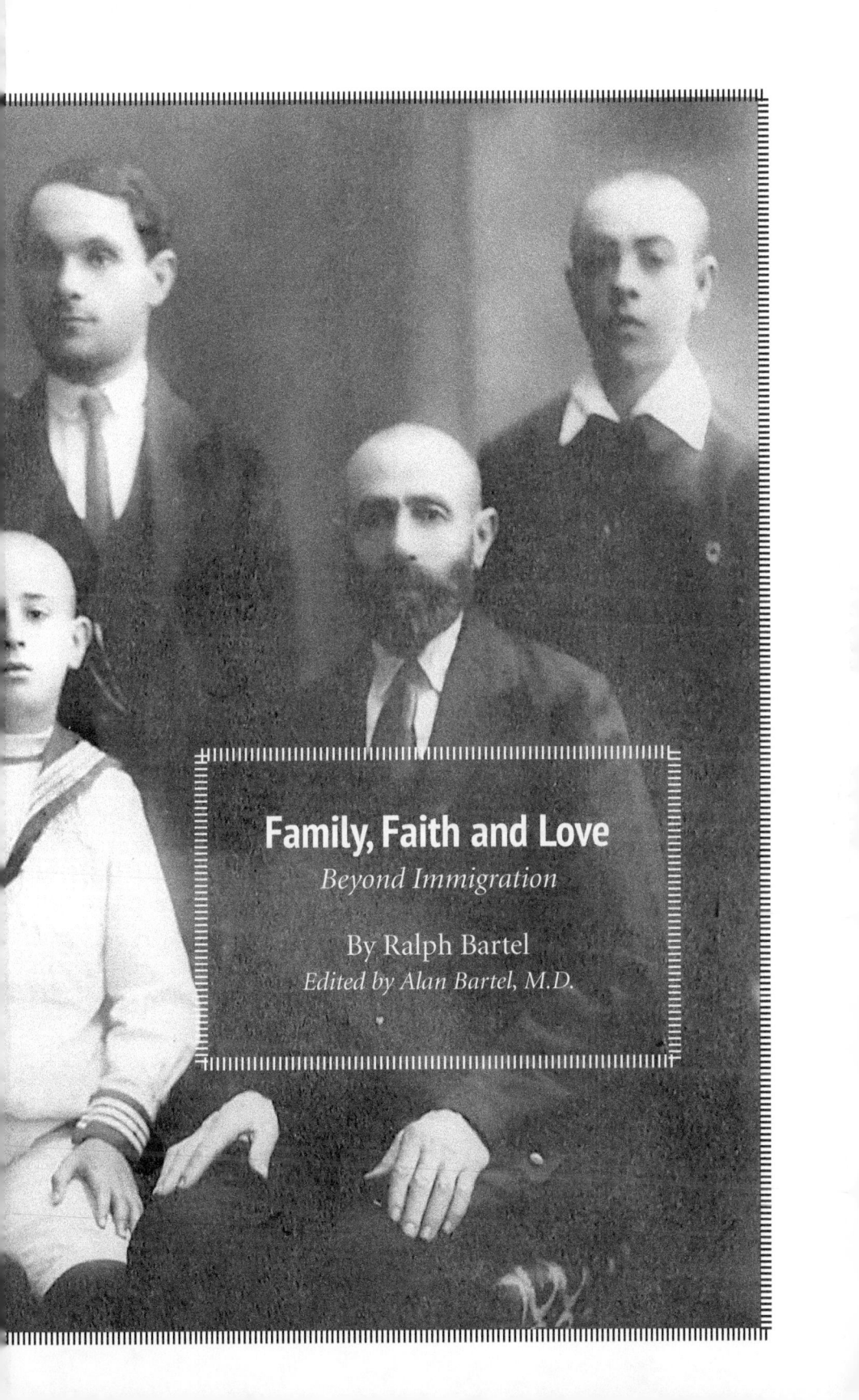

Family, Faith and Love

Beyond Immigration

By Ralph Bartel

Edited by Alan Bartel, M.D.

Published by
PARKE PRESS
Norfolk, Virginia

Parke Press, 129 Conway Avenue, Norfolk, Virginia 23505 • *parke.press@cox.net*

ISBN 978-1-7323105-1-3 Hardback; ISBN 978-1-7323105-2-0 Softback

Library of Congress Control Number is available upon request.

Printed in the United States of America

Title page photograph: *The Bargteil family (L to R): Ralph, Bessie, Chaika, Mayer, Muni Alter, Gedalia, and Velvel Bargteil. Around 1920.*

CONTENTS

PREFACE

by Alan G. Bartel, M.D., son of Ralph and Mollie Bartel

After my father's retirement from teaching, in 1972, his four grown grandchildren (I had two boys, my brother had two boys) naïvely began asking questions, and Dad was encouraged by us all to record stories about his life. He always had an incredible memory for places, names and detailed information about past experiences. So, he began typing all kinds of stories. Each one was typed with two fingers on a regular typewriter, until we got him a laptop when he turned 90. Incredibly, most of the stories were two to 10 pages long. He and my mother even started a writer's club in their retirement community, and she, too, would write. In 1998, the writer's club actually published a book, with each member

Ralph Bartel, early 1950s.

contributing a chapter. The *Miami Herald* and *Sun Sentinel* both wrote articles about their group effort.

Eventually, I copied each of their works, filed them away and later scanned them into the computer. This went on for more than ten years. For Dad's 95th birthday, I presented him with copies of all his stories so he could recall what he had written. In all, my parents wrote more than a hundred stories. He continued to recall stories of many events of the past, and the stories with historical interest are recorded in this book. My mother died at age 92, my father five years later at 98; they were married for 69 years. Their writings have left our family with interesting and wonderful memories and a unique glimpse of the past – I have selected the best of those writings to compile this book.

These writings have been arranged as chronologically as possible in this book to best reflect Ralph and Mollie's remarkable journey – a story of family, faith and love, of persecution, immigration and integration, within the mainstream of American life.

My father and mother, both schoolteachers, raised me and my brother in a middle-class family in Miami, Florida. My mother primarily taught third grade; my father taught elementary and junior high school, then he was a guidance counselor and assistant principal in his later years. We were a small, loving, supportive and stable family. Summers were free for Mom and Dad. So when possible, they took my older brother and me on frequent road trips.

Money was always a major issue during my child hood, as my parents struggled to make ends meet with their

Ralph and Mollie Bartel, 1990s.

teacher salaries. Dad frequently worked odd jobs in the summer, particularly in photography and real estate. I had a typical childhood in many ways, riding my bike to school every day where I got a good public education.

My father taught Sunday school and was engaged in local synagogue activities and Jewish institutions. We were observant Jews and attended synagogue frequently until I got to high school. I was active in Jewish youth organizations, and my older brother graduated from Hebrew High School. Despite having a somewhat small extended family, we celebrated Jewish holidays and traditions together. Judaism was important to us all.

My mother and father had endured many struggles as immigrants to the United States. Mom was actually born in New York (in 1911), where her parents had migrated when they left Ukraine (formerly part of the Soviet Union). In fact, both her family and my father's family came from the Ukraine. My father had emigrated from there as a child, which you will read about. Neither my grandparents nor Mom and Dad would ever talk about their past in front of us; questions about pogroms, "the old country" and even the Holocaust were not discussed.

After retirement while living in a South Florida retirement community, Dad began putting to new uses his incredible memory for details and his talent for writing. In part to keep himself busy, to memorialize family history and heritage of which only he and Mom knew, and as a loving legacy for his children, his grandchildren and the great-grandchildren he was blessed to see, he wrote stories periodically and circulated them to his children and grandchildren who were all adults by then. During major Jewish holidays, he actually wrote and conducted religious services for the residents, all in their 80's and 90's. He condensed all of his services, and provided each participant with a service booklet written in large print, including explanations for mixed marriage couples or non-Jewish attendees. There was no traditional standing during the service, and my father began with a disclaimer stating that he was not a Rabbi. He also taught a Yiddish class in the retirement community. (Unfortunately, other than a few words and the common phrases in so many Jewish homes, I never learned Yiddish. I remember my grandparents speaking Yiddish to each other. My parents only used Yiddish when they did not want my brother and me to understand their conversations.) In addition to leading the holiday services, both my parents began writing stories in their eighties and nineties – about Judaism, about our family and finally about their struggles including their immigrant journey.

During their long life together, my parents traveled extensively to over 50 countries on five continents, and they sometimes did so with their dear friends. This fact is made all the more remarkable because they started doing so while on teacher salaries and then later on during their early retirement while they were fully mobile. But during all their travel years, my father "never wanted to see Russia again." Instead, he did so through my oldest son's eyes: his oldest grandson managed to find and visit the tiny village that was Dad's birthplace in the Ukraine, a story you can read about in this book (page 192).

NOTE: One item that will be helpful for any reader is a list of the most-often-referred-to names and who they are. My parents lived into their 90s, had so many relatives, friends and interactions, that it is good to list out some of the "characters" on the next page.

BARGTEIL (BARTEL) Family Tree

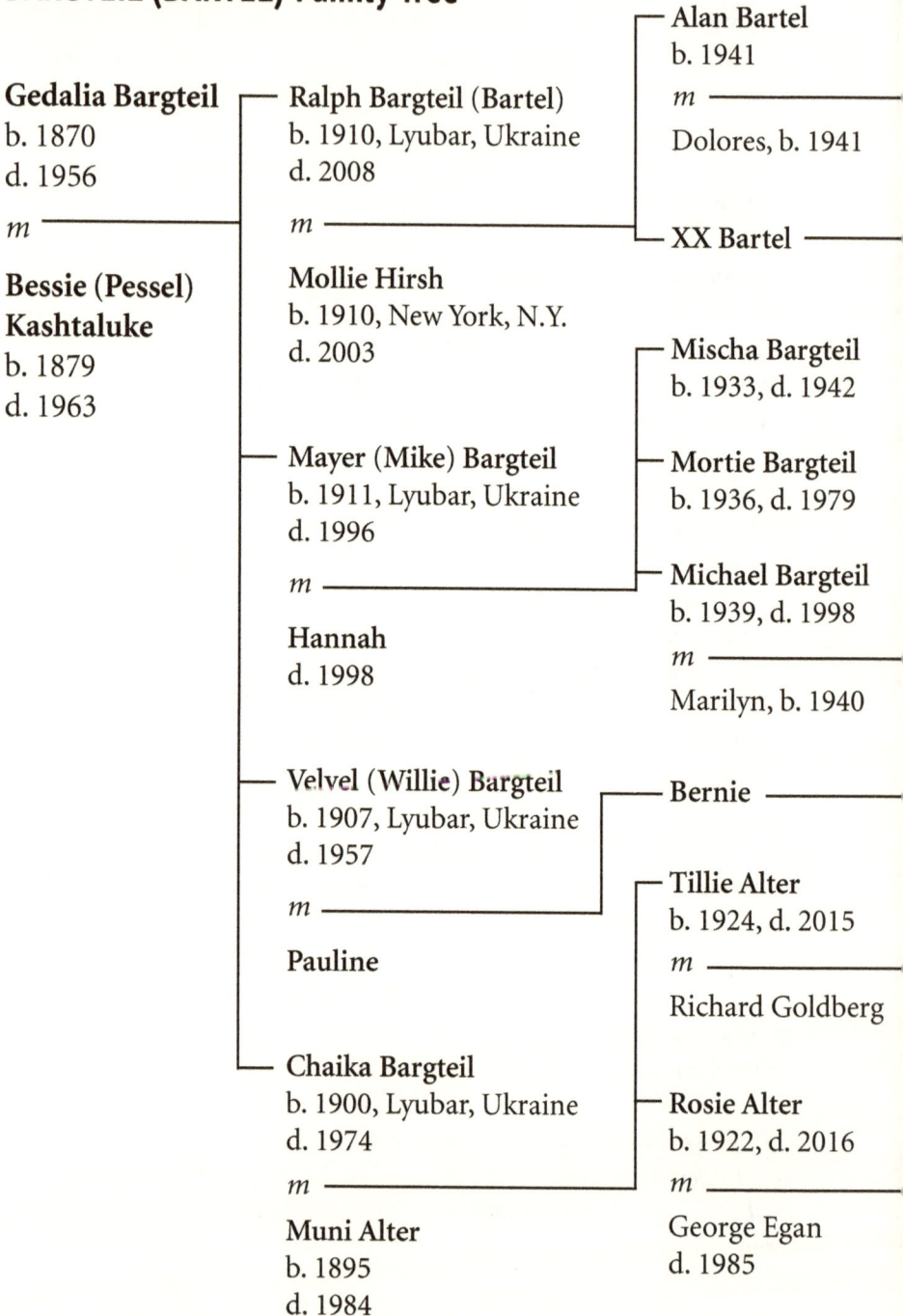

Gedalia Bargteil
b. 1870
d. 1956

m

Bessie (Pessel) Kashtaluke
b. 1879
d. 1963

Ralph Bargteil (Bartel)
b. 1910, Lyubar, Ukraine
d. 2008

m

Mollie Hirsh
b. 1910, New York, N.Y.
d. 2003

Mayer (Mike) Bargteil
b. 1911, Lyubar, Ukraine
d. 1996

m

Hannah
d. 1998

Velvel (Willie) Bargteil
b. 1907, Lyubar, Ukraine
d. 1957

m

Pauline

Chaika Bargteil
b. 1900, Lyubar, Ukraine
d. 1974

m

Muni Alter
b. 1895
d. 1984

Alan Bartel
b. 1941

m

Dolores, b. 1941

XX Bartel

Mischa Bargteil
b. 1933, d. 1942

Mortie Bargteil
b. 1936, d. 1979

Michael Bargteil
b. 1939, d. 1998

m

Marilyn, b. 1940

Bernie

Tillie Alter
b. 1924, d. 2015

m

Richard Goldberg

Rosie Alter
b. 1922, d. 2016

m

George Egan
d. 1985

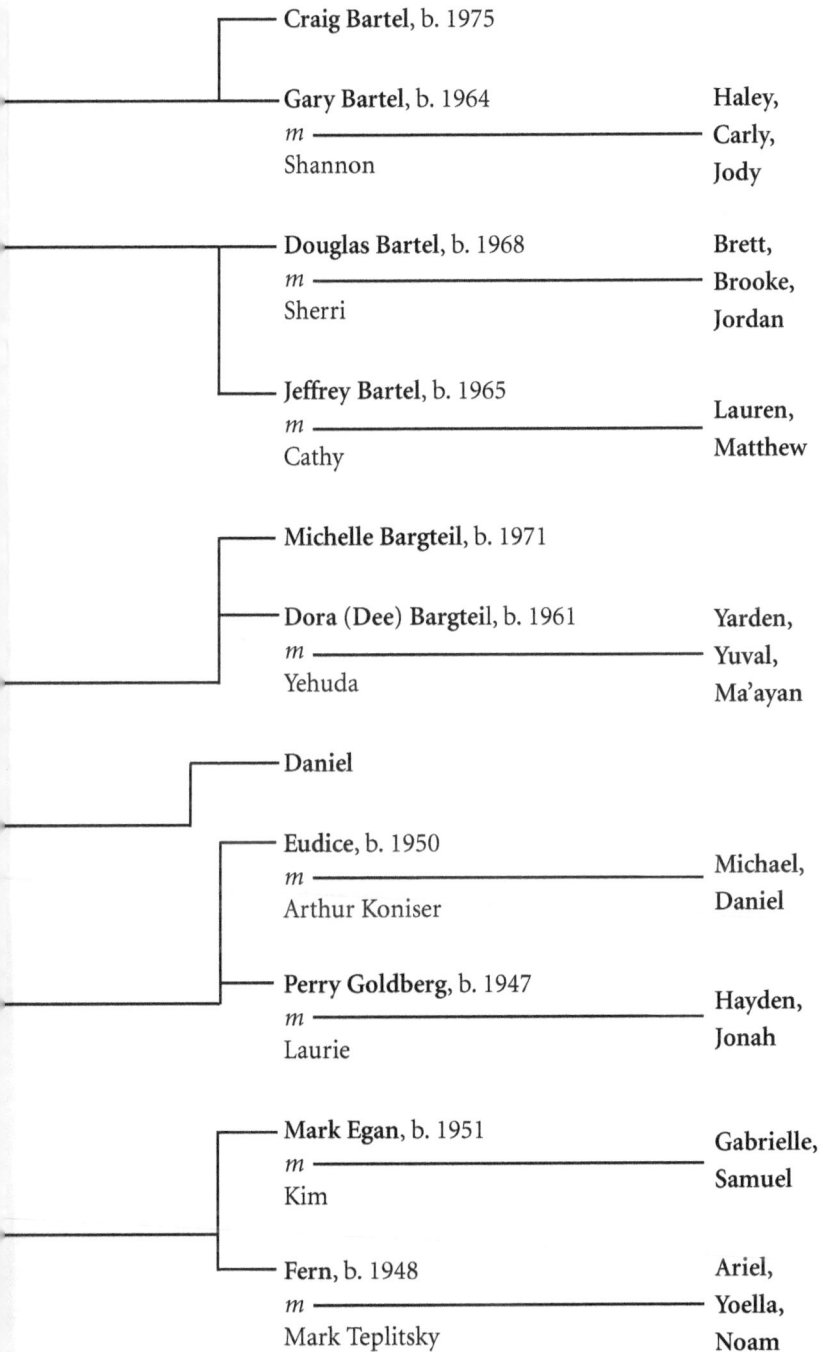

Craig Bartel, b. 1975

Gary Bartel, b. 1964
m ——————————
Shannon

Haley,
Carly,
Jody

Douglas Bartel, b. 1968
m ——————————
Sherri

Brett,
Brooke,
Jordan

Jeffrey Bartel, b. 1965
m ——————————
Cathy

Lauren,
Matthew

Michelle Bargteil, b. 1971

Dora (Dee) Bargteil, b. 1961
m ——————————
Yehuda

Yarden,
Yuval,
Ma'ayan

Daniel

Eudice, b. 1950
m ——————————
Arthur Koniser

Michael,
Daniel

Perry Goldberg, b. 1947
m ——————————
Laurie

Hayden,
Jonah

Mark Egan, b. 1951
m ——————————
Kim

Gabrielle,
Samuel

Fern, b. 1948
m ——————————
Mark Teplitsky

Ariel,
Yoella,
Noam

Short Stories
by Ralph Bartel

||||||||||||||||||||||||||||||||||||||||||||||||||||||||||||||||||||||||||||||||||||||||||||||||||||||||||||||||||||

EARLIEST MEMORIES – OUR HOME (in Lyubar)

Note: For purposes of accuracy, all spelling of words and sounds in this narrative will be as they were used then. Both the Yiddish and Hebrew pronunciations are different from the ones we use today, only because we have adapted to the common usage. I will write as if I were speaking them since many, many years have passed since we left our birthplace. I hope my memories are as good as I believe them to be. The pictures in my mind are very clear, in most matters.

As I sit here, facing the screen of my computer, I can't help but wonder how much all of us take for granted. My earliest recollections of the town in which I grew up, Lyubar, paint such a dismal picture of primitive life that I marvel we survived at all. Our own family circumstances, early on considered the upper middle class, were the exception. Yet, measured by current concept of bare necessities, our conveniences and "luxuries" were remarkably few.

Our house, which was one of the biggest in town, had many abundances that few of our neighbors shared. As one entered our home, a very large main living/dining room extended at least 25 or more feet. It was well furnished, with a comfortable sofa, several restful sitting chairs – used for special guests or occasions – a very large dining table with many chairs. Three spacious bureaus held linens, silver and fine china dishes, used for holidays and special occasions. Large windows on both sides, covered with white lace curtains, provided light and air. Two samovars (a heated metal one used to heat and boil water), a very large shiny "silver" one – for special use – and a regular sized (which we brought with us and is in Canada) for everyday use. This one always had water heated, to make tea available, without notice.

Straight ahead, a hall led to several bedrooms, followed by a large built-in oven on the left side, which heated the entire house. On the right side was the wall of the huge baking oven, where bread and challah was baked, twice weekly. (On rare occasions, we got baked goods from the village bakery.) The baking oven stretched at least ten feet, and could easily bake six or more breads or *challahs* at a time. Halfway down the hall, the upper portion of the wall opened up to the "Pripitchik," a larger cozy, warm place above the oven. It was large enough for a grown person to stand up and to rest, play, study, read or just stay cozy warm. Blankets and winter clothes were stored here, too.

Directly facing the huge iron doors of the baking oven was the kitchen, where we ate all of our meals during the week (On Friday nights and Saturdays we ate in the living/dining room). In addition to the table and chairs, the kitchen had a fireplace, which provided heat and a place for the water to boil. In a far corner was a pot-bellied iron stove used for cooking (and heat, too). A pantry and closets had plenty of storage space for two sets of dishes, as we kept kosher. One set for *milchik* (dairy) and the other for *fleyshik* (meat). Thus, the back of the house had lots of room and plenty of heat for our comfort. Our parents' bedroom on the left, opposite the kitchen, was convenient to the rear door, the outhouse and the stable – facilities that few of our neighbors had.

The stable housed all the animals. The most important occupant was the milk cow, which provided all the milk for our daily needs and enough for cream, cheese, and butter, which we made at home. The cow's stall was separated from the rest of the barn. She was milked early every morning and late in the afternoon, when we brought her back into the barn, from the fields. In the long winter, she roamed the backyard, nearby woods, or was kept tied up in her stall, fed with hay. A large number of chickens ran loose in the fenced-in yard. If any escaped, they were shooed back into the barn at night. Shortly before any Holidays, a few ducks or geese would be added to our flock. These were fed and fattened well, so that – when they were slaughtered by the *Shochet* (a highly trained expert on ways to slay a fowl or animal, according to Judaic Law) – there would be enough fat to render and make Schmaltz (fat), a very important ingredient in the cooking process. A ladder in the barn led to the loft, where the hay was stored for the cow's main feed. The dirt floor was kept carefully cleared of the fowls' droppings, while the cow's manure was always saved and used as fertilizer for the spring vegetable garden.

The spring vegetable garden was a big adventure. One or more peasants, who were customers in our store, in town, or who depended on us for their extra income – so they'd buy their vodka and other needs – cultivated and planted the different vegetables. After they did the hard work, we children were sometimes allowed to pick the radishes or carrots, which came up first. They returned to finish the heavy work of picking the final crops. The harvested vegetables were preserved in glass jars and stored in the cool, dark cellar, which had an entrance, outside – below the kitchen – for winter use.

A well provided water for the animals and garden but it was not fit for human consumption. Water for the house came from two common town wells. Some came from the run-off of rainwater, from the wooden roof, collected in large barrels, located alongside the house. In the winter, snow and ice became other sources of water.

Everyone washed in cold water, upon rising and before eating. (A special prayer, for the washing of hands or face, had to follow). On Friday afternoons, or before Holidays, the water was heated and poured into the large galvanized tin tubs, to be used for bathing or in the kitchen. On special occasions and before important Holidays, we went to the public steam baths, famous for their fragrant scents that lent a pleasant odor, as we sat in the steamy rooms – not unlike modern saunas. Once in a while, when water was being heated for laundry washing, some was left over to use for hands and face. Of course, if we were invited somewhere, to a *Simcha* (celebration), water was warmed for our use.

Each bedroom in our house had a basin under the bed to use during the night or on cold days. My sister, Chaika, and older brother, Velvel (later named Willy), had their own bedrooms. I shared mine with my younger brother Mayer. The boys' bedrooms also had tin pails. In the morning before washing, we threw out the pails' contents in the back or side of the house, and sprayed them. However, since we had our own outhouse in the backyard, we made use of it. During bad weather and clear days, newspapers were torn up and the smaller pieces and placed on a shelf, inside, for our convenience. (In my memories, I can still smell the odors.) A couple of times a year, one of the peasants would clean the accumulations out and we'd have a nice, comfortable place.

Our house always had a peasant do our heavy or "dirty" work. During the very long very cold days of winter, a male took care of our ovens and stove, cleaned the yard and barn, and whatever other chores were necessary. In the other seasons one was always ready to work for us. Every Saturday morning one would come in to put out the lights in the lanterns, left burning from the night before. While not a fanatic in the observance of rituals, Papa always followed them in his daily life. We were taught to conform to all "laws" of Judaic teaching. (Even into my teens, I did not turn a light on or off, or ride on a Saturday or Holiday until I got a job that required work on Saturday. I was 20 years old before I knowingly tasted a non-kosher food – a hot dog – while at work! on a Saturday. This is how we were raised.)

My emphasis on our use of the peasants is deliberate. The relationship my parents established with them was so strong that the peasants deliberately risked their own lives when they sheltered and hid us, during the *Pogroms* (persecution) that followed the Revolution. As they say in the movies, "But, that's another story." Suffice it to say, they were a very important part of our daily lives, in our home and our community. Our home was always a busy place, put to many uses. Except for the one time, when my maternal grandmother died – in our house – and *Shiva* (seven days of mourning) was observed here, many happy events took place, in a busy atmosphere.

My sister Chaika, when home from the University of Odessa, was

Ralph Bargteil sits on a bicycle, in a portrait of his extended family, around 1913.

a very popular girl. Many young men and women congregated at our house for meetings and discussions about politics and philosophy, with me as an always interested but silent observer. Mandolins and balalaikas accompanied the group, with singing usually an integral part of the gathering. Chaika's clear soprano voice led the group in singing the many sensuous peasant and ballad songs. Here, I first heard and sang the French Revolutionary song, The *Marseillaise*, which became the French National Anthem. On occasion, Chaika invited me to sing a duet with her as we led the others, accompanied by the musical instruments.

The large table and many chairs provided ample room for the visitors and family. The samovar, placed in the middle of the table, was used extensively, to serve *tgtheelke* (cookies). I was about six or seven when we were introduced to electricity in our house. The new source of light came from one double strand of wire, suspended from a rafter in the high ceiling leading to a fixture that looked like a large white soup dish upside down, with a single bulb under it, directly over the table. The biggest wonder was the little switch that lit and shut off the light. It was located near the door, miraculously so far away. Compared to coal-oil lamps we had in the rest of the house, the light over the table was the brightest and most cheerful place to be. It was used constantly. It was here that I first learned about the *Chaluzim* (Pioneers) who were emigrating to Palestine, and the hardships they were enduring as they tried to farm the arid land. Stories of the bravery of these young men and women, in the *Kibbutsim* (communal housing and living), were very inspiring to a curious little boy, a very attentive listener.

Our parents loved card games, which were played quite often at one end of the big table, and taken most seriously. Although playing cards for money was forbidden, games were contested as if the entire fortune was at stake. (Mama, years later, said she deliberately "lost," because Papa hated to lose.) A dedicated watcher and listener, I soon learned every game they played, and participated in their love of cards every time they invited me.

Fall brought the greatest use of our big living room. The peasants harvested crops. Since most of them were, in effect, serfs, beholden to the large landowner (known as the *Pooritz*), their only income came from any crops they were allowed to raise for themselves, after they'd satisfied the owners' obligation. Papa allowed many of them to buy what they needed during the year, on condition they'd repay their debts with the vegetables or grains they harvested. Many of them were illiterate and relied entirely on the honesty of the merchants with whom they traded. Because our parents' reputation for fairness was well known and respected, many of them relied entirely on Papa's and Mama's words and advice, even on personal family matters. Letters sent and received by them went through our parents. Their loyalty and trust never varied and we could always depend on them, whatever our needs. Came the fall, and they repaid their debts with the fruits of their labors.

On a typical pre-arranged day, a wagon filled with cabbages would be delivered and brought into the house, where they'd be stacked in a covered area. All the movable furniture had been taken away and a huge "working table" – consisting of carefully picked and scrubbed large planks, laid on several "horses" – waited for the work to begin. A number of friends and neighbors had been invited to participate in the subsequent making of huge barrels of sauerkraut. Using large knives – especially sharpened by the village knife sharpener – Papa would cut each big head in half and pass the cut parts to the other workers. Each one was equipped with a smaller sharp knife and proceeded to cut the halves into three pieces. One person rolled the barrel close to the workers and the pickles were scraped into the brine, already prepared. When the barrels were nearly full, they were carefully rolled onto a homemade dolly and wheeled outside, to the cool confines of the cellar. All the workers shared the sauerkraut during the coming winter.

A similar procedure was followed for pickling green tomatoes and cucumbers. Venturing into the cellar in the fall meant smelling the fragrant odors of the different brines, as the culturing and curing times took place. It was impossible to resist sneaking a little pickle or tomato, or a taste of the sauerkraut or *borscht* (a soup made from beets), long before any of them were fully done. Grown-ups as well as little boys had a happy time. All winter long our own pickled foods were available and served to guests. A visit to a neighbor meant carrying one or more jars filled with our own truly "homemade" foods. In many poorer neighbors' homes, ours was the only source of these delectable but necessary edibles. Thankfully we always had plenty to share. Equally important, our parents felt a personal responsibility that none of our neighbors or friends should ever go hungry. Thus, it was usual to see another family sharing a meal with us, even on an ordinary weekday. Impressions of such acts built a child's character, without

The Bargteil family (L to R): Ralph, Bessie, Chaika, Mayer, Muni Alter, Gedalia, and Velvel Bargteil. Around 1919.

specific Biblical lessons. Two other additional days remain etched in my memory. Mama's mother lived in a small house, on the northern edge of town, near the river. When she became too ill to care for herself, she came to live with us. In less than two years, she passed away. It was a very tragic time for me, a little boy who had become very attached to her and who had spent many hours by her side, helping take care of her.

Mama had one brother and a younger sister, both of whom came to Lyubar for the funeral and mourning period that followed. Before the week ended, discussions started about dividing the few possessions left by her death. Mama told them that they could divide everything between them. It was then that I had one of the most miserable lessons in human behavior. I shall never forget the loud and mean arguments that went on, as they fought over who was entitled to which tablecloths, with or without napkins, sheets, blankets, pillows, dishes, and the other pitifully few items. For a little boy, terribly confused and heartbroken at the loss of the only Bubba he'd ever known and loved, to hear such bickering was an unbelievable but very meaningful experience. Without fully realizing what I was doing I tearfully questioned Mama whether this is how all families acted when a person died. Although reassured that this behavior was not typical, I made up my mind that I'd never do that when – God forbid – Mama or Papa passed away. To this day, I've tried to make sure that our heirs – hopefully – will not act that way when we're gone.

The other memorable event took place shortly after the Pogroms. Chaika and Muni (the man my sister met) announced their engagement. Because of the unsettled times, it was decided to have a *Farknast* (Engagement) ceremony in our house. On the forthcoming Saturday night, invitations were spread by word of mouth to Muni's family and the few friends who'd survived and remained. The most outstanding memories of that night were the crowding and noise. One young man stood up on a bench and made the formal announcements of their engagement, imminent marriage and departure. As was customary, Chaika was introduced as the daughter of our parents' names. Muni got the same treatment. The applause was dampened by the fears, which prevailed. A number of our neighbors were missing because they'd escaped or had been killed or hurt during the terrible times we'd endured. Muni had lost a younger sister, who was killed during a previous confrontation with the invaders. The emcee began to call out the names of family and friends. As a name was called that person called out what gift he was prepared to give the engaged couple. One said he was giving a set of sheets; another, two goose-feather pillows; a third, a down *perena* (comforter). Each gift was listed in a loud voice, the emcee repeated it; apparent bedlam followed, as everyone had a reaction or comment about each offering. This went on throughout the confusing and noisy evening.

April 1, 2007

A CHILD'S MEMORIES

A recent inquiry by (cousin) Mark Egan about Lemberg (now Lvov), in Galicia, Poland, and its relationship with my birthplace Lyubar (in Ukraine), brought back memories of places and distances as best I remembered them. I pointed out to Mark that, since I was a little boy when we left for America, whatever I remembered could be tainted by a little boy's perception of reality. The following story illustrates this fact.

Those of you who've read my descriptions of life in Lyubar remember that our family had a store in the middle of the town, which sold all kinds of dry food items – several kinds of beans, flour, sugar, salt, dried fruits, nuts, etc. Papa (my father, Gedalia) ran the store until items needed to be replenished. Then, he would leave for several days at a time, while Mama (my mother, Pessel, later known as Bessie), took over.

To me, his trip was a great adventure, because he was going away to a mysterious, faraway place in the unknown world of a little boy. The two places he usually traveled to were called Berdichev and Zhitomir, also in the Ukraine.

Kiev, where Papa's mother had lived and died, and where his two brothers lived, was so far away that we only heard about it when one of my uncles came for a rare visit. Odessa, where Mama's father had come from, and where my sister Chaika was studying at its university, was even further away. As for Lemberg or Poland, the only time Papa went there was during the terrible Great War, after Polish or German soldiers had passed through our town. He was away for more than two weeks that time, and Mama was terribly worried when we hadn't heard from him for so long. When he returned, I was fascinated to see Papa's beard all covered with icicles, from the bitter cold Russian winter.

Another mysterious fact that I could never understand was that distances were always expressed in *viersts*, a measurement of distance that I could not compare – and still can't – to anything (it actually equals 1.07 km.). As a result, when Papa or anyone else talked about so many viersts from Lyubar, I was always confused and too embarrassed to ask. All I remember is that both Berdichev and Zhitomir were about 20 *viersts* away from Lyubar. I can't recall ever seeing an actual map as a child.

In the ensuing years, after arriving in the United States, I was too busy learning English, and adjusting to the difficulties of Americanizing myself, to worry or even think of viersts or anything else having to do with growing up in or about Lyubar. So much so, that I'd completely forgotten about those days or those problems. Then – to my utmost surprise – my oldest grandson Gary actually studied Russian on his way to graduating from James Madison University. After that, he'd continued to take Russian seriously, while getting his master's degree from George Washington University.

Gary then went on to Law School at the University of Richmond. He found that the practice of law didn't fulfill his ambitions in life so he decided on a career in business. Mollie and I wished him luck and were happy to hear of his successes. Then he announced he was going into the import/export business and traveling to Russia to set up his first contacts. He began to ask questions about Kiev and the country where I was born.

Meantime, we had joined a group called The Writers' Workshop in the Forum retirement community in South Florida. Mollie and I were asked to write a story about our life during our early formative years. I decided to write about my family's escape from Lyubar in 1920. Much to my surprise and delight, the story was well received by my fellow members. It was the first story described by the local papers, in an article illustrating our writing club's endeavors. The article even included a picture of me, along with leaders of the Workshop.

Proud of my achievement, I sent a copy of my story to Gary's parents (my son Alan and daughter-in-law Dolores). They loved it. Alan immediately e-mailed a copy to Gary, who was already in Russia by then. Gary was also intrigued by what I wrote, and informed us he'd like to visit Lyubar, since Kiev was on his itinerary. Gary wanted to know if I could find Lyubar on a map, or let him know its exact location and anything else I remembered about it – where we lived – etc.? To my deep embarrassment, I realized that I knew or remembered very little about the place where I was born. I hadn't seen its location on a map. What to do?

I went right to our local library. Their reference section couldn't help. My friend, George Getz, a part-time teacher at our community college, suggested I try the Boca Raton Library on Glades Road, west of Lyons. I found exactly what I was looking for in their excellent reference room.

The young librarian on duty in the reference room was very helpful. Without hesitation, he typed my request into his desk computer and directed me to a shelf holding the world atlases. He even told me which number atlas and what page I'd find what I needed. Sure enough, I found Lyubar nestled in the southwest part of that page. Not only that, but, I remembered Berdichev that was located due north, and Zhitomir was almost the same distance south of Lyubar. Some 75 years after we'd left Lyubar, I'd finally see its name on a map. And, to top it off, there was Kiev (about 160 miles to the east), and Lviv (then called Lemberg), in the southernmost corner of the same page.

It was a most satisfying conclusion to the faint memory of a little boy, even though it took almost 75 years to verify. The lesson derived from this little tale is that one never knows how much we've retained from our earliest days until some little question or event re-awakens the sleeping, past experiences that lie dormant in our minds, patiently waiting to be told. Even more important, during the retelling, other related early parts of our lives, which we weren't even conscious of, spring up to refresh our memories.

My point, if this little tale interests you: it also tells you that you, too, have hidden memories – both happy and sad – that make interesting stories to be told to your family and friends. The trouble it takes is well worth the results, if mine are any example. Do it! It's fun!

Love, Ralphy

A SUMMER LESSON

A headline in yesterday's obituary (in 2001) noted the passing of Larry Adler, celebrated harmonica virtuoso. It reminded me of my summer session of 1927, when I took an Advanced French class to enable me to enroll in high school in Baltimore (as told in my "Education" story).

Students were seated in alphabetical order, starting on the window aisle. Larry Adler sat right of front of me (A before B) and I soon got to know him very well. He was a tall, lanky kid and a born comedian. His clowning around, before our teacher Dr. Uhlig came in, was a source of delight to all of us. When Larry tired of cracking jokes, he'd pull out a harmonica – ranging in size from the tiny one that he would hide in his mouth to a large one, double the usual size. Every morning he'd entertain us, surrounded by a group of us boys watching and listening. My desire to listen to Larry, as soon as I arrived at school, almost cost me the chance to get credit for the course.

The summer course in French lasted six weeks. At the end of the fourth week, Dr. Uhlig told us that our assignment for that weekend was to study the section on irregular verbs in our assigned textbook. On Monday, there would be a quiz that would help determine our final grade. The assignment did not worry me at all. I already knew the material, and a quick skim of the chapter later that day confirmed my feelings. Even so, I did take the time to review the chapter and forgot about it for the rest of the weekend. I came to class on Monday morning and saw Larry and a couple of other boys quietly gathered around Ed Gersuk's desk, in the next aisle. Curious, I walked up to the group and saw that they were looking at something in Ed's hands. "What's that?" I asked. "A crib," explained Ed, pointing to a small folded piece of paper in his hands. With my limited vocabulary of English, I knew only that a crib was a tiny bed for babies. "May I see it?" I begged. "Sure," he replied, and handed me the mysterious folded paper.

As I opened it up someone yelled, "Put it away, here comes Uhlig!" Hurriedly, we all took our seats and I slid the piece of paper inside my desk. Before Dr. Uhlig reached his desk, he pointed a finger in my direction and said, "What's that you're hiding?" Feeling my face turning crimson, I said it was nothing. "Bring it right here" he shouted in his thick German accent. Shamefacedly I complied. "Did you write this?" he demanded as he unfolded the paper. "No, sir!" I said. "Where did you get this?" he insisted, repeatedly, while I refused to tell him. "In that case," he said angrily, "you might just as well not take the test and leave the room since you'll fail the class!"

No matter how much I tried to explain – in my own thick accent – that I'd never even seen the contents of the paper and had just asked to see it out of curiosity, he ignored my pleas. I just as stubbornly insisted that I was innocent, knew my subject, and did not need any help from any source. Grimly, with what I knew was now an ashen face, I returned to my desk and proceeded to take the test. When I handed in my paper we said nothing to each other.

I continued to take the class for the remaining two weeks without exchanging a word with Dr. Uhlig or any of my classmates. Worrywart that I was – and still am – I spent many sleepless hours in bed, trying to think what I'd tell my parents if I failed that class. After the class ended, I had to wait three weeks before I received my final grade. Much to my relief, he'd given me a "C." Considering the fact that Dr. Uhlig had a reputation as a very tough grader, this brought unashamed silent tears of thankfulness. The word "crib" became a very meaningful and memorable part of my vocabulary. As did the names Larry Adler and Ed Gersuk.

Ralph Bartel
August 14, 2001

CLOTHES QUESTION

Ever wonder why (my wife) Mollie and I often get attention by wearing coordinating colors? It's probably because both of us, although raised under different circumstances, were denied the pleasure of choosing what to wear while growing up. Let me tell you about my circumstances, and what I think are my reasons for being so "clothes conscious."

During my earliest years I had – for a boy growing up in a small "shtetl" – a comparatively good selection of clothes to wear. (A shtetl or shtetel is a small town with a large Jewish population, which existed in Eastern and Central Europe before the Holocaust.)

Early on, our parents provided us with good, clean daily garments and even used the town tailor to make well-fitting clothes for holidays and special occasions, for me and Mayer (my little brother, as he was then called). The Big War and Revolution and pogroms that followed changed everything. From then on, survival became the only thing that mattered, certainly not clothes.

During our 1920 voyage from Lyubar, all of us in the family had cardboard in the bottoms of our boots, because the soles were so thin. We wore our warmest everyday clothes and sweaters under our heaviest overcoats to try and overcome the bitter cold Russian winters. Arriving first in Poland, satisfying our constant hunger was our only desire. It didn't get any better when we got to our first stop in America, Canada. Again, our daily struggles were food and a roof over our heads. The farthest thing from anyone's mind was what to wear. Each of us wore the same pair of knickers, long black stockings and cheap shoes until they wore out completely. We wore the same "union suits" (one-piece underwear) every day. It only came off when it was washed – once a week – while we waited for it to dry.

Conditions were not any better after we came to Baltimore. Papa's draw of $8.00 a week certainly did not go for clothes. In fact, as we began to grow and my feet became so big, I had to buy high-top sneakers to use for everyday wear. (They only cost a dollar a pair.)

Mike (Mayer had changed his name once we settled in the States) and I continued to wear our knickers daily, to school and to deliver the orders, after school. When I tore a hole in my stockings – while trying to roller skate – Pop forbade me to skate again or go out for sports, to prevent another such catastrophe.

Mom spent over an hour mending the tear so I could use them again the next day. The most important event in Mike's and my lives occurred when Willie – our older brother – decided to get married. Pop decided it was time for our first long pants!

Fortunately, a store called Brager Eisenberg's Bargain Basement had a special sale. With each sale of pants and sport coat, we had a choice of a free baseball bat and ball, or glove. As a result, we each got our first brand new pair of long pants and attractive sport coat, plus we came home with one bat, a hardball, and one glove between us!

The matching jackets and pants were to last us for several years and were put to good use by both of us. For the first time, we had something to wear when we were invited to a party or for the Holidays. We wore identical outfits, although Mike was 17 months younger than I, he had sprouted up and eventually was about an inch taller.) Since I was now going to high school, I even bought another pair of pants.

My attire became very important as I attended high school and normal schools (the historical name of teaching colleges). The proper clothes finally allowed me to attend parties and have dates. Since most of my peers were better dressed than I, it became a matter of great concern for me to try to emulate them. I saved every penny for more and better-looking clothes, albeit bought on sale or at a bargain basement. When I began teaching, in 1931, all male classroom teachers always wore practically identical suits and ties, either blue serge or oxford gray. The blue serge usually left a shiny sheen after every wearing, while the Oxford gray's black color was perfect for funeral directors. I felt that, as a teacher, I should not portray myself in such somber and solemn colors, and determined that I'd dare to do something about it. Unfortunately, I couldn't afford to spare any of my earnings on such luxuries.

My first chance came during a post-Christmas sale, after I was married. Mollie, too, decried the austerity and sobriety of male teachers' dress and urged me on, when I noticed an ad for men's clothes at Brager Eisenberg's Bargain Basement. The sale featured two three-piece suits for $25. A dark green suit with white pinstripe came with two pairs of pants, while a navy blue suit with a narrower pinstripe offered a coat, vest, and pants. I could buy both for the sale price of $25. We couldn't resist! Then, Mollie saw an off-white – almost a cream color – summer suit, reduced to $10. (Our photo album shows me wearing this on a visit to Washington, D.C. during Cherry Blossom time.)

The first day of school after the New Year's holiday, I wore my new blue suit, with a matching striped blue-and-white tie. It created a sensation. Before the day was over, it seemed every boy and most teachers, male and female, found some reason to pass me as I stayed on patrol during the change of classes. My own boys couldn't stop staring at me and asking questions. "Are you going away? Why are you all dressed up?" And, on and on. When I came to school the next day, dressed in my new green-and-white striped suit, the buzzing grew. It was some time before the whispering stopped, as I alternated between blue serge or oxford gray and my two new suits.

Before school ended in late June, the continued hot weather "forced" me to wear my new white suit. I wished I had a camera to record the stares and examinations I caused as I stood in the hall and when I walked from my class into the cafeteria for lunch.

Even the students who normally skipped school seemed to be enticed to come back by and see the man teacher, dressed in white, teaching. Quite an event! Unquestioningly, I loved every minute of it. The "ham" (you should excuse me!) in me just glowed with pleasure. I knew I had succeeded in breaking the barrier when Sid Chernak, my mentor and very good friend, who was also my boss, came to school one day wearing an attractive brown suit for the first time. That made it official.

Later working in Becker's Men's Department store, before we left Baltimore, exposed me to new styles and colors of shirts and ties. I took advantage of the many opportunities to expand my wardrobe, always at reduced prices. I even bought a pair of silver-gray spats (spatterdashes, a footwear accessory that covered the ankles) to wear on special occasions. By the time we left for Florida I had an extensive variety of clothes for every normal occasion, or so I thought!

The move to Florida, in 1944, revealed a totally unbelievable new world. The vistas of palms, beaches, and blue-green waters of the Atlantic Ocean were surpassed only by the myriad of multi-rainbows of fashions in both men's and ladies' apparel. We were in a dream world of light and brilliant colors, displayed in window after window on the world-famous Lincoln Road in Miami Beach. Night after night we'd gaze in awe and wonder at these dazzling sights. Did ordinary people actually wear such clothes? When the "season" began and the visitors strolled along with us, attired in these brilliant arrays, we mentally drooled at our options of buying new clothes.

Unfortunately, our first year's experience in Miami Beach did not permit us to indulge in any of our fantasies. Money was tight and we struggled to just survive the year. With the end of World War II, our luck changed, and the year 1945 more than made up for our efforts. Before we left for Atlantic City that summer, I took advantage of the spring half-price sale at one of the best men's stores on Lincoln Road and bought a gold sport coat with blue pinstripes for $50, the most I'd ever splurged on a suit or jacket before. My oldest son, then about 10, was so impressed with the suit, he asked to wear it when he grew up.

Mollie also indulged herself in a new outfit that matched my colors, and we bought new identical brown plaid sport coats for both two sons.

When the four of us paraded on the famous Boardwalk in Atlantic City during that summer of 1946, wearing our Florida outfits, all eyes turned to admire us. From then on, Mollie and I began to buy coordinating outfits, whenever our budgets permitted, and dressed in matching colors – a practice we have continued all these years.

The end of the tourist seasons in Florida always brought great reductions in the prices of clothes. Each year we'd wait till the crowds left and – whenever we could spare a few dollars – stock up on the beautiful fashions that became available at very great discount. Little by little, our wardrobes expanded, so that when we traveled anywhere and got dressed in our colorful outfits, we were noticed – both by family and strangers.

Mollie always packed our suitcases when we traveled, and she invariably insisted on including many more changes of outfits for me than I thought necessary. This often resulted in interesting experiences.

Two incidents stand out. During one of our summer visits, (daughter-in-law and son) Dolores and Alan took us to see a new mall in Virginia Beach (where they had settled). As we passed a men's shoe store, one of the salesmen ran out and stopped me.

"Where did you get those shoes?" he asked, pointing to the light blue suede shoes I was wearing. When I answered, "Miami Beach," he shrugged and said, "Oh! I thought so," and turned away.

On one of our many trips abroad, we toured several countries using the same bus and driver. We became quite familiar and friendly with many members of the group. One day I overheard one young man say to another, "I wonder what colors Ralph's going to wear this morning?" I laughed and said, "Turn around and you'll see." Red-faced, he started to apologize. I assured him I was flattered that he noticed and we laughed it off. Inwardly, I was thrilled. Thanks to Mollie, I still am clothes conscious.

August 8, 2000

THE CHEDER

My earliest recollections of attending *Cheder* (Religious School) are of enjoyable days. The boys ranged in age from three or four to six-year-olds, to learn the basics of *Aleph Bayz* (ABCs). Learning consisted of repeating, by rote, the words or sounds of the *Rebbe* (Rabbi/teacher), as he pointed out the lesson of the day, using old, tattered notebooks. The lucky ones, like me, whose parents were willing to spend the money, had their own booklets, to follow, read, learn, and write in. Every lesson was the same. The Rebbe would read a sound or word and the group would repeat it over and over again, till he was satisfied. Homework consisted of reading or writing the letters/words learned that day. Woe unto the boy who was not paying attention! Physical punishment was an expected daily occurrence. If one became too difficult for him to handle, the boy would be sent home, where additional punishment awaited. The shame of not doing well, in Cheder, became a source of gossip through-out the town. Fortunately, that never happened to me.

After the alphabet was conquered and words recognized, learning continued with the use of old copies of the *Siddur* (Prayer Book) as the text. Again, all learning took place by repeating, word for word, the daily prayers. Those of us with a grandfather, father, or older brother at home – who said his prayers, daily – could repeat them, orally even before starting Cheder. Now, we were given an opportunity to learn to read the words we knew. For others, this was a very bad time. The Rebbe showed little patience for anyone who could or would not learn the Siddur – the backbone of our daily lives. The monotony of "learning," by repeating the meaningless prayers, turned many youngsters away from learning Hebrew, unless they were exposed to it at home. Although most retained some semblance of the routine and order of the prayer service, many practiced it without any meaningful reason or did not say their prayers often. It wasn't unusual for an old man to ask a little boy on what page or prayer we were on, if he came in late for services. Sometimes, I would have to point out the exact line that the Cantor was reciting or singing. A surprisingly large number of men did not even know how to read their prayers and depended on their memories when reciting them. Some had never gone to Cheder. The brighter boys learned the meaning of the words they read. As their fluency progressed, they were "promoted" to the next level, which included the *Machzur* (special books used for Holidays). By the age of six, their parents celebrated the honor of the son's admittance to the study of the *Chumosh* (first five books of the Bible). Memories of the wonderful party given at our house, when my younger brother Mayer was admitted to the Chumosh class at the tender age of five, are still vividly clear. All our relatives and family friends were invited. The boys who were in our Cheder class, along with their parents, also came. The Rabbi, Cantor, and all the influential men of Lyubar honored us with their presence. It was a very exciting and noisy evening. The main event, of course, took place when Mayer displayed his maturity by reading a passage from the Chumosh and translating it into Yiddish. The family beamed with pride, as we were congratulated by each of the visitors. It was a *Simcha* (Celebration) long to be discussed and remembered.

Our parents had decided to dress my younger brother and me alike. Both of us were measured by the town tailor, who made us identical navy blue knee-high pants and white blouses, with collars edged in blue, while a blue anchor was prominently sewn in the corners – for a nautical motif. On our heads were round, white sailor hats, with the same design. From then on, we were always dressed alike, well into our teens – even when we bought our first pair of long pants, with sport coats to match, when our older brother, Velvel (Willie) was married.

Those of us who studied the Chumosh had the opportunity to learn the translation of the Bible portions, which were read each Saturday, in *Shul* (synagogue). As we progressed, a selected few were allowed to learn *Rashi* (a commentary on many passages in the Bible) by a very learned sage. Suddenly, the Shabbas Torah passages became very meaningful, when the Rabbi or a very important traveling scholar or *Magid* (Storyteller) would lecture about the week's portion and its hidden meanings. After the Service, we were allowed to listen; and, if we dared, even comment on what was being discussed by the learned elders. (Papa would be very proud of us, when we made a point or asked a question.) This marked the beginning of our involvement in the study of the

Talmud, a large group of commentaries, discussions, and debates that cover every aspect of Jewish lore, study, and laws. The ultimate aim for a father was to see his son become a Talmud scholar! The highest level of learning in our Cheder was the study of the *G'morra*, an interpretation of the laws of Judaism (part of the Talmud), that is the basis of all Judeo/Christian moral teachings. Many of our current common laws are derived from these teachings. In this class, the teacher would pose a problem – not unlike law school – and ask different students how he'd solve it. Invariably, after one had given an opinion, another student or the teacher would show a different possible interpretation or solution. For an eager, inquisitive youngster like me, this was a very happy time. Discussions were often lengthy but indecisive. Unfortunately, the effect of the war in progress, and the revolution brewing in Russia, led to an interruption of my Cheder studies. Much of what I was exposed to, in my early years, remained – even though I never returned to the serious study of our heritage.

No discussion of the Cheder would be complete without some description of the place where we studied. The dimly lit two rooms of the Synagogue, attached to the main Shul, were used for daily prayers three times a day. In between, Cheder was conducted. They had no conveniences or facilities. Light came from small windows on one side of the room. During the long, harsh fall and winter, kerosene lanterns hung from posts, and shed a limited amount of illumination. There was no provision for water or toilet use. If one could convince the Rebbe of an emergency, he might permit the well behaved to go outside and use the nearby woods. Otherwise, one had to wait till he, himself, needed to go. At recess, there were only a few minutes. To wash our hands, there was a bucket of water outside. The result was that all the smells – food, body odors, and unclean or wet clothing – were exaggerated by the proximity of our seating arrangements. Most of us wore heavy suits of underwear that were not changed until the cold weather ended.

The class sat on long benches of plain wooden planks on both sides of a large bare wooden table, as close together as possible, in order to hear the Rebbe and follow the reading or saying. Still, for some of us, it was fun. That's all we had!

EDUCATION
Part I

In addition to attending Cheder in Lyubar, I also had the opportunity to start *Ghymnazia*, which is the equivalent of a combined elementary and high school. After one has reached the age of six, you are permitted to take the examination – to see if you are prepared. Jewish children had to excel in order to be accepted.

Many parents deliberately refused to let their children attend or even try for the exam. In addition to saving the cost of extra clothing and supplies for school, the reason given was that it was sacrilegious to be exposed to the Gentile atmosphere of the Ghymnazia. It was far more honorable for a Jewish boy to study, to be a scholar or, hopefully, a Rabbi. Thus, attendance at the Ghymnazia was not a common Jewish experience in a small town or village. Our parents felt that we should have that privilege. My memories of my studies – for only one year – at the Ghymnazia, are very hazy. It was a very happy time for me. I was very attentive and retained the lectures well, so that my grades were excellent on tests and I was frequently called upon to read out loud in class – considered an honor by students. We were given a chance to take a foreign language during that year and I chose German. The chance of learning a strange new alphabet, and reading and speaking another language was a challenging experience. Unfortunately, World War I and the unrest leading to the Revolution in Russia disrupted the educational system and our school had fewer and fewer teachers and classes. Thus, I have no memories of any formal Russian education beyond that one year. Although I remember reading papers in original German, I have long since forgotten what I knew and have never had the desire to renew. My best guess is that I learned at home. My older brother, Velvel (Willie), had been a good student at the Ghymnazia, My older sister, Chaika (Ida), had not only finished Ghymnazia but had attended the University of Odessa until the Revolution forced her to flee and come home. Both my parents were literate – an unusual situation in a village like Lyubar. In fact, Mama was called "Pessel, Mayer Odessar's," meaning the daughter of Mayer, who came from Odessa. My grandfather Mayer, who died about a year after I was born, was reputed to be a great scholar and was a highly respected man in our community – reportedly held in higher esteem than the Rabbi as a student of the Torah. My younger brother was named for him. When we went to services, a crowd of women would actually surround Mama to sit near her and follow her. She read the Hebrew prayers in her Siddur fluently, as well as newspapers in Yiddish and Russian. I recall many occasions when folks would bring a letter or notice to her in our store, to read and explain. If a reply was required, she'd oblige, too. Many peasants came to her for this service. I'm certain that these acts helped to form the bonds of friendship that later saved our lives, during the pogroms and revolutionary strife.

As for Papa, he was quite an unusual man. At the age of thirteen, he and his older brother were forced to start working to help support his mother and a younger brother and sister. Still, he not only knew how to read the Hebrew prayers he recited, but could translate them into Yiddish, when asked to explain. It was probably from him that I learned what little Hebrew I was able to master. He also read and spoke Ukrainian, Russian, and Polish. The most likely source of my early education was my exposure to the many heated arguments and discussions that took place in our home when Chaika returned from Odessa. She was a beautiful and popular young lady, well-educated and knowledgeable about the Revolution, the Zionist Movement, and the general turmoil prevailing in our country and the world. Her singing voice was considered outstanding, and her ability to play the balalaika and mandolin – both of which were in the house – added to her attraction. The result was the constant presence of a group of young men and women in our living room. Many nights, after I was supposed to have been in bed, I would crawl, in the dark, to my door, so I could listen to the discussions. It was here that I was first attracted to the Zionist cause and determined that someday I too, would become a *Chalutz* (pioneer) in Palestine. I learned the words to the French Marseillaise without knowing their meaning. All the popular revolutionary songs, as well as the local peasant songs – later made world-famous by the Russian Cossack Choir singers, in the '30s and '40s – as well as the Hebrew songs, became part of my daily vocabulary. Sometimes, I was invited to add my soprano voice to the group. The acquisitions came about without conscious effort on my part, but remained with me for many years afterwards. By the time we left Lyubar, I was comfortable with Russian, Yiddish, Ukrainian, some Hebrew, and a little German. When we came to Poland I had difficulty with the Polish language and, particularly, with the Galician pronunciation of Yiddish initially. Gradually, I absorbed both, so that in a matter of weeks I was able to understand and converse in them. By the time we left Warsaw on our way to America, I was fluent in Polish and had no difficulty in speaking the language when I came in contact with Poles. It came in very handy during my first year of teaching, when I made visits to my students' homes, since the majority of their parents and grandparents spoke only Polish.

Our family arrived in Canada during the second week of August, 1921. Instantly, we were confronted with learning not one, but two new languages. Worse yet, we were confined to a slum area where the little of the new languages that we encountered were slurred by the various accents of the motley group of immigrants who were our neighbors. Since none of us knew any English or French, and, since the community did not help us learn either one, only Mayer (Mike) and I had a chance to learn them during our enrollment in school. Conditions beyond our control, related in another story, prevented us from starting school in the first months after arriving. By the time we finally were admitted, we had missed much of the early orientation given to new immigrants and were not accepted too graciously by our overworked native French teacher in the overcrowded classroom. My teacher walked me to a broken-down desk in the back of the room, motioned for me to sit down, and proceeded to ignore me for the rest of the day. We had been through so much misery that this action did not even bother me. I just sat there, probably reflecting the numb feeling that permeated my entire body. At least, nobody bothered me. Yet! The large number of students in my class was made up of an unbelievable mix of boys and girls of native French speakers, poor and a conglomeration of a dozen different countries' immigrant children. Most of us were dressed in castoff or threadbare clothes that barely covered our scrawny bodies. We differed considerably in size and age. Apparently, it was the practice to put all newcomers into the same room, without regard to their age, ability or experience. The poor teachers who were thus burdened had to try to assess each new entrant and establish some means of communication – in order to give us some semblance of instruction. Looking back at my experience of those early years – after having been a teacher for so long, myself – I can't help but marvel at the amount of success my first Canadian (and later, my American) instructors had. The school day was divided into two sessions. The mornings began with an hour of French lessons. Since the class was constantly adding new members, the lessons were usually repeated about once a week. I paid strict attention. It wasn't long before I had picked up the words and meanings of the beginning lessons, in French. On Fridays, the lesson ended with singing French songs. When the Marseillaise was started, I immediately joined in the singing and surprised both the teacher and classmates by knowing the words and melody. With the help of a little girl, who spoke Yiddish, I explained that I'd learned the song in the "old country." When the teacher asked if I'd like to lead the class in singing that song, I blushed and timidly shook my head. It would take several weeks before I found the courage and confidence to do so. Although still faced with the difficulty of learning both English and French, I soon found a way to enjoy classwork. As a part of doing arithmetic, the teacher would write several columns of two-digit numbers on the blackboard and call on volunteers to see who could add the columns fastest. This didn't require any knowledge of language and, since I had good addition skills, I became one of the teacher's pets during those drills. The ability to sing and do arithmetic helped acclimate me to the daily routine and it wasn't long before I began to look forward to going to school. At noon, all the classes were dismissed for lunch. We had to go home, eat, and be back by one o'clock for the afternoon session.

The afternoons were spent with instruction of English, History, and Geography. Geography became my favorite subject, because I had begun to save stamps and had practiced finding where the different countries were located. My eagerness to learn helped me pick up enough of both new languages to get good marks in my studies. Both daily sessions were broken up with a 15-minute recess. Since the entire school was let out at the same time, there was usually bedlam – whether outside or indoors, in the huge gym. I was a typical "scaredy-cat": shy, timid, and weak, physically. It didn't take long for the big French bullies to size me up and decide to have some fun with me. One would "accidentally" bump into me. Of course, he immediately would cuss me out with the first two French words I'd heard upon my arrival in Canada: "MOUJI JUIF"

("DAMN JEW"), he'd yell, and push me into one of his friends. The friend, in turn, would push me into another, making me a good dummy to play with. I didn't dare try to defend myself, for fear of getting a terrible beating, so I cried while the others watched and laughed until one of the teacher-monitors finally came by and broke it up. It finally ended one day, in the gym, when a Chinese classmate – as big and tough as any of them – came over and grabbed the leader. "Leave him alone" he yelled, "or, you'll have to deal with me." Like the cowardly bullies they were, each one of them skulked and moved away. They never touched me again. My hero, the son of the Chinese laundryman on the corner, became one of my best friends till we left Montreal. With no one at home or in our neighborhood able to guide me to speak English correctly, and (unbeknownst to me), with the strange guttural dialects I picked up with their contacts, I found that I had to unlearn what little facility I'd acquired when I came to the United States. My accent, pronunciation and vocabulary were so bad that my classmates soon labeled me "the mad Rooshian", when I enrolled in Public School #63, in Baltimore in April, 1923.

Compared to my experiences in the short time we had spent in Canada, things were much better at the schools in Baltimore, for a "Greenhorn" immigrant boy. There was still a lot of catching up to do, but a much brighter future faced me in the "Land of Opportunity." Compared to the schooling I had in Montreal, P.S. #63 in Baltimore, was an exhilarating experience. I was the only immigrant pupil. The classroom, while full, was not as crowded. The teachers seemed truly interested in helping me and went out of their way to accommodate my needs. It was the best of all times, in spite of my language problem and the prejudices of the predominantly Gentile peers. Perhaps because of my difficulty in communicating, I was placed in the second grade upon my enrollment in April of 1923. I did register as Ralph Bargteil, after I learned what the English name for Rachmil was. However, when asked for my date of birth, I gave the date upon which I'd become Bar Mitzvah, in Montreal (which was the Hebrew date observed by my parents). Thus, I was forced to accept March 22 or 23 as my "official" birthday, when I applied for my own citizenship papers many years later. Back to P.S. #63, after a couple of days I was moved to a fourth grade class, where I remained till the end of year.

Our school had classes from the first to the eighth grade. The

Naturalization certificate of Gedalia Bargteil in 1928, when the family moved to Baltimore, Maryland.

grading system required that a student attain a certain level of achievement in each grade before promotion. Thus, it was quite common to see children – boys, usually – who were considerably older and larger than their classmates in each room. I was not the biggest student in my class. My teacher, an elderly, kind lady, noted my difficulty with the fourth grade books and suggested that I go to the public library about a half mile from where we lived, and get some "easy" books to learn how to read. The equally kind librarian pointed out a row of Uncle Wiggily Adventures, which I devoured in a few days. It worked, and between them, they gradually increased the level of the books until I'd be back for more, two or three days after I had checked out my limit of five at a time. I became an avid reader of any and all the famous series of paperback books of that time, from the Horatio Alger series, Zane Grey's westerns, Frank Merrival, and many other popular series. Reading became an obsession with me, to the point where I was never without a book in my hand. I'd bring my book to the table to read while I ate. I'd take it to bed with me and read till all hours of the night. Some of the worst scolding from my father came when he caught me reading – at the table or in bed. No matter where I went, for a walk or to visit someone, a book always came along. There were always a couple of books for me to finish, while I had a few minutes of free time working in the family store. Even though I was learning to read and understand English words exceedingly well, my diction gave me a lot of trouble. It was hard for me to pronounce some sounds ("th" was "d," "v" and "w" were commonly confused and interchanged; vowel sounds, mispronounced – the list was long). It would be several years before I could improve my pronunciation enough to be able to speak to anyone without feeling embarrassed about my accent. Even in my late teens I would occasionally lapse and mispronounce a word before catching and correcting myself. Without a mentor to constantly help and correct me, this area of adjusting to English was difficult. I would be 19 years old and ready to graduate Baltimore City College – the name for my Senior High School – before I had the ability and confidence to speak English without fear of mispronunciation.

Part II

Thanks to the genuine interest of my many teachers, I found school a very gratifying part of my life. When the 1923-24 school year started I went into a fifth grade class (in Baltimore), where I remained for only two weeks. The teacher suggested that I be put into a sixth grade class and I was moved into the only class where I can remember my teacher's name. I shall always be grateful to Mrs. Chambers for her kindness and guidance in shaping my educational progress. (Regrettably, I did not realize it till many years later and never took the opportunity to express my thanks to her.) It was her encouragement that made it easy for me to excel in academic subjects. With her help, I also was permitted to skip 6B, the lower half of the sixth grade and complete 6A, including 7B in the one year.

Unfortunately my physical attributes did not match my academic skills. Although I had put on some bulk to my skinny torso soon after arriving in Baltimore, I was still a gangly string bean of a kid, with long, skinny arms and legs attached to a small body, who knew nothing about the games being played. The result: whenever teams chose up sides. I was the last one picked, reluctantly, by the unlucky last picker. My awkward attempts to play games that were strange to me, along with my poor physical skills, made me unpopular when the class went to recess or played a game like baseball. That, too, was a part of the learning process. I had to try that much harder to attain some modicum of mediocrity. A star or even a good athlete, I never became.

The 1923-24 school year played a crucial role in shaping my future education, following a new development soon after we settled down in our temporary living quarters above the store. We were enrolled in a Hebrew school at the Har Zion Synagogue – not far away. By the end of a couple of weeks, the director of the school came to our house and told our parents that both Velvel (Willie) and I were far too advanced for any classes they had to offer. If we wished, they could arrange for us to receive scholarships to the Yeshiva University, in New York. If not, it would be better for us to apply for admission to the Baltimore Hebrew College, located within a 30-minute ride on the local streetcar.

Papa left the decision up to us. I was very much against going to the Yeshiva University. I had no desire to study to be a rabbi; did not want to live among strangers in a faraway city, and, wanted to stay home, to study in an atmosphere where I could get rid of my terrible accent – which was the cause of so much teasing at school and even beatings in the neighborhood. If we were to live in America, I wanted to speak like any other American, without shame.

We enrolled at Baltimore Hebrew College (on free scholarships, since we couldn't afford it, otherwise) for a year, at night. The courses were dull, lecture type, and quite boring to children who wanted and needed to learn so much. After a year we persuaded our parents to let us stop. It wasn't hard to do so, since both of us were needed in the family store. The people who were our customers of kosher food products were very scattered in the Fallbrook section of Baltimore, a predominantly Christian area. This meant that, to accommodate them, we had to deliver their orders regularly. Since we did not have any other means of delivery, all orders had to be carried in bags or baskets daily, and on foot. Since Papa and his partner Uncle Bilich, were busy and too old to drag the orders, my brother Mike (as he'd become, by now) and I became the delivery boys – whenever we were not in school. We'd deliver some orders before school and the rest after we came home.

In the fall of 1924, I started another year of school life in a brand

new school. Forest Park Junior/Senior High School was an unbelievably fantastic place for eager knowledge-hungry students. It was huge,
stretching several blocks long with a tremendous green campus surrounding. It was three stories high, with large, airy classrooms, opening from long halls stacked with lockers: a cafeteria, with endless large
tables and chairs, with a gleaming huge silver and glass counter filled
with all kinds of tempting foods (I knew I'd never taste them, since they
weren't Kosher, and I was very observant.) The mirror-like Olympic
sized indoor swimming pool with crystal clear water was very intimi-
dating to a boy forbidden to swim by parents who were afraid he might
drown. The gymnasium could accommodate several classes of boys or
girls (separately) simultaneously. It was awesome and very frightening
to one unused to such luxuries. Add over 200 students in grades 7 to
12, and the noise and confusion became pandemonium! But, it was my
school so I could go home and brag to other kids in the neighborhood
that THAT'S where I was a student! Unbelievable!

My 7A schedule was waiting for me. I was assigned to a homeroom
teacher, as well as five different teachers, for four academic subjects and
my gym class, all in five different classrooms located on different floors
and sections. In addition, we had a period assigned to the cafeteria,
plus one marked study hall. The teachers were very understanding and
tolerant of stragglers when we arrived late for class. In spite of the overwhelming early confusion, school soon became routine and enjoyable
again. By the time I started the eighth grade, in February, I was a couple
of months shy of my 15th birthday. The lunch period and study hall
served as an excellent time to do my written homework so that I could
catch the first streetcar, to rush right home to help in the store. If there
was any additional reading or studying to be done, there was always time
to do it either in the store or at home, in the evenings after dinner.

The summer of 1925 brought several changes in our lives. Uncle
Bilich, who started the store as Papa's partner, was a very good butcher,
but a poor public relations person when it came to handling customers.
The complaints got so bad many refused to let him wait on them.

Finally, Papa and he decided that only one of them could operate
the store. Since my uncle was older, he was persuaded that he'd be better
off retiring. With the rent due him as owner of the building, and the payments for his share of the business, he didn't need the aggravation and
he sold us his interest. That put the burden on our immediate family. I

would have to be in the store every day. Both Mike and I had learned how to cut meats, knew each kind of meat and their prices, as well as all the other parts of the grocery business. Now I had to start working full time, daily. (Willie had never worked in our store, since he'd gotten a job when we first came to Baltimore at the age of 18.)

When school started in September of 1925, the burden of deliveries fell on Mike and me. Both of us had to get up before six. Mondays, Wednesdays, and Fridays. On Tuesdays and Thursdays, I had to get up before four to go on the streetcar with Papa to the markets, buy live chickens, go to the *Shochet* (ritual chicken killer) to kill them properly; while they were being killed and feathers plucked, get fresh vegetables at produce market. Then we had to gather everything together and lug it home on streetcars. On Thursdays, we also went to the fish market, to buy fresh fish for the Sabbath business. I'd rush into our house, which was not too far from the store, wash, change my clothes, grab a glass of milk and a piece of cake or roll for breakfast, then back to the store to get the deliveries made up. When that was done, Mike and I would divide the baskets into our delivery zones and take them with us on our different ways to school. By the time school started, we'd done a half-day's hard work. Neither one of us thought this was any big deal.

As the days of fall progressed, the burden of carrying on the work in our little store became harder and harder on all of us, Mom's abilities were limited and her health precluded her from doing much more than help wrap something up, get a loaf of bread or an item off the shelf, to serve customers. We couldn't afford to hire anyone to work. No matter how hard each of us tried, it became too much to handle. Papa had to have someone in the store that could take orders over the phone, fill them out, and deliver them, as well as help him wait on customers and fill their needs alone. Finally, in desperation, he told me I would have to quit school and work full time!

Baltimore labor laws prohibited a child from quitting school before age 16. If, however, a family could prove the need, a child over 14 could get a work permit and leave early. Since I was already in 8A, I begged permission to finish the session. In February, I would get my work permit and stop. All of us put in the extra hours and struggled to satisfy our very limited number of steady customers. In February, we promised, our service would be prompt and better.

My classroom work was my real joy and I hated to have to give it up.

When my homeroom teacher learned I had to leave school in February, she suggested I contact the night school to see if there was some way for me to continue with my studies. She arranged an appointment for me with Dr. Otto K. Schmied, the principal, who became my mentor, before I'd ever heard of that word. After checking my grades, he said he'd be happy to help me. Thanks to him, I enrolled in two ninth grade classes in February, at night, to complete two half-units of the sixteen I would need to finish High School. Dr. "O.K.," as he was known to everyone, (a name I'll never forget) also urged me to go to summer school and complete the second half of both classes. I promised him I would, and did. Mike took over during the summer in the half days I was in school and I got my two units credit, then.

Summer school mornings lasted only six weeks and didn't interfere too much with my work. Before school was over, Papa had decided that since our customers were so scattered, the only way we could service them properly would be to buy a car. We'd not only use it for prompt delivery, but also could use it to market – to buy more things more cheaply, and, not have to lug it all on the streetcars. In 1926, when one bought a car, the salesman had to teach the buyer how to drive and to help obtain a driver's license. It was decided that, since I was already 16 years old, and, since I'd be the one doing the deliveries full time, I'd learn how to drive first and get my license. He'd get his chance to learn how, some day, when he had the time. In August, 1926, Papa became the proud owner of a new Chevrolet and I, with him at my side, drove it slowly and carefully home – for all the family, neighbors, and customers to inspect and admire.

My desire to continue my education did not abate. I compensated for not attending school by becoming on even more avid reader. My exposure to American and English Literature opened new vistas for me, and I read anything and everything that I heard or read about. I discovered the Baltimore columnists like H.L. Mencken, to satiate my summer literary appetite. By the time night school opened in the fall, I was ready to take more classes. I decided to consult my advisor, Dr. O.K. Dr. Schmied suggested I go slowly – after learning of my busy daily schedules, particularly of my early hours on Tuesdays and Thursdays, he recommended that I not take my classes till I solved how much time I had for school.

Disappointed, I complied, only to learn that his judgment was wise.

My responsibilities in the business increased and I had less and less free time. Still, I was determined to go back to school and told my family that often. Frustrated but aware of the family needs, I continued to work. My luck changed early in 1927 when Mike came home and said he was tired and bored with school. He would quit and work full time in the store, and let me go back to school.

It was true that Mike was a very bright boy who could easily do any assignment that interested him. But, he was bored by the mediocre level of teaching in the average classroom. Most of the time he'd grasped the point the teacher was trying to make early in the lesson and would just stare out the window or do something to disrupt the room. Being disciplined for inattention or disruption became a regular routine. Since no one ever took the time to challenge Mike, he was truly tired of and disinterested with school. Our parents' disappointment with his decision was tempered by his promise to go to night school and take high school courses, just as I had done, to finish. But then Papa reminded Mike, that he wouldn't be 16 till September and couldn't drive the car."

"Don't worry!" he replied. "I can take care of that. I already know how to drive, and I've got a friend who got me proof that my sixteenth birthday was last year." With that, he pulled out an official-looking paper, certifying that his school record incorrectly listed his age and that he was already past his 16th birthday. It was notarized and sealed and looked genuine.

How and where he got that paper, Mike wouldn't say. Apparently, he'd given this a lot of thought and was well prepared. Upon promising to finish the school year and stay out of trouble, Papa agreed. Since I was a licensed driver, Mike could get a learner's temporary license and I'd take him down for his permanent license when school was over. A person with a learner's permit had to have a licensed driver beside him. When he drove, Mike was Mike. Before school ended, he could be heard and seen driving a car, usually alone, well above the posted speed limit! (But not ours!)

Elated at the turn of events, I again consulted with Dr. Schmied. After congratulating me on my good news, he informed me that he'd be glad to plan my three-year schedule with me, since I needed 14 more units to complete my high school requirements. Aghast, I informed him that I couldn't possibly wait for three years – that I'd be 20 years old, when I finished.

Wasn't there some way that I could expedite it? I'd be willing to go to night school, also, if that would help. He pointed out that the high school classes had seven period days. With five devoted to subjects, a lunch period, and a study hall, there was no way we could squeeze 14 units of study into less than three years. Undaunted, I made a proposal to him: Could he help me get into summer school, to take both halves of a unit, simultaneously? Then, if I passed them, I could go to a high school and take six units one year and seven the next – skipping both lunch hours and study hall and graduate in two years, not three. He had never heard of such a plan and didn't think it was possible. But, if I were truly determined, he would try for the summer school. Then, we'll see.

Part III

My plan was to take French, both the first half and the second, at the same time (to satisfy the Foreign Language requirement) since I was certain I could handle them easily, given my lack of study in Montreal. It took some time to convince Dr. O. K. and, he warned me, there was no guarantee this plan would work. The head of the foreign language department at Baltimore City College – where summer school was to be held – was a stubborn old man and would probably not agree. In spite of his misgivings, he agreed to accompany me to Dr. Uhlig's office to see what would happen.

He was right. Dr. Uhlig was indeed a tough customer to convince. In a distinct German accent, the old man kept on saying, "No!" This was ridiculous! He'd never heard of such a thing! He would allow me to take the first half, but I would have to pass that before I could take the second. When I broke out in protest, in my bad English accent, we all laughed. That seemed to break the ice. I quickly spoke out, in French, to show him that I could handle it.

Finally, he agreed to let me register in both halves – on a two-week trial. If my teacher in the first half (Dr. Uhlig was teaching the second half class and would have me in it) would say I was making good progress, I could stay and finish both parts. He, of course, would have the final say. Happily, I thanked him.

The classes were a snap. Practically the entire classes consisted of boys who'd failed and were repeating the course. (Larry Adler, the famous harmonica genius of the coming years, and Eddie Cersuk, who was to become a famous educator and Assistant Superintendent of Baltimore City Schools were both in my class as repeaters, as was a classmate of Mollie's at Normal School. I stood out like a sore thumb, by comparison. After a wait of two weeks, my two "68s" came in the mail, a big surprise, since I'd been told that Dr. Uhlig gave only "68s" and "Cs" for passing grades. Elated, I tried to contact Dr. O.K. to see if he'd keep his promise to help me.

My friend was away on vacation and would be back the second week of August. When I finally reached him and told him of my success. he congratulated me and calmly told me not to build up my hopes. He would make some phone calls and get back to me. I couldn't wait for his call. Every time the phone rang, I ran to answer it. Finally, the call came.

We were to see the Principal of Baltimore City College next Friday morning! The next two days seemed to take forever to pass. I was so nervous, I could hardly sleep. Each night I would go over all the things I would say, all the arguments I would counter, all the statements that would convince the principal to let me do the impossible. When sleep finally came, I was exhausted.

Dr. Edwards, the new principal of Baltimore City College, had been a very popular vice principal for many years and had been lauded in the newspapers as an excellent choice for the job.

There I was, a very apprehensive *lenger-loksh* (long noodle) – as my mother used to call me – accompanying Dr. O. K. to his office to await my fate. I was told to wait on the bench, while they conferred. The agony of not knowing what was being said and not being able to contribute to the arguments were devastating. It must have been then that I developed the ulcers and nervous conditions that were to keep me out of the Armed Services many years later during World War II. After what seemed an interminable time, I was ushered into Dr. Edwards' office. Although he towered more than a foot over me, his voice was gentle and pleasant to the ear. He proceeded to inform me that he was quite impressed with my background information that Dr. Schmied had conveyed. He thought I had made a great deal of progress in the short time I'd been in the United Sates, but what I wanted to do was unheard of. He regretted to have to deny my request.

Notes: The reader should realize that this took place more than 70 years ago. My vocabulary and means of expression were hampered by my limited contact with American educated individuals. When one adds a distinctly horrible accent, easily aroused by anxiety, fear or disappointment, the words I spoke are not repeated here. The gist of our discussion is a true portrayal.

Paled by the terrible news, I nevertheless had the good sense to thank Dr. Edwards for the time he'd spent considering my problem. Politely, I begged him to give me a couple of minutes more to plead my case.

Breathlessly, I explained, my plea could not be compared to anybody else's. I was not the typical high school student. My future and, perhaps, my family's future depended upon my getting an education. (So, I exaggerated a little bit. I was desperate!) I had sacrificed my schooling before I was sixteen and got a work permit, in order to help my family. Now, my family was willing to sacrifice its health and welfare for me. Both my parents worked hard all day and both are attending night classes, studying to become American citizens. My younger brother dropped out of school so that I could pursue my studies. My grades showed that I could work hard daily and still get high marks. I'm already past 17 years old. If I take three years to finish high school, it will be that much harder for me to realize my dream of going to college, and on and on. Finally, I asked, did anyone ever take six units of study in one year and pass them, successfully?

I was told that there had been several instances of that, in the past, but – in each case – the person had completed all other requirements and needed only those six to graduate. I needed three units of Latin, three of English, World History, American History, one and a half of math, and one unit of science – all as the basic courses, plus two and a half of electives, in order to graduate in two years. There was no way that Dr. Edwards could think of, that a schedule to meet those needs could be made up, to fit into all this into a two-year plan.

Well, I countered: suppose I were to take an examination, in Latin, to show my proficiency in that language, and pass it. Would I get credit for it? I could then take third-year Latin (Cicero) during one year, and fourth-year Latin (Virgil's Iliad) the next. Would that be possible? Yes. that could be arranged, he said. All right, then, I added, if I pass the Latin requirements, I could take an English literature and another

English course the same year. If I were to pass my six units in my first year, I could then be assigned the last six missing classes in the following year and graduate in two years!

My "couple of minutes" request lasted more than an hour, and my persistence (along with a few encouraging words from Dr. O.K.) persuaded Dr. Edwards to let me take the Latin exam. If I passed that, he'd work out a schedule for the next school year, to start in less than two weeks.

The story of the next two years can fill an entire chapter. Suffice it to say that I overcame every obstacle that tried to prevent me from reaching my goal – including a tyrannical homeroom and history teacher who made anyone who came to class even a minute late, stay an hour after school. I had a backbreaking schedule of early risings on Tuesdays and Thursdays to drive to the markets, plus daily deliveries on the streetcar, on my way to school before I started my school day. At the end of the last period, daily, I could be seen running for the first streetcar to get me to the store, where other work waited for me. I made it! Proudly, I wore my 1929 class ring, when I received my high school diploma, in June, at age 19!

Like the vast majority of immigrants, my parents envisioned a grand plan for me. A high school diploma was only the start of a successful professional career. After I finished that, I'd go to college and study to be a doctor. Although getting into medical school was very difficult, due to the quota system – for Jewish applicants – in vogue at the time, they were sure I'd make it. All I had to do was continue to get good grades. They even found a solution to the high cost of tuition.

At the time, pre-med requirements could be met by a two year course in pharmacy school. Both Johns Hopkins University and the University of Maryland in Baltimore, offered this course. It was settled! When I finished high school, I'd go to pharmacy school. If I couldn't get into a medical school, at least I could always make a good living as a druggist, an honorable profession. With pharmacy school tuition in mind, I made a determined effort to save every penny. Delivering cleaned and pressed clothing for our tailor neighbor brought me $1.25 a week, plus an occasional nickel tip. Grudgingly, I received permission to work Saturdays at a large A&P store, where I made three dollars (for a 14-hour day). By the time I was ready to graduate, I had saved up over $190 in my savings account in the Chesapeake Bank. That was almost enough for one year's cost of tuition. But . . . even the best laid plans have a way of not coming to fruition.

Every week Papa conscientiously wrote a postcard or letter (in Yiddish) to my sister Chaika and her husband Muni, living in Montreal. He inquired how they and their two young daughters were doing, and how business was at the Old Rose Printing Co., owned and operated by Muni. It was Papa's habit to let Mama and the rest of us read both his writings and any replies received. All of us were thus kept aware of family matters. About the time I was ready to get my diploma, we received a letter from them saying that Muni was on the verge of losing his lease and his livelihood. Earlier cards and letters had mentioned that they were struggling to make ends meet. We had heard similar stories of struggle from my Aunt Soorka (Sarah, Papa's sister) in New York where she lived with her children; also from Uncle Chaim (Mama's brother) and his family in New York; and from others. This time, we all agreed, after reading Muni's latest letter, it seemed to imply very dire conditions. Their silent cry for help was felt by all of us. We could not let them lose their only means of making a living.

Without hesitation, I told my parents I would withdraw some money from my savings account and send it to them. Warning me not to take it all out, they reluctantly agreed. I got a cashier's check for $150 and sent it special delivery. (Many years later, Muni told me how much it meant for them. He reciprocated by later lending me money, when I needed it.) Both of us repaid the other, of course, in due time.

My parents were devastated when they heard how much I'd sent. How could I do this? How could I now go to pharmacy school? Where would I get the $200 for the first year's tuition? It took quite a while before I could calm them down and explain why I'd sent so much and what my new plans were. First of all, I explained, unless Muni received enough to pay off his past due rent, we'd be wasting my money. Besides, they probably needed any extra there was to live on. As for me, I didn't think I could ever be a doctor or a pharmacist. To do that meant taking many science courses, which I never liked. In addition, I had been talking to my good friend, Sid Chernak, the choir leader at Har Zion Synagogue, where we were preparing for the holidays. He had just finished his first year teaching and loved it very much. He advised and encouraged me to enroll at Maryland State Normal School (again, what teaching college was formally called). The yearly cost is only about

$30-$35. At the end of two years, the top 75 graduates are assured of a job. A teacher!

Unlike in the United States, the teaching profession is highly respected by Europeans. The Jewish people have always encouraged their sons to become a scholar. To become a teacher was an even higher sign of achievement. In practical terms, the thought of being able to reach such a goal for so low a cost made a lot of sense. In fact, I pointed out that I even knew of a summer job where I could pick up enough money for spending purposes, so I would not be a burden to them. It did not take any more to persuade them and the new plan was adopted.

Encouraged by their final acceptance of my change in plans, I went right back to the bank, withdrew $35, and gave it to Mama, to save for my school fees. I can't explain why I did that. About ten days later, I was in the store when Papa returned from the bank with the deposit bag in his hand. He took out the cash and handed it to Mama, telling her to take it home and hide it.

"What happened?" We questioned. Why didn't you make the deposit?"

"When I got to the bank," he said, "I noticed an unusually long line leading inside. Curious, I asked why. A man said that this was a 'run' on the bank. Everybody was trying to close their accounts because several banks had failed and closed and people thought the Chesapeake might, too. So, I decided not to make the deposit and came back." Luckily, he had a very small balance in the store checking account. My savings account balance was less than $10. The Chesapeake Bank of Baltimore never reopened. The Yiddish word, *Bashert*, is very apropos.

The Thursday before Labor Day was registration day at Maryland State Normal School, the two year teacher training center located on the outskirts of the City of Baltimore in the town of Towson (it's now Towson State University). After a long hour's ride on two streetcars, I joined a large contingent of freshly scrubbed teenagers, eagerly, perhaps pensively, awaiting a new scholastic experience. Looking around me, I was sure that I was the oldest registrant on the luxuriously green campus. I couldn't care less! This was my first day at achieving my new goal and I was anxious to get started.

The contrast between high school and Normal School was quite dramatic. About half of the entering class – labeled "Juniors" – of over 300 students came from Baltimore City, with the rest coming from rural towns scattered all over the state. A majority of the City contingent was Jewish. In a total enrollment of some 600 "Juniors" and "Seniors," there were only about 70 males, in contrast to an entire school of over 2,500 boys at Baltimore City College. The large number of non-Jewish and female students made it very difficult for a shy young man, unexposed to such a group, to adjust. Fortunately, I knew a couple of the Baltimore City boys and they helped me with answers and suggestions. Before long, I felt at ease and started to enjoy the classes. It was too good to last.

After a couple of weeks of classes, a notice appeared on the main hall bulletin board stating that there would be no excuses from classes for the forthcoming Jewish Holidays! By then, I had become friendly with a number of the boys from Baltimore and several approached me to get my reaction. Although I had worked on Saturdays, occasionally, I was still an observant Jew and did not hide my beliefs. I ate only kosher food and still brought a sandwich with me for my daily lunch. About the only food I bought in the cafeteria was milk or ice cream. Therefore, the notice was a terrible shock to me and I expressed my violent opposition to it. As usual, there were a lot of opinions among us. Some feared possible repercussions if they raised objections, others, like me, vowed to protest. The upshot of our talks was that I was delegated to file a protest and attempt to get the notice rescinded. Upon inquiry, I was told that this matter required a meeting with the Vice President of the faculty, and I made the necessary appointment.

HANDY FOREIGN LANGUAGE

It's gratifying to get a positive response to my latest essay. My grandson Doug's assurance that – even though he'd read about some items before – there were still some interesting things, new and different, that he learned. It made me realize that the memories we recall are, as a matter of fact, not always 100% reliable. Since many "facts" are second or third hand, they may only be partially true.

In her book, "Total Recall," Sara Paretsky (Delacorte Press Random House, 2001) has a couple of characters that debate the value and/or the accuracy of therapy, by specialists, in memory recall. I'm not about to go down that road. All I can tell you is that – no matter how carefully I try to relate my memories, honestly and completely, I'm certain they are facts missing. Of course, this is especially true of my stories about Mollie, her brother Herman, and her parents, Alexander and Pauline Hirsh. Can any of you doubt that my Mollie, whom I knew since 1930, and knew so well for more than 73 years, kept some intimate secrets from me? Can anyone of you swear you told someone – no matter how dear and close – EVERYTHING about your past? I know I can't. Let me give you a better "for instance:" Let's try with Alexander (no known middle name) Hirsh, Mollie's father and my father-in-law. By far, most everything I have written about him came second or third hand. I was told that his real last name was Gershkowitz (sp.) and that he had studied engineering at Odessa University, in his hometown. Later, to avoid serving in the Russian Army, he fled to Berlin, Germany, to get his second engineering degree from the University of Berlin. Can anyone of you conceive how many years it'd take, or how much it'd cost, to verify – even if such records are available – just these items, as examples? Of course not! So, as long as you accept my story as reasonably correct, I am willing to share it with you. Let's enjoy. But, what's all this got to do with the title above? Everything! Every time I think about the questions raised about a story or the comments made, something is suddenly reawakened in my memory bank. And, it's only fair that I share my memories with you. And, that topic rules! I'll try to show how the ability to utilize a foreign language affects our lives. Since I can't possibly be mistaken for a "Venerable Dowager," I rely entirely on my "old age" as an excuse for all commissions or omissions. Let me therefore preface this offering by reminding you that – if any of you are not mentioned – it's only because I'm not sure of your history of the use of a foreign language. Honestly! No slight intended. By the same token, the order in which I describe anyone is not deliberate/important. Today's "something" has to do with incidents in which ability to use a foreign language has played a part to some of you or me – that I happen to remember.

Before I start with my experiences, let me tell you about what I remember about some of the other family members. Alexander (Alex) and Pauline Hirsh (Mollie's mother) both came to the U. S. in the 1905 immigrant wave. Both were both fluent in Russian and Yiddish and made use of both languages while learning English. (Pauline continued to call her husband *Elyushah* – the Russian version of his name – during the years I knew them, from 1930 on.) Both of them read and wrote in Russian and English. Both were fluent in spoken Yiddish. I never saw Pauline read or write Yiddish. While all of you may think there's nothing so unusual about that – it should be remembered that many, many, early immigrants were totally uneducated – not even able to sign their names. There was no such thing as universal education, either in Europe or in America. I even saw people in the bank sign documents – deeds, checks – with an X, simply because they'd never learned how to read or write. So, to say that a person was able to read or write a language – any language – was a compliment. (As a child, I had to show grown men what page we were on, during services in the synagogue, because they couldn't read. They simply memorized the prayers, orally, and mumbled along during services. Mama was always surrounded by many women, who cried, mumbled, and followed along, as she read the Hebrew prayers in the women's section. None of them could read.)

I've written how Mama, when she was in the store, would often be asked to read people's mail and write their replies for them. Since Mollie and I moved to the Forum retirement community here in South Florida, I've been asked to read Yiddish letters by residents on several occasions. Now it's time to get back to the Hirshes. They often conversed in Russian, whether in the kitchen or at Pen Mar Park (a scenic mountain park and

A postcard showing PenMar Park, from the 1940s.

resort area in the mountains near the Pennsylvania Maryland border). They spoke Russian, especially if they wanted to discuss personal matters. Speaking Yiddish at home was typical of most immigrants living in a Jewish neighborhood. Alex was far more literate in all his language skills, probably because of his college studies. He was also proficient in German. He often acted as interpreter and switched easily from one language to another. No problem for him! Mollie knew a few Russian expressions, but predominantly spoke Yiddish or English to their guests in their Glendon Heights Hotel in Pen Mar. Interestingly, my father used to write his postcards and occasional letter every Thursday, to all our family. When I received my weekly postcard, I generally replied as soon as I had a little free time. One afternoon, as I was writing, Mollie asked me to add her regards. "I could only write it in English, and you're writing in Yiddish," she said. "'Would you like to write them in Yiddish?" I replied. "I wish I could," she said. Believe it or not, I wrote out the Yiddish alphabet, transliterated the sounds of the word formations; and, in less than an hour, she was able to *"greese"* (send her regards) to my parents, in Yiddish! You can't believe the pleasure it gave them to see her words, written in clear, legible, Yiddish. They proudly boasted about her prowess for a long time. During our teaching days in Florida, after the influx of the many Hispanic refugees, the School Board initiated regular Spanish lessons into the curriculum. Like most teachers, Mollie learned to use many phrases to communicate with the parents of her Spanish students, who guardedly brought their precious youngsters to school every day, happy to greet their teachers. It played a great role in helping the eager children adjust to their new environment. Both Mollie's and my parents attended night school classes in order to learn the rudimentary early history of the U.S. and to learn enough English to pass the exams required to get their citizenship papers. None of you can possibly understand or appreciate the sacrifice it took for most elderly people to apply themselves to the task of learning a new language, especially since they had to do so after a hard day's work.

My oldest son had a very close friend in high school named Phil Catalano. Both of them strove to reach the top of their class, scholastically, and enjoyed a friendly rivalry. They were the best of friends in high school, and would call each other after school to continue their conversation. To ensure that their parents did not know the subjects of their discussion, they spoke in Spanish, a language in which they were both fluent thanks to public school education in Miami. I can't vouch for Phil's parents, who were fluent in Italian, but it worked for us. Neither Mollie nor I had the faintest idea of what they were talking about. My son went on to take Italian and French while at Harvard, to help him understand the lyrics of Italian and French operas. As a young lawyer in Miami, he represented Iberia Airlines in a big lawsuit and would travel to Spain for depositions and hearings in Spanish. His oldest, our grandson Jeff, is exceptionally fluent in Spanish. It came in very handy, when he worked for the Mayor of Miami during one summer of college. He too attended Harvard. This led to a lengthy association and eventual job as Chief of Staff for the Mayor, and many subsequent successes. He was able to resolve many problems for Spanish-speaking callers and to speak with Spanish groups when called upon, in the absence of a busy Mayor. He, too, went onto Law School and Spanish has come in handy for him. His younger brother, Doug, minored in Spanish in college, and has used it in his career. Doug did surprise me when he requested some information about a Yiddish expression, at the time he was an Executive Producer for a local TV news station. If I remember correctly, I didn't help him much, so I suggested he get an English-Yiddish dictionary. Big help, wasn't I? Only he can finish this.

The biggest surprise of all awaited us when we were invited to attend Gary's graduation from James Madison University. Until you have experienced the birth of your first grandchild you can't believe the joy and rapture that suddenly fills your life. Gary was born in Gainesville where Dolores and Alan lived while Alan was in Medical School at the University of Florida. Our cup truly "ran over" whenever we drove there to visit our enlarged family. Our pleasure watching Gary grow, always happy and lovable, was dimmed when we found he'd been born with hearing loss. Fortunately, his loving parents, determined to overcome this problem, found a wonderful speech teacher and Gary was finally able to overcome so many challenges with his hearing and speech. We carefully followed his school progress, while we secretly worried. We swelled with pride every time he went from elementary to junior and to senior high school- and with good grades, too! When we were invited to attend his graduation from James Madison – which I'd learned was rated as one of the top 100 Academic Schools – our pride knew no bounds. Imagine my surprise when I found out that Gary not only graduated but had also successfully passed RUSSIAN as his foreign language require-ment!. Unless any of you have tried to learn Russian, or German, or Turkish, or Greek, or any of the Slavic languages, you cannot possibly believe how hard these are to learn. Unlike the Romance languages of Italian, Spanish, or French, from which a great part of the English language is derived, the earlier mentioned languages are a prodigious challenge to learn. Yet, in spite of that, Gary chose Russian! Wait! He wasn't finished! He went on to use Russian to fulfill his foreign language requirement while pursuing his Master's degree at George Washington University! Surprised? Why should I be surprised? Could he possibly have any more surprises? Guess what! Gary did get his Master's at GWU. Then, he passed his language requirements in SPANISH!! (He used his Russian during his venture, in 1995, into Ukraine, which I will write about) So, don't be surprised if he can speak Portuguese, after dealing with the Brazilians. And now, after his several visits to China, I wouldn't be a bit surprised if he broke out in Cantonese. Then, Gary went on to marry a woman who taught French!.

Mentioning all of this reminds me of my younger brother, Mike, and his wife, Hannah. When they first met, neither could care less about Jewish customs and practices, which involves the use of Hebrew – the ancient and revered language studied by millions of people throughout the world, both Jewish and Christian. I witnessed their change from total non-believers to ardent, practicing and involved members of Synagogues and eventual emigration to Israel. Yet, that alone was not the ultimate joy of their lives. They told me that their greatest pride came when their older granddaughter announced her intention to come to Israel to study for her master's degree, after getting her undergraduate degree from Brandeis University. "Yes!" they told me, "Dee planned to study for her degree IN HEBREW!!!" To them, that epitomized pride. The story of Dee (our lovely niece who brought her beautiful family from Israel to visit with us this past July) and her progress in Israel became a part of Hannah's fabulous almost-poetic descriptive letters of their life in Israel. Hannah's beautiful American-born granddaughter was so proficient and fluid in Hebrew – the same old foreign language that was still being used as a means of oral and written communication, today – that she was earning extra, unexpected *shekels* (Israel's currency) as translator for some of her professors! Think of that! A professor is so impressed with your skills, in both Hebrew and English, that he offers you money to translate material from Hebrew to English or visa-versa! Is that an honor or what?

I must also include Wally and Bobby Hirsh in this, our nephews and sons of Mollie's brother, Herman. Both of them were pioneers in becoming American professional players of the Spanish-originating game of Jai Alai. Long, long before South Florida became a mecca for the many current popular sports, Jai Alai was a very important source of entertainment for both tourists and residents. Mollie and I joined our friends quite often to watch these excitable Spanish professionals play this fast-paced sport. Imagine our surprise when our nephew Wally announced that he was going to play Jai Alai, as a professional. Bobby quickly followed his older brother. It doesn't take an Einstein to understand that – if they were going to play a game with Spanish-speaking players on a daily basis – they'd have to learn to speak Spanish, too. There is no doubt that speaking everyday Spanish affected their lives.

I can't possibly omit my parents' ability to speak, read, and write foreign languages. You must understand that, unlike urban-dwelling people, most residents of typical "shtetls" like Lyubar, where we lived were unlikely to be literate on any level. How come? In most cases, boys' going to *cheder* (religious schools), so they learn to participate in the required daily prayers was the prime motivator for learning. By far, the struggle to make a living was so great that few families could even afford the small cost of schooling. Remember, too, many parents were also illiterate. So, at the urging of the local Rabbi, most boys were sent to the cheder at the age of three or four, to see if by chance they had a bent to learn. The highest honor a parent – from the richest to the poorest in town – was to be able to brag that their son had become a learned man!

The emphasis, however, was that the achievement was to be in the field of religion. While Papa agreed with those goals he also knew that the sectarian world outside of Lyubar required the ability to speak, read, and write Russian. Since, at the time, he could afford to send his children to the Gymnazium, he saw that each one of us studied and prepared ourselves. (All of his children passed the exams. For Mayer and me, World War I intervened.) This is the place in my attempt to recall when I become so mentally frustrated, desperate, and annoyed with myself. Why? Why did I wait so long? Why didn't I ask somebody? There were so many people around me who could have filled in the gaps in my memory. Imagine how much help either of my parents could have been to me, if only I'd asked! How about Chaika, my bright, older – by ten years – sister? Couldn't she, wouldn't she have had answers to my many questions? Willie? Even Mike, who was so much more gregarious than I? Mike, who visited our relatives much more often than I. And, as smart as he was, could surely have known things that would fill in the gaps. All I had to do was ask. Why did I wait till I joined the Writers' Workshop to start to tell you about our family history???? There's nobody left to ask, only my memories.

Maybe there is a moral in all this. Maybe I can arouse some of you to start a diary, if you haven't already done so. If your reaction to my stories is any indication of how descendants treasure the details of family history, think of what your recollections and experiences could mean to YOUR children, Grandchildren, and GREAT-children!!! For YOU, it's not too late. Especially now, with all the innovative means of recording the current technology offers you. DO IT! You can't possibly leave them with a better legacy. Listen to one who knows! DO IT! NOW!

Interestingly enough, today, August 24, 2007, I received a copy of a newspaper article describing a trio of musicians, calling themselves the North End Trio, picturing and naming flutist my son, Alan Bartel, as a member. On Thursday last, I spent a wonderful Thanksgiving Day at my grandson Doug's home, together with our local family members. Doug had saved a newspaper article for me, which pictured two of my great-grandchildren (Doug's two youngest girls, Jordan and Brooke), while they were out selecting a pumpkin for Halloween. There are two perfect examples of family history – fun and cherishable – that all descendants of the Bartel Family will love in days to come. I'll certainly add these to my treasury of memories.

Finally, I can get back to my parents. Although they both declared their place of birth as Lyubar, on the false passport we carried on our way to the U.S., I'm inclined to think that neither one was born there. Why not? Common sense. Only my maternal Grandmother is buried there. Upon reflection, maybe my argument may not be valid. I should have said we (children) were not allowed to go to a cemetery. Many practices that were prohibited had been established out of silly superstitions that were followed for so long that they eventually became "sins" or "laws." My parents – Mama, especially – were not any different. In spite of her sophisticated educational background, she followed and enforced many of these prohibitions religiously. And, they applied to grownups as well as to children. Thus, my arguments must be based on more reliable logic. In Lyubar, Mama was known as "Pessel, Mayer Odessar's." Translation: "Pessel (Bessie), the daughter of Mayer, who lived or came from Odessa." My maternal grandfather was revered as a distinguished and learned man, one of the most desirable honors a man could attain. All four of his children (Mama had two sisters and one brother) were not only literate but also well educated. It was a matter of great pride that townspeople came to her to read and write letters. Her space in the synagogue was always surrounded by crowds of women, who followed her voice as she recited the prayers in Hebrew. Her help and kindnesses to the illiterate peasants was appreciated so much that they – at great potential harm to themselves, if caught – hid our family during the pogroms. There was no place in Lyubar where she could have attended to become literate in Russian, Ukrainian, Yiddish, and Hebrew. How could she have been born in Lyubar and acquired this background? It seems logical to say that she and her siblings must have spent their youth in some large city that offered them such opportunities. Being "Pessel, Mayer Odessar's," Odessa springs to mind as probably the city of her origin. In any case, being the daughter of a highly recognized, learned, and wise man, how she attained her background and education is not surprising.

What has always been mysterious and surprising to me, however, is how Papa came to be so well versed and knowledgeable. Again, how could he possibly have been born in Lyubar? Unfortunately, these questions never seemed to be so important to me, in my youth, that I'd have the nerve to raise such a question. I was always too timid to try to pry in my parents' personal and early history. Still, I often wondered. I knew that Papa was only 13 years old when his father died and he was forced to go to work to help support his widowed mother and siblings. I also knew that one of his brothers was older then he, and, that all of them lived in Kiev – the large city that was so far away from Lyubar – in a small child's mind – that we never went to see them. I can only remember seeing my uncle, Papa's older brother, visit us a couple of times. He was taller and heavier than Papa, and always brought us kids the absolutely, most delicious, and beautifully wrapped, chocolate candy bars. (Since I cannot remember candy being available in Lyubar, those long-lasting, delicious, surprises are still vivid in my memory.) So, based on what little I knew of Papa's early life, I can only conclude that he probably got his early education in Kiev; was either a traveling salesman or otherwise involved in some kind of trade or some form of merchandising; and, thus, acquired some fluency in other languages. I should mention that Papa often went to Poland, where he acquired his Polish fluency.

Back in Lyubar, Papa was addressed as "Reb Gdalia," an honorary title, in respectful recognition of his linguistic accomplishments. Naturally, I'm proud. And, from him, I learned. It took me long enough, didn't it? I'm finally up to how I utilized foreign languages. But, again, I must remind you that I was never a "great" scholar. School and learning came easily to me. One might even say that I learned in spite of my minimal effort. Believe it or not, I had a great ear for sounds and could repeat songs or sayings after just hearing them once. Any wonder why I get so frustrated, now? I was told that the first words I spoke/babbled were Ukrainian (because I was nursed by a peasant woman shortly after I was born?) Funny, I don't remember any of that part. Naturally, Yiddish was the first language we spoke at home. Like most children I didn't learn to read or write until I started Cheder at age three. There we learned how to read and write Hebrew, the language in our prayer books.

Papa could afford to buy us notebooks, so we soon began to write our homework assignments and practice writing at home. Writing and reading Yiddish I must have acquired at home. Papa always had a Yiddish paper in the house and wrote his letters there, too. To gain admission to the Gymnasia I had to pass an exam. I did. During the first year I had to choose a foreign language. For some reason I chose German. The original German alphabet had several letters that were different from the Cyrillic Russian. Maybe I was a "quick study" for I had no difficulty learning and reading German. Unfortunately, WWI intervened; and, I never returned for my second year. I had no occasion to use that language again. I soon forgot what little I'd learned. When Chaika came home from Odessa University, she had a constant flow of friends. They sometimes lapsed into French – aping the aristocrats of Russia, who used French, to differentiate themselves from the riff-raff. By listening to them I learned the Marseillaise and a few common expressions. They came in handy when we came to Canada. By then I had learned how to read and write Russian, Yiddish, and Hebrew. In addition, I could speak Polish (street talk), which I'd acquired in the nine months we'd spent there after leaving Lyubar, but had no occasion to read or write it.

The French I acquired while at school in Montreal was to serve as the basic reason why I continued to study French in the United States. The third-floor cold-water, walk-up flat over the stable – that we rented in Montreal – was part of an old building that had been converted into a warren of dark, sparsely furnished cubicles that catered to the poorest of the poor. Naturally, its main occupants were the latest immigrants, who struggled to make the few dollars monthly rent. Our neighbors' children became our playmates. In the course of time we were exposed to languages, words, expressions, and pronunciations that, if anything, made our attempts to adapt to our new surroundings more difficult. Still, we learned from each other. Because we were all so poor, we improvised ways to play games. One of the first things I learned was how to barter.

Although as a group we represented different European back-grounds, we all found English a very daunting challenge. However, most of us enjoyed the multi-colored "Funny Papers" (comics) that appeared on Sundays. The antics of the famous and popular characters portrayed (*Mutt and Jeff, Barney Google, The Katzenjammer Kids* and many others, were funny – even if you struggled to read the words in the balloons above). Problem: How can we get the Funnies when we have no money? Solution? Easy! Wait till the people finish with their Sunday paper and throw it in the garbage piles in the big yard down below. The Challenge? See who could find the most funnies. By Monday morning those of us who had found (and laughed at) any funnies were ready to barter our find with whatever was available: a different set of funnies, a ball, a marble, a half-broken toy, or anything that no longer interested you.

One day a boy came down with his pockets bulging with his hoard of treasure. As the offerings and haggling began he reached into one of his pockets and came out with a fistful of multi-colored scraps of paper. My eyes must have bulged with curiosity. Although I had seen a few stamps on the letters Papa received or sent, I had never seen so many different ones so closely. I was immediately attracted to the variety of beautiful, colorful stamps from so many different places, most of which I'd never even heard of. I had discovered a new love! No matter what it took, I was determined to get some of these attractive, interesting stamps. Yes, the funnies I'd salvaged from the depths of garbage piles would be the source of my new and sudden desire to start the collection of stamps. What irony! Talk about contrasts. From the dirt, stink, and filth I went to a hobby that requires using gloves, tweezers, special envelopes, and books, to preserve and handle the delicate stamps that flow from all corners of the globe. I can't touch a stamp with my bare hand or I'll damage its value. The pleasure of admiring their beauty and variety of shape and design was well worth the many hours I spent handling them. Unfortunately, the greatest deterrent to my accumulating a truly valuable collection was one I couldn't control. I soon found out that only the rich could afford to be a collector of stamps or any other item of material value. Still, I was determined to pursue this hobby as much as I could. Which leads to the tale of a couple of interesting events.

By the time we brought Chaika and Muni to join us in Montreal we must have moved to a larger, nicer place to live. I believe that, at first – before their daughter Rosie was born – Chaika and Muni lived with us. At any rate, Muni played a close part in our lives, as I remember. During the summer of 1922, after we'd finished our first year of school, we found out that Montreal not only has cold winters, but also has a long, boring and HOT summer. One morning Muni heard us – Mayer and me – complaining about the heat. Calling us over to him, he took out his "buytel" (coin purse); extracted two nickels; gave one to each of us; told us to wait awhile; then, go to the confectionery store across the street; buy a bottle of soda and walk over to Mount Royal Park. "There," he said, "lay down on a shady grass spot. You'll find it's much cooler, then." What wonderful advice, and with a whole nickel, each, too! We couldn't wait to follow his suggestions. "What flavor are you going to get?" Mayer asked,

The vista in Mount Royal Park, in Montreal.

as we started to cross the street. "Sarsaparilla!" I yelled back. "Me, too!" He agreed. When we rushed into the store, the elderly owner was busy, trying to sell an old lady a paper fan. "Aren't they pretty?" "They're two cents each, or three for a nickel; and they work well, too," he added, as he waved one in front of her face. Suddenly Mayer, always the entrepreneur, nudged me in the arm and motioned me away from the two old people. "I've got a great idea," he whispered. "Why don't we share one bottle between us and buy four fans with the rest of the money. We can take them to Mount Royal and sell them for a nickel apiece!" Calculating quickly that if we did as he suggested, we'd end up with 10 cents, each, I grudgingly agreed.

We shared our drink in front of the proprietor (otherwise, we'd have to leave a penny for deposit, for the return of the bottle) and selected four colorful fans. Armed with two fans apiece, we quickly ran and walked to the huge, beautiful Mount Royal Park. As soon as we got to the park, Mayer took charge. "See that big shady tree?" he asked, as he pointed to one about a half-block from the entrance. "As soon as I sell my fans, I'll come back there and wait for you. If you sell yours first, you wait there for me. O.K.?" I agreed. We discussed our spiel to our expected buyers and separated. He took the right side; I, the left. It was an easier job than I'd feared. Although I was a little hesitant in my approach to the people trying to find some comfort – away from the hot streets of the city – I, somehow, was able to sell both of my fans for the 5-cent price we'd agreed on. Sure enough, when I breathlessly rushed to the designated meeting place, there was Mayer, sitting with a great big smile on his face. With triumphant grins on our faces, we made our way back to the confectionary store, to restock our supplies. We were in business. Not surprisingly, we both invested our entire fortune of a dime in buying more fans. And, not surprisingly, again, Mayer was able to bargain with the store owner and we each ended up with seven – count them – fans for our dime. In a quick mental calculation I visualized the unbelievable hoard of money I'd end up with – if I could sell all seven fans! Imagine! I'd have 35 cents of my own! Can you picture the look on Mama's face? On Papa's? He'd want to know where and how I'd gotten so much money. What was I going to tell them? How much of the truth? Just as I was getting ready to rehearse my speech, a nudge from Mayer woke me up. He quickly reminded me that we still had a job. We had fans to sell. Disappointment, worry, and unbelievable joy awaited me. Exultant over our good luck this morning and fantasizing of the upcoming exploits, we anxiously wended our way to the now-familiar park. As I gazed around "my territory" I realized that many more people had decided to use its cooler areas. Perfect, I thought. It should be a cinch, now, to sell all my fans. I'd better get started. Then, the bad news hit me. Several people already had fans! The nerve! How could they? Suddenly I was not so sure of myself. Had I lost my touch?

It took what seemed like a long time before I made my first sale. The next appeared to take even longer. I wondered what time it was. As I looked around for a possible person to ask, I noticed a Chinese gentleman seated on a shaded bench. Unlike the many Chinese I'd seen in Montreal, he wore a beautiful pressed suit and tie. Even his shoes were highly polished. He was sure to have a watch. Sliding over slowly towards him, I excused myself and asked if he could tell me the time. He looked at his watch and, in excellent English, told me what "the correct local time" is.

I was so intrigued at his command of the language I was struggling with that I wasn't aware he had asked me a question. Raising his voice slightly, he said, "I wondered what you were doing with those fans?"

as he pointed to my hand. I could feel myself blushing – which I did constantly when I did something wrong or embarrassing – as I excused myself for not listening and told him I was trying to sell them. In short, he ended up buying all five of my remaining fans! I could not believe my luck! Instead of worrying about my stock, I was now richer by 35 cents! Elated by my sudden good luck I hardly heard his continuing questions.

He noted that I spoke with a strange accent. Where was I from? When did I come to Canada? Did I come alone or with my family? I ended up sitting on the bench with him. In spite of my horrible accent and lack of understanding of his fluent English, we managed. He was on a diplomatic mission for his (Chinese) government and was going to visit many places around the world. When he learned that I was interested in foreign stamps he promised to send me some stamps during his travels. He wrote down my name and address and I hurriedly went to meet Mayer.

My new Chinese friend was as good as his word. Within a month I received a letter with a note, identifying the new, breathtakingly beautiful stamps. I don't recall any particular country, but only remember my sheer joy at receiving them. From then on my interest in geography grew immensely. He sent me several more letters before we left Canada. When we came to Baltimore, I was so busy adjusting to my new surroundings that – when I didn't get any more letters from him – I figured he'd gotten tired and decided to stop. More than six years later, in the summer of 1929, when I hitch-hiked to Montreal, a surprised Chaika told me she had received a number of letters addressed to me but threw them away – because they looked strange and were from different places. What would a little boy want with mail from such strange places? Besides, she was a young mother of two little girls whom she was trying to raise at a time of great suffering and struggle. She had her own problems without worrying about her little brother's strange letters. You can imagine my chagrin. In the excitement of my leaving Montreal, I'd forgotten to tell her about my new hobby. Who knows what treasures might have been lost? Anyway, the past cannot be changed. What's done is done.

I was a guest – a very welcome guest – and became too busy enjoying my adventure to worry about stamps. Their sincere pleasure at my visit and enthusiastic efforts to entertain me soon overshadowed any ill feelings I had. The week passed quickly and my thoughts reverted to planning my return hike to Baltimore and the new problems facing me upon my return. In a couple of weeks I was due to start my biggest challenge yet – enrolling at Maryland State Normal School and preparing myself to become a teacher. One of the great advantages of hitch-hiking is that the long empty days give your mind plenty of opportunities to rehash the plusses and minuses of your latest adventure. On the whole, I decided, my visit to Chaika and Muni and their two delightful little girls was a definite plus. Still, I couldn't help but recall how terrible I'd felt when Chaika told me of my missed letters from the Chinese diplomat. Worrywart that I was, I couldn't put it out of my mind. In my serious attempt to try to forget about it, I reminded myself that I had a hidden treasure of stamps at home. Gee! To think I'd forgotten all about that! I'll have to check it. In 1928 Papa bought our first home at 2790 West North Avenue, an old house that had been repossessed by the Building and Loan Association in which Papa had a savings account. In spite of the fact that the house was old, it was in excellent but neglected condition.

When we took possession, we found that the former occupants had left it dirty and full of junk. Our first job was to go through the place from top to bottom; to save what might be useful and throw out all the rest. Mike and I (by now, we had Americanized our names to Mike and Ralph) joined Mama in the full, big, dry basement. Whoever had lived there had been a '"collector." It seemed like every inch of the dry and spacious basement was filled with worthless or broken objects. Talk about a mess! It took several days of hard work before we finally were finished clearing all the accumulated boxes, barrels, and baskets of waste. But, sure enough, when you go through a dirty job like that, you're bound to find some things that might be used again. We did. Dozens of dust-covered Mason jars, of various sizes, proved to be useful. All they needed was to wipe the accumulated dust off and they were good as new. A couple of barrels, full of broken torn or broken objects, turned out to be useful for Papa to use, when he pickled his cucumbers into the delicious pickles.

Among the unexpected treasures, I discovered an old, ordinary notebook – not unlike the ones I'd used in school. Curious, I opened the cover and discovered a hidden treasure! Every page was filled with hinged Confederate States stamps, issued during THE CIVIL WAR OF THE 1850s! Mind you. I had no idea of the value of those stamps. But, even so, I knew that they represented a short time in the history of the U. S., and, therefore, might be worth something because of their scarcity.

I'd check this out later. We have important work to do now.

To make sure I'd get back to it, I put the notebook on one of the higher shelves, along with the Mason jars, and promptly forgot about it! Cleaning up the basement was our top priority. It wasn't until I was on my way back from Montreal that I remembered when and where I'd put it. My first job, I told myself, would be to find it again. In spite of my travails in getting home safely, I remembered to go downstairs and check my forgotten treasure. Talk about surprises. Talk about disappointments. Talk about chagrin! Try as I might, searching for what seemed like hours, I couldn't find the missing notebook! I felt I was going to pass out from sheer despair. How could this terrible thing happen to me? After the tragedy of losing all the stamps that Chaika had thrown out, now I can't find my Confederate stamps! With sweat pouring down my face from the long search in the hot, muggy basement, I ran up the stairs and confronted Mama. "What happened to my notebook that I left on the shelf with the Mason jars?" I hollered.

Mama, who had just returned from her two-week vacation at "The Hot Springs," looked at me as if I were crazy. She hadn't the faintest idea of what I was screaming about. It took a long time before I could explain to her about my lost "treasure." It took even longer for her to explain that she knew nothing about its disappearance. It finally dawned on me that Mama – in her desire to clean up the mess in the basement – must have seen the old, dirty notebook stuck among the Mason jars and promptly added it to the trash that we were removing. NOBODY NOTICED and NOBODY KNEW! If anyone was to blame, it was yours truly.

I never thought it important enough to tell anyone about my find. Blame me. As my beloved old stories that helped me learn to read might have put it: "The moral of this story is – if you discover what you think is a treasure, let someone know. It might help preserve it." Let that be a lesson to you. Some people claim that one can profit from a loss by finding something positive in all losses. I can't argue or defend that. I can only tell you that these two "tragedies" in my plans to build a stamp collection made me even more determined that, someday – when I became rich enough to afford it – I was going to start my collection again. And this time, I'd be careful. I'd make sure that someone knew about it.

I did come back to it. And, even if I didn't accumulate a "treasure," I enjoyed doing it. If you're still with me, I'm sure some of you are asking yourselves, "How do all these sidebars of adventures fit in with the title of this story?" The answers are of course, "nothing" and "everything."

If you'll take a moment and look at the title on page one, you'll find it's called "HANDY FOREIGN LANGUAGE." That was my real intention – to show how a foreign language can come in handy in one's life. Honestly! After sending you a long, serious, philosophical, and fearful dissertation on the dire outlook of the financial world, to me and to your future, I decided to lighten up a little. In my long life I have experienced a number of ups and downs. And, I have learned that no matter how miserable life is, sometimes; somehow, most people find the strength to overcome these miserable times, and, somehow, too, most people find a way to rise up and succeed again. Pick your own explanation for these "somehows."

As for my HANDY FOREIGN LANGUAGE theme – it's true. Even though I never tried to be an expert in any language, the bits and pieces of the various foreign languages that I accumulated during my lifetime often came in very HANDY. Especially after Mollie and I started to travel seriously. True or not, it was fun. I hope you, too, find it was fun to read this "not-so-important" tale.

Be well and enjoy.

Love, Ralphy
(just in time to wish you all a very enjoyable celebration
of the Holiday Season)
December 1, 2007

HERMAN HIRSH

Note: This story and a few others references PenMar (PenMar park). This area of Washington County, Maryland near the Pennsylvania-Maryland border opened in the late 1800s as an amusement park and resort area. The mountain area was a popular summer place with parks, hotels, a roller coaster and carousel, plus a dining and dancing place. It closed in the 1940s, then reopened as a county park in the 1980s with simply pavilions and basic park facilities.

Herman Hirsh, born in 1913 and two years younger than Mollie, was a typical youngster growing up in a first generation American home. Like his mother Pauline, Herman's ready smile and cheerful, happy-go-lucky demeanor were traits that would last him a lifetime. He made it easy for everyone to like him. He early portrayed his bent towards physical and mechanical skills. Even as a little boy his neighbors on East Baltimore Street would call on him to fix a problem with the electricity, furniture, or plumbing. When not in school, he could be found at the ballpark. He loved baseball and softball best, although he enjoyed all sports. Their family moved so often that Herman had little opportunity to make any long lasting friends. Because of his interest in mechanics, he attended Baltimore Polytechnic High School, the most prestigious school for boys ambitious to study engineering or science. In spite of his parents' involvement in PenMar (he always had to leave school before the term ended because his help was needed at the hotel there), he finished high school successfully, as well as two years in the Johns Hopkins School of Engineering. However, again because of the family business at PenMar, he never finished college.

Herman hated the Glendon Heights Hotel business with a passion. Although he loved to fix any problems related to the building, he despised working as a waiter and gave his parents – especially his mother – daily fits. After the bell rang for breakfast, Herman would wait till the very last second before he'd rush down the steps and be ready to work. Mollie or Mom Hirsh (as I called her) would stand at the foot of the stairs and call him, repeatedly, to come down – all in vain. Sometimes it seemed as if he did it deliberately, to provoke. But it was just his way of showing his dislike for the job. Once he came into the dining room, he was a most competent worker. I worked there too, helping my wife's family. Between the two of us, we could serve an entire dining room full of people, smoothly and efficiently. In all the years we worked together, we never argued about his part of the work. He just plain hated waiting on tables and while he felt obligated to help his folks, Herman found every means possible to delay doing it as long as possible. Just as soon as he finished serving and set the tables for the next meal, he'd generally disappear, without explanation, only to return again, wearing his cheerful smile, when it was time to serve. All the guests liked him and his service (though never enough to tip him) for, after all, he was the son of the owners.

Most of our guests came from Baltimore or Washington. We got to know them quite well, even making lifetime friends. It was a family style of operation, where everyone soon felt at home. One year a man who'd watched Herman at work told Herman that he'd help him get training for a manager's job with the Kay Bee chain of men's clothing stores. "Call me, after the season's over," he said. The prospect of getting away from the drudgery of PenMar and its hopeless future for him, while being independent, found a willing young man. Herman begged his parents to let him go. They realized that this was an opportunity for him and reluctantly allowed him to follow through.

In the fall of 1932 Herman went to Johnstown, Pennsylvania, the historic town of the Johnstown Flood. Following training, they sent him to Durham, North Carolina to manage the Kay Bee store. He made friends easily and wrote glowing letters of his new life. Although he'd been away from any form of athletics for years, he soon joined an amateur softball group on Sundays. He rekindled his exceptional skill as a very strong softball pitcher very quickly. Before long, he joined a semi-pro team and became their star pitcher, earning $15, some Sundays – quite an excellent extra income in those days.

During the years he was away, Herman seemed content to just stay in Durham and showed no desire or intent of going anywhere else or do anything else. Between his job at the store, his friends, and the weekly softball games, he had no complaints or ever expressed any need for change, or to come back to Baltimore.

The outbreak of World War II changed many people's lives. Herman knew he'd be called to serve his country before long. When his call came, he returned to see us and decided – with the shortage of cars because of the war – he'd best leave his 1937 Chevrolet with us, till he returned. We could use it, meanwhile, if we wished. None of us could foretell how handy that would be.

The Armed Forces got it right and assigned Herman to do what was best for him and the country. He was sent to the Navy and made a part of the Sea Bees, the unit assigned to solve the engineering problems on the islands of the Pacific. He worked to rebuild roads and airport facilities damaged by Japanese air raids, temporary and permanent bridges over rivers, new airstrips needed by the military, and help move men and equipment where needed. Although he must have seen many new and exotic places during the time, he never wanted to talk about his years of service. When the War finally ended and he received his honorable discharge, we were already living in Florida, on Miami Beach. Herman joined us in 1946 at the Sinclair Hotel (which I had leased to operate and earn extra income).

Among the souvenirs he brought back was a miserable case of malaria. Although he said it was in remission and of minor intensity, its occasional return attacks were frightening. He'd forewarned us and we watched, helplessly, as he struggled during its seizures, which – fortunately – were of short duration. As he'd told us, they went away. . . eventually.

During his stay with us at the hotel, we insisted he just relax and enjoy the beach and climate. Herman, despite his outward cheerful attitude, seemed unsure of himself and undecided as to his future plans. By early May, I'd sold the remaining three-year lease on the Sinclair Hotel, effective in the fall, bought a home in Miami. Our older son stayed with me to finish school, while Mollie and Alan went to Atlantic City to get ready for the summer. Meanwhile, Herman continued his rest and recuperation.

Despite all our best efforts, there were few people who stayed at the Sinclair. Oceanfront hotels offered rooms at as little as $12 or $15 a week, just to keep their places open. We sat around daily with nothing to do. My father insisted that he could take care of the place until we came back and urged us to go on to Atlantic City. I arranged for a tenant, who was paid up for the entire summer, to keep an eye on my folks; and, on the day school ended, the rest of us (my mother, Herman and our oldest son) took off for Atlantic City. We didn't let Mollie know, just in case we were delayed. This turned out to be one of my most harrowing experiences.

We left in the late afternoon. Herman and I planned to take turns driving. Since I had driven this route before and knew the best roads to take, I drove till we'd get out of the congested traffic in South Florida. (In 1946 there were no express or divided highways in Florida.) It took a couple of hours before we passed through Palm Beach County on U.S. 1, the only road that led north. Every tiny little town along the way had at least one traffic light. I noticed that Herman had become very quiet. One glance confirmed my worst fears. A malaria attack! I pulled into the first gasoline station to find the nearest doctor or hospital, only to be told that Ft. Pierce was the closest place that had a clinic. The next hour seemed to last forever. By the time we got to Fort Pierce, Herman had recovered enough to tell us that we shouldn't bother. The person in charge at Fort Pierce told me they weren't equipped for malaria and suggested we put Herman on the train, due shortly, to get him to Philadelphia, which had a veteran's hospital and could probably help him. Ignoring Herman's protest, I drove to the nearby railroad station. I bought a ticket and explained the situation to the conductor, who promised to watch out for him. As soon as the train pulled out, I told Mom that I planned to drive straight through to Atlantic City, without stopping, just in case Herman decided to call Mollie and get her worried.

There were only two "better" ways to drive north in those days. One was to follow U.S. 1, the other way led along the east coast towns (U.S. 17 and 17A) and led toward Cape Charles, Virginia, which had a ferry across the Chesapeake Bay to Delaware and New Jersey. Although both ways were only two lanes and had stoplights in every town, U.S. 17 offered the fastest direct route if you could make the right connections. Since I planned to drive without stopping, I figured to encounter the least traffic during the night. By the time we stopped for dinner at a Howard Johnson's restaurant in Jacksonville, it was quite dark. Driving at night on a narrow two-way unlighted highway is not a pleasant way to travel. Even on a clear night, without rain, the only light on the thin road comes from your own headlights. The "shoulders" on each side of the road consisted of a gravel strip some 10 inches wide, that easily scattered when disturbed by a wheel going off the macadam road. A driver needed all his wits about him, just to stay on his side. If one grew sleepy or tired or was drunk, it was easy to lose control. So, in spite of being distraught over Herman and mentally and physically exhausted, I had to concentrate on driving on a predominantly deserted "highway." When the distant lights of an approaching car or truck gave warning of possible danger, every effort went to make sure I looked only at the road in front of me and stayed on my side, gripping the wheel as hard as possible (no power of any kind, then), away from the coming vehicle. The sudden whoosh of the wind as we passed made our light car sway and often left a spray of dust in my face. It was never relaxing. The monotony of the endless drive in pitch-black darkness was finally relieved by the sight of the huge rainbow of lights that formed the arc of the bridge over the Savannah River.

After paying the toll, I faced the huge span rising precipitously over the large body of water. A sudden feeling seized me – that the top of the rise was open, and that all of us could die from the drop into the water from the top. I was afraid to move and just sat there! As if in a dream I became aware of the man in the toll booth shouting at me to go on. The continuous blare of a horn in the car behind me finally aroused me from my fears and I put the car in low gear and crept slowly up the seemingly unending high rise to the top. It was only when the car started to level off and I saw the lane continuing ahead that I changed gears and increased my speed. Whatever the cause of my phobia, it disappeared when we reached level road again. In fact, I seemed to get my "second wind." All my anxieties were swept away by my determination to get to the Cape Charles Ferry. The rest of our journey became same monotonous trek through dark towns, an occasional stoplight, and the meeting of oncoming cars or trucks. It was well past midnight when we pulled on to the dock and got in the long line stretching to board the waiting ship. The slow movement of the vehicles ahead of me only awakened the reality of my exhaustion. We had left Miami Beach some ten miserable hours ago, with hardly any rest.

With great anticipation I waited my turn to park the car on the ship and stretch my legs, before I found a place to rest. From the lights on the dock I could see how each car and truck was waved into the two lanes on each side of the ship. Slowly but surely we were drawing closer. We were only about ten vehicles away from going aboard when I saw an officer on board wave to the two seamen who served as guides to the drivers. Only five cars ahead of us; only three; only. . . suddenly, the movement stopped. They had dropped the guard rails on the ship; the ship's whistle shrilled a loud warning, and it began to move away from the dock. Wearily, I got out and stretched my aching bones. Now I knew how it felt to be completely exhausted! Every bone in my body seemed to hurt. Still, I had to find out where the next ferry was and how soon it was expected. Quickly and painfully I wended my way to the booth near the water. The old attendant opened the door as I approached. "When does the next ferry leave?" I asked. "At six o'clock in the morning," he replied. My questions and protestations fell on deaf ears. Nothing was going to change their regular schedule. After talking to the fellow in the car ahead of me, who quietly assured me this had happened to him before, I concluded that we'd just have to make the best of it. The pre-war cars were not built anywhere near the comfort of our modern vehicles. Herman's 1937 Chevy had little room for a driver. The seats were not padded. There were no power steering, windows, brakes, or transmissions. Cars were built strictly for utilitarian purposes, as means of going from one place to another. The more time one spent in a car, the more uncomfortable one felt. So, unless one was used to hard, crowded, uncomfortable surfaces, sleep was out of the question – except for the very young or older people.

Yet, somehow, I napped on and off till the noise of newly arrived autos woke me about 5 a.m. The three of us made use of the restroom and washed our hands and faces before boarding the ferry. The long voyage across the Chesapeake Bay to the northern landing was broken up by having a good breakfast in the ship's lounge. Because of our place in line during the night wait we were the second car off the boat. The rest of the trip was uneventful and, less than 24 hours after leaving Miami Beach, Florida, we pulled into the spacious lot of our guest house in Atlantic City, New Jersey. Mom and I had discussed what would be the best way to tell Mollie about what had happened to Herman. Prepared with all the details we trudged wearily up the steps, only to be greeted by a smiling Herman at the door. Amid the excitement, confusion, and greetings of a not-surprised Mollie and Alan, we learned that Herman had felt so much better by the time his train got to Philadelphia that he just took the next train to Atlantic City and walked in on them before noon. He explained what happened and they just waited for our arrival. All our anxieties and concerns about him had been for nothing! My determination to drive straight through was entirely unnecessary. He was fine!

Nothing cures aches and pains and anxieties caused by a long drive than a couple of days of comfortable rest and being together with a loving family. We decided that our next project was to find something for Herman to do. The long summer facing us could be terribly boring for a "healthy" – he said – young man in a strange place, with no friends or work. Looking through the classified section of the local paper, I saw an ad for a "House for rent on Atlantic Avenue, for the summer." After telling Herman of our experience in 1944, with the Murphy sub-lease, I offered to rent it if he was willing to operate it. He agreed. The place, the second floor of a row house about a mile closer to downtown, only had five rentable rooms, sparsely furnished but adequate for summer tourists, and seemed made to order for Herman. It would give him something to do and was not a big investment for us, the new-rich business entrepreneurs from Florida.

Every morning, after breakfast, Herman went the short distance to the Atlantic Avenue house and waited for possible tourists or guests. We put an ad in the local and Philadelphia papers while he waited for inquiries. To sum up, it was a flop. He rented one room to a working couple for the summer and had an occasional weekly or shorter guest. The income didn't cover the entire cost of the rent. It, however, did give Herman something to do. Late in the afternoon, when I came to relieve him so he could go to our place for his supper, I'd find him poring over the daily "Racing Form," trying to decide what horses to bet with the bookie in a store across the street. That seemed to be his sole means of recreation and occupation. We gave the place up after Labor Day. When we returned to Florida, to our new house on S.W. 16th Street in Miami, Herman came, too. Herman still did not have any plans. He didn't know anyone in Miami other than Joe and Mary Weinstein, who'd bought a home not far from us at the same time we did. We didn't know anyone else in the area, either. In addition to teaching during the school year, I always had other jobs or investments, a necessity to try and make ends meet.

Herman had no idea of the kind of work he wanted to do. I had noticed a fellow came around in an open truck and sold vegetables and fruit from it to our neighbors. I told Herman I'd be glad to get him an old truck if he'd like to try his hand at it. He did and, for awhile, was able to make a few dollars a day, peddling fruits and vegetables. Although none of us liked his work, he stuck to it, because it made him feel somewhat independent and productive.

Meanwhile, I had become a real estate salesman at Harold Winchell's office on Flagler Street. After a year, I was told, I could qualify for a broker's license. With the profits I'd made when I sold the lease of the Sinclair Hotel and its operation in 1945-46, I became Joe Weinstein's partner; and, together, bought three lots on Flagler Street near S.W. 27th Avenue which were all zoned for business. We planned to put a building on it and erected a big sign, offering to "build to suit or lease" it. Herman was still living with us and as a diversion, built a beautiful addition to our house. It was the entire width of the little building and included a 24'x9' screened back porch, a half bath and shower, and a closet with the plumbing hookups for future conversion into a kitchen. Our neighbor Joe Weinstein, seeing Herman's worth, and learning of his background and experience, suggested Herman get a contractor's license. With him as a builder, me as a real estate broker and Joe as the money man, we'd form a team and develop vacant lots. When my year as a salesman passed I took the exam and got my broker's license. Herman took the courses needed and got his contractor's license. We were ready to become developers.

Since we couldn't get anyone interested in leasing our land on Flagler, Joe suggested we put a small building on one of our lots, for my real estate office. In 1947, the Ralph Realty Company opened its doors, a lonely little building, one of the first built by Herman. It was located in the 2600 block of Flagler Street. Actually, this was not the only building Herman had started to build. When we decided to go into the construction business, I'd asked Herman to draw up plans for the best possible use of a 50-foot lot, with the most usable or rentable space, at our lowest cost, on a lot zoned for business. He came up with a plan to build three 15 plus-foot stores on the ground floor, with three apartments above. It was a simple but excellent use of space and we all liked it very much. (Zoning restrictions were very liberal then and we could build on the entire area without worrying about green space, parking, etc., which are required now.) Joe, our money partner, liked it so much that he insisted we stop work on my office and use this plan on a 50-foot lot I had acquired in the 3600 block of West Flagler Street, also zoned for business. Herman went right to work on that and built this little building at the same time he worked on my office. While it was being built, we had an offer to sell it – at a profit – which Joe eagerly told me to accept. "You can't go broke making a profit" he said. I felt we could have made more holding on and renting it ourselves, but we couldn't fight the partner with the finances, so Herman and I went along.

Herman then built a two-bedroom house on NW 5th Street and a 10-unit apartment building on a deep lot on around the 1900 block of NW Flagler Terrace. These projects were to be our Waterloo. The aftermath of the War had caused a severe shortage in building materials and our projected costs of construction kept creeping up day by day. The house on 5th Street cost us so much more to build than planned that I was glad to get our money back, just to get rid of it. The big job, on Flagler Terrace, turned out to be a disaster. I had found this almost 200-foot-deep lot, zoned for apartments, at a good price. Herman had drawn beautiful plans for ten efficiency units, estimated to cost us about $28,000 to build, complete with stoves, sinks in the 8'x14' kitchen/dining areas and the Bahamas couches that converted into beds, in the 14'x16' living/bedroom areas. Herman got the permits to build them. Then, everything went wrong. Remember, Joe was our partner and the only source of funds. He had the final say on all details and decided to take charge. First, he did not like the simple type of roof (the cheapest), which Herman had chosen. "This building" he said, "should reflect his corporate name (The Merit Corporation). When anyone sees our building, it should show 'merit.' To do that, it should have a red tile roof, not an ordinary one – like all the others around here." We got bids on a tile roof and added $4,000 to our costs.

Before we were finished with the new roof, Joe came back with another brilliant idea. He had seen a one-piece, self-contained unit, including the sink, refrigerator and stove that would fit into our kitchens and, again, make our units outstanding. We had no choice but to change our plans again. We had to drop our orders for individual sinks, stoves, and refrigerators that we'd spent weeks to obtain and buy Joe's picks. Ordering those units not only delayed completion of the project but caused another increase (some $5,500) in our costs. Meanwhile, I began having other problems. As broker and leasing agent for this building, I had leased all 10 apartments with first and last month's rent prepaid. My involvement in the projects included finding lots plus getting goods for Herman. We even had to buy our own truck to haul building materials.

In my spare time – Herman could not leave his work – I became a truck driver, hauling building materials so the work could go on. I had so little time to spend at my office and no other source of income, so I had to use the money from the advanced payments to feed my family and pay the mortgage payments on my own home. To top everything off, Coral Gables Federal refused to honor our committed mortgage loan because of the changes in our original plans.

To add to our problems, at that time, Joe and his wife Mary had to go north for some mysterious reason. Before leaving, he told me that – if anyone inquired – I was to say that Mary, his wife, had personally lent us the money for our projects. With no source of income, I had to get a new mortgage so the building could be completed and rentals start to come in. Irv Sherman, the real estate man who had handled the lease on the Sinclair Hotel for me, found a private lender for a $25,000 mortgage. It would cost me $2,500, discounted from the amount lent, payable monthly, with the entire balance due in five years. In desperation, I was forced to take it. With the new mortgage we were able to finish and our tenants moved in. Our monthly Flagler Terrace income was $760. After deducting the mortgage payment there was barely enough for me to draw anything just for my family needs. It certainly left nothing for Herman and Joe. I had neglected my office so much that I had practically no income from there and resorted to helping fill out income tax returns from passersby who saw my window sign.

One day I had a visit from the FBI, who wanted to know how Joe fitted into my firm, and the source of his funds. I explained that we became friends in 1945 and had bought the land under my office together; that as far as I knew, his wife Mary was the source of the money. They had never told me where it came from. Upon their return from New York, Joe told me that the government claimed he had overcharged them on some of the projects he had sold them – as subcontractor – during the War and wanted a rebate of $80,000. He never explained how the matter was settled. Since Joe now had to become a silent partner, and, since our latest project did not generate enough funds for all of us, we finally had to sell the property on Flagler Terrace. When one is desperate to dispose of a piece of property, it generally ends up as a loss sale. After paying off the mortgage there was little left to divide between us. The Merit Corporation was dissolved.

Not long after that, our son Alan contracted polio and I closed my office for good to go back into the hotel business. The Ralph Realty Co. was also dissolved. Joe knew the rough time I was having. One day he came and offered to buy my interest in the land we owned jointly for $5,000. I knew the offer was far below its value but had no alternative. While we ostensibly remained friends, we had little in common from then on and gradually drifted apart.

Herman, a licensed general contractor, had no trouble getting jobs with several different contractors and became financially independent. Mollie and I had become close friends with another couple, Peter and Mollie Glazer. When we met their daughter, Sue, the two Mollies (encouraged by Mom Hirsh) decided that Mollie Glazer would make a good match for Herman. Thus, in the summer of 1950 – while I was the resident manager of the Atlantis Hotel on Miami Beach – I engaged Rabbi Morris Skop, a friend of ours, to marry Herman and Sue in the hotel's Grand Ballroom. The reception entertained the few guests present. With both of them working (Sue had a job as a bookkeeper), they soon had enough to buy a little house in West Miami. This is where their two sons, Wally and Bobby, were born and raised. Again, Herman's skills were put to work and he built an addition to the back of that house,

A postcard showing the Atlantis Hotel in Miami Beach, Florida.

which practically doubled the size of it. The huge patio and workroom became the most used part of the house – for recreation, work, and storage – as well as for sleeping accommodations, occasionally. After the boys were born, Sue stopped work and Herman became the sole breadwinner. They lived the life of a typical lower middle class family, with two healthy sons, and the usual good and not-so-good times. Sue's younger brother, Leonard, loved the boys and was a constantly available babysitter. Even as the boys grew older, Leonard seemed to be always there, to keep them company. Both Sue and Herman became interested in bowling and it became a very important part of their leisure life.

Herman not only looked a lot like his father but also resembled Alexander in many other ways. While both of them had remarkable mechanical abilities and inventiveness, neither possessed good business skills. As a result, Herman's venture into business for himself – to build additions to people's houses – did not make enough money for a living and he had to go back to work with other builders. When that slowed down, he became a contractor for Sears, doing replacements for kitchen cabinets and sinks. The quality of his work was unquestionably superior and he always managed to earn enough money for them to get by. Again, like his father, he found it difficult to save for a rainy day. When Mollie Glazer, Mom Hirsh, and my Mollie and I formed a partnership to buy and develop land in Hialeah, I hired Herman to build our first apartment building on one of the three lots we were buying. My understanding with him was that he'd get a nominal salary during construction. After the building was finished he'd get a major interest in our partnership, without investing any money. (Our partnership provided that all income was to be used for paying off the other two lots and develop those, too.) The first building rented out so quickly that we made plans to build the second one right away. Meanwhile, Herman and Sue decided they needed the money now and asked me to give them cash for Herman's 10% interest. Much against my protests that they'd eventually get more, Sue insisted that they wanted their money as soon as possible. The amount I borrowed to pay them off was a tiny fraction of what they would've received had they waited. In due time, I paid him extra money for other "work" he did for me. Herman and Sue decided to separate and the friendly divorce resulted in Herman's keeping their house on 16th Street where he would continue to raise their two sons.

Herman always encouraged the boys to maintain the close

relationship that they had with their mother and with Leonard Glazer and his family. It's to their credit that both boys continued to do so as long as both of their parents and Leonard's family remained alive. The striking resemblances between Herman and his father remained a constant in his later years. Both Herman and Alex Hirsh loved horse racing and could spend an entire night going over every entry in every race scheduled for the next day at a local track. Both could spend most of a day at the track, just to wait till the horse(s) they'd picked ran. Once their selection(s) had run they'd go home. If you asked them how they fared, the answer was always an "O.K." with a smile. The ever present smile and the happy-go-lucky manner lives on in my memory. In every sense of the word, Herman was a "good" guy.

Ralph
May 7, 2000

JUDAISM AND ITS IMPACT ON MY LIFE

I've tried to clarify how Judaism affected my life by showing the influence of my Jewish upbringing. I could probably have saved time and paper by simply saying that early teachings of Biblical commands and admonitions – as practiced and taught by my parents, especially – were the root of all my eventual behavior. Although I gave up many of the Orthodox customs and practices from my early childhood, all of my moral and ethical beliefs essentially stem from historical Jewish teachings. Here are a few examples.

CHARITY – Of all Jewish influences in my life I believe that CHARITY is probably the most important. From my earliest recollections of practices, which my parents taught us, this stands out as the bulwark of Jewish life. Our greatest responsibility is to help those less fortunate including family, friends and the community. I could fill many pages with details of my involvement in Jewish charities and causes. My contributions pale in comparison with those of our son and daughter-in-law, Alan and Dolores. I swell with pride each time I hear of their work to help children and families with disabilities. My grandsons are each active in a number of charities as well.

FAMILY – Perhaps an even more important Jewish influence in my life has been the emphasis on a strong belief of FAMILY. My greatest joy is to see the members of our family getting together as much a possible. Even more important, in my opinion, is the belief that each of us should always be available to help each other out in every possible way. Regardless of the need, whether it's to help one who needs financial or sympathetic aid, we should always be ready to give each other a hand. I have to believe that my family's help was a very great contribution to what little success I achieved in my lifetime. By the same token, I hope that I, too, helped my family members in their time of need. Curiously, I don't regret or miss a single dollar of the thousands I've "lost," in helping the various members of my family. I'd do it again, without a moment's hesitation. That's what FAMILY is all about.

A very important aspect of family life is the acceptance of each and every member, regardless of his or her strengths or weaknesses. Even if one of us does not meet our own standards, it's our obligation to accept that member as he or she is.

RELIGION - Of all things related to Judaism the subject of RELIGION is the most controversial. My father believed and practiced Orthodox customs and traditions in every phase of his daily life. He taught me - early in my life - to tolerate others' beliefs and practices. As I grew older and read and learned more about Judaism and other religions, customs, and practices, I gave up many of my early opinions about other faiths. My ultimate conclusion is that RELIGION is strictly a private matter and that each one of us has the absolute right to believe or nor believe in whatever he or she chooses. More important, to me, is that each one of us has the obligation to never question the others' rights or beliefs. Each one of us should respect the others. The obligation of parents is to expose or teach their children their own customs and practices and acquaint them with others' beliefs, to allow their children - when they're mature enough - to choose for themselves. Always with the importance of tolerance of others' rights and beliefs. All my efforts went to set an example for my sons and grandsons

MUSIC - My exposure to Jewish music - both at home, to my mother's and sister's singing in Yiddish, and to the beautiful Hebrew melodies in the Synagogue - left me with a love that endured till I lost my hearing in my old age. Even now, when I lead in the commemoration of our various Holidays, I still "hear" those sounds in my mind, although I don't dare try to sing them out loud. Still, the rhythm and beat lives on. Thanks to my wife, Mollie, I was exposed to opera and classical music and found much joy in those, too. Music, Jewish and in general, has enriched my life tremendously, I think it's an important duty of all parents to expose their children to music in its many forms, both vocal and instrumental. It's a source of great pleasure to all of us, young and old.

ISRAEL and our bond to Jews everywhere - From earliest childhood the bonds of the Jewish people to the land of Israel and to Jews throughout the world, has been instilled in me. First, in Biblical teachings, followed by the constant referral in our prayers to "Next year in Jerusalem," and songs, until it's become a part of our beliefs and expectations. The tendency to associate ourselves with the Jewish peoples' achievements in all fields of endeavor – ranging from all the way from Nobel prizes to politics and sports – is inbred in me. I swell with pride to hear or read that a Jew has made the headlines. Vicariously, that achievement by a member of our extended "family' is a cause of celebration. If a Jew is being hurt or wronged, anywhere, I, too, feel the pain To this day.

MORALS and HONESTY – Without a doubt, all of my behavior throughout my life has been guided and molded by my parents, and, through them, by the Jewish Biblical teachings that they believed and practiced. I've tried, both by word and example, to leave this as my legacy. Judaism has been my rock and foundation.

JOBS

Mollie and I began these writings, at this point, more than a dozen years ago. Between us, we've compiled so many articles, stories and poems; we've covered so many topics that it takes some effort to come up with a new title or topic, unless there is specific request that comes for a story from one our grandchildren. I thought that some of you might be interested to know how many different jobs I've had, at one time or another, since coming to this country. Hey! It might inspire some of you to think about your own experiences and actually get you to share them. But, that's later. Not now. This is my story.

My first job – meaning something I did, for which I was paid – was when I was still going to school, at Forest Park Junior/Senior High School in Baltimore. As you will remember, I started there in September of 1924, when they skipped me to Grade 7A – the upper half of the 7B grade – from P.S. #63. Using the streetcar, I helped to deliver orders (for Papa's store) to people who lived around Fallbrook Junction – the end of Line 13 – before school. I was able to get a transfer to line 31, which continued north past Liberty Heights Avenue where I got another transfer to go west to my new school. Are you confused? Imagine how it must have been to an immigrant boy who was just trying to cope with learning a new language, customs, school and neighborhood, and strange people. I worked for Papa before school, but there was little to do when I came home in the afternoons, and I was bored. I asked Papa's permission to see if I could pick up a part-time Job. In spite of my terrible accent, I found a job at Goldberg's Dry Cleaning & Pressing Store, near our house. They offered me a job delivering finished clothing. My pay was $1.25 a week, working Monday through Friday afternoons. Of that, I saved $1.00 a week allowing myself a nickel a day, to buy milk or ice cream, on the days when my lunch-bag was dairy. (I still observed the kosher restrictions of not eating meat and dairy foods at the same meal.)

I saved up my nickels from the restricted days. And, sometimes, I splurged and treated myself to a 10-cent chocolate sundae, when I had cheese sandwiches or salmon croquettes for lunch. On rare occasions I got a tip of a nickel. Those were always saved for Saturday afternoon, when I'd walk to Druid Hill Park (about three miles from the house) to watch a game of baseball or football. Later, on my way home, I indulged in a special ice cream treat, near the park, where they had the most delicious chocolate sundaes with nuts for 15 cents. I should mention that I never got any pay or allowance for working in Papa's store. He never offered and I never expected it. When I finally heard that some boys had a weekly allowance, I just assumed that their parents were very wealthy. It never occurred to me to ask Papa for any spending money, except when I needed to use a streetcar to deliver orders or go to school. If I decided to walk home from school, the money I saved became my "spending money." My first job at the cleaners lasted till I got my working permit in February, 1925. From then on, when I wasn't delivering orders, I helped serve the few walk-in customers, while I was learning how to "traber" ("kashar") meats and chickens, so they'd be Kosher to sell.

During some afternoons, Papa found time to take a nap. My brother Mike had offered to work for me at the store, when in 1927, I went to summer school and night school classes full time so that I could graduate from high school by June of 1929. So, I only helped out in delivering orders on my way to school and helped in the store after I came home from school. We observed the Sabbath and only opened the store after dark on Saturday evenings. On Sundays, we were open for walk-ins and got ready for the coming week's business, staying open until one or two in the afternoon. I relieved Mama on Sundays. Many banks had failed or closed at the time, including the large Chesapeake Bank where we had our small savings accounts and Papa's business checking accounts. I decided to look for a summer job in 1929, after I graduated from high school. I'd need money for Maryland State Normal School in the fall. My older brother, Willie, got me a job working in a grocery store for six dollars a week It was a long way to get there, more than an hour on the streetcar each way, plus a 12-hour work day. But I could save more than five dollars a week, so I took it.

One day I ran into Ralph Smelkinson, one of my high school classmates, who told me about his hitch-hiking experiences. It sounded very intriguing and I wished I could try that, but knew my parents would never let me. Two things happened to change things for me. The grocery store was a busy mom-and-pop operation in an all-white neighborhood. The owners had an older fellow who'd been working for them for a couple of years. When I came along he warned me to watch out for one of the owners, "the old lady" who'd come into the store midmorning. "She's the real Boss," he said, "and complains all the time." He was right. From the moment she came in she'd find fault with everybody and everything, including her husband. Even though I was constantly enraged at the petty faults she found, I needed the money too much, and kept my feelings hidden. I did my best to placate her. It was a thankless job. Nothing pleased her. It didn't take long for me to start wondering how long I could take it.

Meanwhile Mama was getting ready to take on a new adventure. One of the customers at our store had told Mama that there was a place called "Hot Springs" where people came from all over to get rid of their ailments. Mama had brought many of her ailments along with her to America. She really had some legitimate ones and decided that she'd try to see if the Hot Springs would help rid her of some of them. Papa agreed and they made plans for her to go there for two weeks in mid August. As soon as I heard that, I made up my mind that I, too, would try a new adventure, in her absence. I should mention that I had already saved up the $35 fee for Normal School. The summer job was strictly to have some spending money. During the second week of my new job at the grocery store, I'd started complaining about the woman's constant interference. Still, I was determined to stick it out as long as possible. But now, with Mama's plans to be away, I had a new idea. If I quit at the same time Mama left, perhaps I can get Papa to let me hitchhike to Montreal to visit my sister Chaika, her husband Muni and their two daughters. It had been six years since we left Canada and I longed to see them. As I told you in my 1929 summer story, I had a very interesting experience going to visit them. But, I had no spending money left for the trip by the time I paid for Normal School.

After I became acclimated to my new environment, I decided I needed another part-time job. Again, Willie came to my aid. I got a new job at I. S. Shapoff's grocery store. Yes, Mr. Shapoff – the same man who, 17 years later, was the real estate broker who helped me buy my first home in Florida. If I ran, after my last class, in time to catch the 3:05 streetcar, then made the right connections with the two other transfer cars, I'd get to my job about 4:05 p.m. and work until the evenings. On weekends, I worked 7 a.m. to 9 p.m., earning $6 for the week, paid on Saturdays. While the pressure was constant at the Shapoff's store, the atmosphere was a pleasure compared to my former job. The Shapoffs treated me like family. And, the $6.00 a week was enough to meet all my needs. I kept the job till I started student teaching. Meanwhile, I had met Mollie.

Mollie and I had first become good friends when I was offered a chance to become a waiter at her parents' "hotel" in PenMar Park. I had spent a week at Camp Airy in 1927, my first experience at a pre-paid "vacation" in the United States. While there, we visited Camp Louise in Pen Mar, on a Friday night. It was a once-in-a-lifetime experience for me and I'd enjoyed it very much. Working for Mollie's parents was a great opportunity. Not only would I be doing something other than working in grocery stores, I would also have a chance, Mollie assured me, to go to Camp Louise on Friday nights – with Mollie, of course. It was a perfect win-win for me. My folks were duly impressed and urged me to go. A week after school ended, I bought a one-way ticket at the Western Maryland Railway Station to PenMar, to start my new job. Mollie was an excellent teacher and it didn't take long for me to learn the art of waiting on tables. Oh, yes. I should mention that my pay was $6.00 per week, plus tips. I was dependable. You can figure out how good the tipping was when I tell you that – at the end of the summer – I had the total sum of $93 in savings. That's after 12 weeks of paid work! Believe me! I was a real spendthrift! Other than an occasional night when we went bowling (two lanes in the lone games area of the park) at a cost of 3 games for a quarter, and, an even rarer excursion to the nearest town (Waynesboro, Pennsylvania, 5 miles down, in the Shenandoah Valley) there was no place to spend money.

I should remind you that the Great Depression had already begun. In the year before (1930) Mama had spent two weeks vacationing at Glendon Heights, at $15 per week – which was about all we could afford. During my first year at PenMar, guests were so few and hard to get that Mollie's parents offered deals – two weeks for $25. This was for three full meals a day, plus snacks and drinks in between, mornings and afternoons! So, how much in tips could I expect to get?? I was surprised and thrilled when I got 50 cents at the end of a week, on a rare occasion. The biggest tip I got, ONCE, was A WHOLE DOLLAR, for waiting on a family of six FOR A WEEK! But, I did get a "thanks for being such a good waiter," a few times. So much for the value of my services. Truthfully, I did benefit a great deal – worth far more than money – during the summers I spent at PenMar. My first summer was the only time I received any pay, as I would later become part of Mollie's family. I knew how hard everybody was working and how little they had left at the end of the summer – which they needed to live on, till next summer.) Yes, even in that converted, big house, with its miserable, make-do facilities, I learned the rudiments of hotel operation, food preparation, bed-making, people handling, salesmanship, and family relations, that helped me become whatever I was and am. Of course, I left out the best for last. I married the boss's daughter! Eventually! Meanwhile, many of the guests acted as if Mollie and I were already married. How else can you explain the fact that – with no pay – they believed I was not entitled to less tips than the few I got in my rookie year of 1930? I know. Some of you guessed that we were in such bad straits that most couldn't afford. Just my luck. Regardless of the fact that we were in the midst of a deep depression, all I knew was that I did not make enough to take Mollie bowling, either from my pay or tips! Luckily I had fortified myself by bringing some $30 from my savings with me – just in case! (In case you forgot, I'd just finished my first year of teaching, during which I earned $1,200, of which I'd given $900 to Papa, to keep his tiny business afloat. I kept the rest, $300, for expenses and savings. What I did see was how hard we all worked and how little remained for them to live on at the end of the summer.

Luckily, Mollie had finished 19th in her class and was due to get a job the day after Labor Day to join the teaching field. If so, she'd be getting $1,200 for her first year, just as I did. As luck would have it, she did get a job, but not at $1,200 a year. Because of the Depression, school board budgets had been cut so much, so all the new hires would be listed as substitutes, temporarily, and their pay would be $3.00 per day. They would only get paid on the actual number of teaching days in the month! Talk about luck. Most people felt lucky just to survive. And, the Hirsh family – in spite of all their struggles – managed to do so, also. The only reason I added the plight of the Hirsh family was to show that the financial struggles were not hurting just me. By far, most people were struggling, just to exist.

Getting back to me – my luck, to be getting a check for $120 a month as a teacher ended abruptly. All teachers were soon notified that our pay would be cut. So starting in September, I got $100 a month for the next five months. By February, we became "regular" substitutes, at $3.00, a day. The class after us, the 1932 group that included Mollie, was demoted to "temporary" substitutes and received $2.50 a day. And now all of us only were paid for the actual days taught. We were the lucky ones who at least had a job. In the successful graduating classes of 300 to 350 Baltimore City teachers of the early 1930's, only the first 20 of each year were chosen to teach full time, but again at substitute's pay. And, again, by far, all of us lucky ones were given the most difficult jobs available – in the poorest neighborhoods, in Special Education classes, without any prior training or experience – or, in any other troublesome classes, like mine. My first job was to teach a class of boys only, ages 13 to 17, who'd failed to adjust to their regular classes. I replaced a man who'd been beaten up so badly that he refused to return to this job. In spite of our limited income, Mollie and I – like most people who had any kind of a job – helped our respective parents and survived.

By the middle of 1933 we'd decided – after "going steady" for three years – it was time to get married. You know the rest. We married in 1934 and moved in with Mollie's parents in their small three-bedroom rented house. Papa had closed his store by then and moved to a new job and small apartment in Washington, D.C. We rented out his house so he no longer was dependent on me. Between our jobs, even as substitutes, PenMar, and Ma Hirsh's frugality, Mollie and I managed well, comparatively. In February, 1935, the school board restored all of teachers to our full status and. My pay was raised to $150 a month, instead of the $60 or less I'd been getting. Mollie's pay became $140. The wise guy who wrote "What fools these mortals be" must have been referring to us. No sooner had we gotten our first big checks than Mollie informed me she was pregnant. As I explained in my story of the ridiculous, antiquated rules of the Baltimore City School Board, Mollie was required to request a leave of absence no later than the third month of pregnancy. Failure to do so would add a third year to her leave, before she could return to work. What a dilemma! If she could work just a few more months, we could save up some funds to get ready for the baby and pay for the doctor and a week's hospital stay. We'd need at least $300, which we didn't have. After much deliberate discussion, Mollie decided – since she didn't "show" that she was

Ralph and Mollie were married in 1933.

pregnant – that she'd work as long as she could get away with it, while we put away at least some of her pay. In May, with about three months left in her pregnancy, Mollie's principal made her quit.

Our plans to save did not work out quite as well as we'd expected. First of all, we had to find an apartment, since we couldn't continue to stay in the one room we used in the Hirsh's house. The few dollars we'd saved were lent to Ma Hirsh, to buy supplies for the summer business in PenMar. With a baby on the way, I had to start planning for a part-time job, to supplement my teaching income when we returned from PenMar. And the only trades I'd had were working in a grocery store and working as a waiter.

Prior to the summer of 1935, I'd enrolled to take two summer classes at the University of Maryland in College Park, eight miles from Washington. My endeavor was to get my B.A. or B.S. so that I'd be able to get a full college degree. Maryland State Normal School gave us excellent training in preparation to become a teacher, but the program was only two years, which meant that I only had half the number of credits for a Bachelor's Degree. It'd take me till June, 1938, before I could get my B.S. diploma at the University of Miami. We were living and working in Florida by then. And Mollie would also go on to get her Bachelor's at UM.

Back to 1935. My home base during the week base was my parents' apartment in Washington. Mollie suggested that, if I really wanted to get a different kind of job when we returned to Baltimore, it might be as a shoe salesman in a ladies' shoe store – where many young men worked on Saturdays. To my utter dismay – in spite of all her meaningful efforts – I found it impossible to grasp what Mollie was trying to teach me about shoes. The words describing ladies shoes, were all "Greek" to me – high heels, pumps, etc. Nobody in PenMar – where roads were unpaved or rough – wore anything but flat walking shoes so I had no idea what Mollie was talking about as she tried to "educate" me.

Eventually, my part-time work as a shoe salesman was a very useful experience. When I started to work in Washington's Hahn's Shoe Store, I not only earned a much-needed additional income but also became subject to withholding Social Security taxes. Schoolteachers were not subject to withholding S.S. taxes before 1970. By the way, this became the base from which my earnings were calculated for my first Social Security check of $113 a month, which I received when I retired in 1973. High finances, eh?

While teaching in Maryland, I'd also been selected to give demonstration lessons to teachers, at $100 a lesson, which added to my yearly income. I'd also been transferred to the largest school for Industrial Education – some fifteen different shops provided excellent training for the boys who were misfits in their regular classes. I became a member of the teachers who taught the boys their regular related subjects. I would later be promoted to do the demo lessons for principals and school supervisors (still at the pricey sum of $100/lesson), as well as the income from working at a shoe store in Washington. I was earning enough to take care of my family, by myself. Meanwhile I'd been taking graduate courses at the University of Maryland in Baltimore City and classes in guidance at Johns Hopkins. The vice-principal-in-charge (the school board saved money by appointing leaders of schools and naming them thus, instead of principals) was Sid Chernak, one of my best friends and mentors. It was a mutually satisfactory situation. He became very impressed with my skills as a teacher and – before my first year ended – had me installed as Teacher-in-Charge, in his absence. There was no pay for that honor. In 1941, World War II broke out. This affected the school's faculty because most of the shop teachers were men. With the draft in force, we kept losing one teacher after the other. A colleague, Mr. I.U., was a Major in the Army reserves and was one of the first to be called to the service. He'd been in charge of the school cafeteria, so

Sid asked me to take it over. In addition to the men who were being called, much of the staff of women were working at fairly low wages at the school. They soon found a need for their skills at considerably more pay in the industrial parts of our community, so we had to find replacements for them as well at school. Fortunately, by then I knew much more about kitchen operations. Ma Hirsh had catered affairs in Baltimore, after they came back from PenMar, and I'd been very much involved in those catered weddings and Bar Mitzvahs, held on weekends. In addition to teaching a full schedule of classes, I had to handle all the business of running a school cafeteria that prepared food for about 300 kids a day. That included hiring housewives who'd never worked before and who didn't know how to make even a large container of tuna or other salad to feed 50 or more hungry kids; or, to make 75 or more sandwiches of ham or bologna. Others were shown how to portion food in a plate, to find time to meet with salespeople, to order the makings of the menu for the five days of the week, teach the cashier how to handle cash or tokens (we sold a week's tokens for 60 cents a meal). Most important was my supervision at the start of each day's lunch period, to see that everything was going smoothly. It was a trying, time-consuming task, with no compensation. Meanwhile, Baltimore was the home of many industries that converted their former businesses to a war priority, and the city had started a demand for more and more workers at higher wages. Between the draft and war, every able-bodied person – male or female – was needed to fulfill the nation's needs. Boys from our school, 16 or 17 years old, who had been trained in our machine shop, found good paying jobs. Because I had taken graduate courses in guidance and counseling, Sid appointed me to act as Placement Counselor, since the former teacher who handling that had been drafted. Now, in addition to my regular job as a full-time teacher, I was also the cafeteria manager with a direct telephone to my room in case a problem arose. I was also the placement and guidance counselor. And, just in case, I was the teacher-in-charge during Sid's absence. Of course, when school let out on Friday afternoon, I drove straight to Washington and my job at Hahn's Shoe Salon where I worked till 9 p.m. I would stay at my folks' apartment overnight, worked from 9 to 9 selling shoes. Then I would drive to our apartment in Baltimore. I was just a young fellow in my early 30's, so "no problem." I must admit that I was embarrassed when one of the boys I'd placed at the Julian P. Frieze Co. (which had converted to manufacture replacement parts for Armed Forces) showed me his pay envelope. After two weeks of work, including overtime, his pay was greater than my monthly check as his former teacher! And that's since I'd reached the top of my salary schedule of $220 a month for ten months! I'd been teaching for 11 years and was being paid less per month than my 17-year-old student got for two weeks! In spite of the war effort and the scarcity of teachers, the school board still stuck to its antiquated pay scale. Why didn't I quit teaching and find a better-paying job? Good question! Simple answer: I didn't dare. First, I was sure that the Draft Board – whose chairman lived next door to me on Maine Ave. – would call me up for service. Who'd take care of my family? My supervisor had arranged exemptions for me, because I "was contributing to the war effort" through my work at school. Second, I was still earning an average of $14 a week, selling shoes. Plus, I earned $100 for the demonstration lessons, which I was still doing. On top of all that, someone arranged for me to receive an increase in pay the next year – so that I was making as much as a vice principal. Even Ma Hirsh insisted on paying me $7.00 a week, as "her costs" of our family food bill. She and Pa Hirsh had been living with us, as they could no longer go to Florida for the winters. When Pa Hirsh was hospitalized, Ma Hirsh remained with us until after his passing. In truth, her help with the shopping, cooking, and housekeeping lifted a big load off Mollie's shoulders. When our son was born, she saved us even more. But, she was a very independent and proud person, and felt better when she "paid." So, we accepted. In all the years we knew each other and lived together, either in PenMar or elsewhere, I'm proud to say we never, ever had an argument. Both of Mollie's parents were most pleasant and undemanding, and certainly never a bother. We had the room and they cost us nothing extra. Sure enough, it was too good to last. During all these years, I had been living with pains in my stomach. Dr. Larry Adler, our family physician, could not do much for me. He sent me to a "specialist" who took X-rays and decided I had stomach ulcers. In addition to going on a very restricted diet, they both agreed I was under a lot of stress and I should give up some of my activities and get more rest. Since school work was a must, the only solution was to give up selling shoes in Washington. For the first time in years, I actually was free to be a husband and father with my family – for two whole days a week! What's more, we could look forward to a free summer, since I had convinced Ma Hirsh to sell the guest house in PenMar after the summer of 1941.

We'd had a very difficult two summers, with Mollie assuming all of her late father's work in the kitchen, added to all her other responsibilities. Plus, she was pregnant. With the help of Pearl, the farm girl whom we'd brought from PenMar to help Mollie while we awaited the birth of our second child, along with Ma Hirsh, life on Maine Avenue went smoothly. I went back to my school work. Pearl was a gold mine of action. Though only 16 years old, she knew every phase of housework, cleaning, canning, laundry, and yard work. She was a wonderful, devoted, and happy – a whirlwind of activity. She wouldn't let Mollie lift a finger without her help. She had never been in or seen a big city like Baltimore and found everything exciting and wonderful. After our son Alan was born, Pearl took over, taking care of him as if Alan were her own child. Pearl was one of 18 children in a farm family and had obviously had plenty of experience. In any case, she relieved all of us from many worries.

Hey! Before I forget, this is supposed to be about my jobs. Sorry!

It didn't take long for me to get bored that fall, without all of my extra work, hanging around the house with little to do. After school, I had managed to join a group of men who played pick-up baseball games on Sundays to relieve their stress. One day, I learned that Bernie, a friendly guy, was from the well-known Becker Family Men's Department Store. I used to pass Becker's daily when I attended Normal School. One word led to another and he invited me to work for them on Thursday afternoons until 9, and all day on Saturdays. Thus began a new experience, working as a part-time employee in a high class men's store. I learned to appreciate finer brands of men's merchandise and gradually accumulated a better line of clothes and men's accessories. I also became friends with Allen Becker, Bernie's older brother, who was in charge of the high-class clothing department of the store. He was also one of the most famous amateur photographers in the country. When Allen later came to Miami Beach in the early 1950's, he called me and I helped him start his first famous and most successful photo studio on 41st Street on Miami Beach. It was Allen who taught me whatever little I ever knew of basic photography. That's another job I had, another part of the story. Oh wait, I just remembered that I also worked in another grocery once. During those years in Baltimore, there were very few supermarkets as we know them today. Most grocery stores were "Mom and Pop" operations. The two exceptions were the J. M. Crook chain of about 50 stores (one of which occupied the ground floor of the Bilich home, above us) and the nationally known chain of the Atlantic & Pacific (A&P) Tea Company. Before I became a shoe salesman, I tried to work in one of those A&P stores, which offered $3.00 for a Saturday job. I couldn't resist the opportunity to make that much money in one day! It was the hardest work, physically, that I've ever done. I was on my feet, constantly, from 7 a.m. to 7 p.m., except for two 20-minute breaks for lunch and supper! When I finished and took the streetcar home, I was so tired I remained standing all the way, for fear I'd fall asleep past my stop. During the Christmas holidays of 1943, while exchanging greetings with our next door neighbor, he told me that the draft board was planning to call my number up shortly. We had decided – whether I was drafted or not – the family would move to Florida. Both Mollie and her mother had urged me to do so for years. They were prepared to rent a guest house and support themselves in the business we all knew so well. This led to our ending up with the Sinclair Hotel lease in Miami Beach. Here I must stop to make a complete confession. When I leased the Sinclair I WAS A FAKE! I KNEW ABSOLUTELY NOTHING ABOUT OPERATING A HOTEL! NOTHING AT ALL!!! Did I ever hire or fire a staff of any kind? NO! Did I have any bookkeeping experience? NO! I should write a book of questions about hotel operations that I had no answers to. None of us had ever had enough experience lo undertake the operation of a 50-room hotel, with all the complexities it involved! How I managed to raise and invest over $25,000, which I needed to take possession, is beyond my comprehension. An even more important question is, how could Mollie, family and friends back me so much without hesitation? Remember, I not only lacked the experience of the operation of such a large enterprise, but I was asking them to back me and lend me so much money without a single source of security or guarantee of success. It boggles the mind to understand how so many people could put so much faith in an untested and inexperienced person. My parents and Ma Hirsh cleaned out their entire savings accounts, which they had scrabbled together after many years of toil and struggle. They turned it all over to me! My friend, Jack Sapperstein, who worked hard for years to build up his pharmacy, lent me $5,000! My brother-in-law Muni, friends Sol Dantzig and the Barber sisters – everybody helped. Just thinking about it, now, is overwhelming! Isn't it amazing? Happily, I'm proud to say that everyone was remunerated, in full, with interest.

Every phase of hotel operation requires knowledge and experience.

Poor or neglected service is the easiest way to fail. But, when you add the facts that the country was still at war and that all items of consumption were either very limited in supply or missing altogether, one's ability to operate was reduced manifold times. EVERYTHING WAS STILL RATIONED. Common, everyday needs – linens, soap, toilet paper, cleaning items, gas, and on and on – were just not available! In spite of it all, we managed to overcome and eventually succeeded. Everybody helped. Again, everybody helped, including people whom we'd never met before – Irv Sherman, the agent who helped me lease the hotel; Morris Margolis, one of the owners of the Sinclair; some local hangers-on who regularly stopped by the hotel; guests, like the Weinstein family. Everyone either knew the answers or knew someone who had answers. And, they were always available with free advice and references and help. Thanks to all our family and friends, plus the strangers who chipped in and became friends, we were able to overcome our problems and learn hotel operations. I actually became a knowledgeable hotel operator. As nerve-wracking and trying as our first year at the Sinclair was, the second year more than made up for our efforts. The end of WWII, in Europe, in 1945, unleashed the withheld desires of our citizens to spend some of their wartime accumulated funds. In spite of the continued rationing, people sought every means available to spend, spend, and spend – on anything, anywhere! Cash flowed like rain in a storm. All the people who had ever been to Florida or had ever heard of Florida, all decided to come visit. The same for people who'd never heard of or been. We were flooded with guests at the Sinclair by people able and willing to spend whatever we asked for accommodations. Unfortunately for us, we were limited by regulations to a maximum rate of $12, double, per day, for all our rooms. And, unlike some other hotel operators, I complied with the law. What can I tell you? In all my fanciest dreams, I never imagined I'd make so much money in one season. Before the season ended, we decided that the Sinclair Hotel was not the best place in which to raise our two fine sons. Now we could afford to find an apartment or house of our own. Furthermore, we, too, had had enough of the hotel. I called my friend, Irv Sherman, and told him I wanted to sell the remaining three years of my lease. He found a buyer. The sale of the lease lifted a big load off our shoulders. I not only made a smart profit on the sale, but I also got back the $15,000 that I'd paid for the fifth year of the lease as our security deposit. Added to the profit I'd made from operating the hotel during that season, I now could pay off the mortgage I'd held on our guest house in Atlantic City. Plus, I had enough left over so that I bought a home in Miami and we could live comfortably till I decided what my next venture would be. As the interpreter said in Jonathan Safran Foer's novel "Everything is Illuminated" – "My ebullient atmosphere was ominously anticipated." In plain English, we were very happy in our new home in Miami. In short, life couldn't be better.

Even a happy home has its limits. After we'd furnished our home as best we could – due to the limited supplies caused by the war – I was 36 years old and found the summer leisure to be quite boring. What to do? It made no sense to just sit around an empty house all day and use up our savings. The only solution was for me to find a new job. Of all the jobs I'd ever had, none made me want to go back to the retail world of selling. Should I return to teaching now that we were in Florida? With credit for my nine years' experience from Maryland – the maximum credit they allowed – I'd be earning the big amount of $2,700 per year – the top of the salary scale at the time for Dade County schools. Ridiculous! I'd made several times that in one season at the Sinclair. One day I passed a storefront on Flagler Street that said "J. Winchell & Co., Real Estate and Insurance." That sounded interesting. The idea of selling real estate seemed intriguing. What did it take to qualify? I went in and found a man named Harold Winchell to be very friendly, and glad to talk to me. Before I left, he offered to sponsor me in his office, to get a license as a real estate salesman. This was a family-operated agency. Harold was the licensed broker; his wife was the receptionist, bookkeeper, and licensed insurance agent. His son-in-law was the top-producing salesman. The other men seemed to be busy and happy. I became a real estate salesman. My job with Winchell did not produce any sales worthy of note. It served primarily as a means of learning how to evaluate real estate for purchase and sale, which came in handy later on when I began to invest in properties. At the time, more importantly, it trained and prepared me to take and pass the broker's exam and led to the opening of my own office.

I must interrupt here and elaborate on several events. When the Japanese finally surrendered and the War ended, Mollie's brother Herman had returned from his service with the naval engineers in the Pacific. He brought home very little as souvenirs and was reluctant to discuss any of his experiences. As I think I've mentioned, he did bring home a mild case of malaria, which deterred him from work. He joined us at the Sinclair and in Atlantic City. When I bought our first home in Miami, in 1946, I didn't realize how bad a deal I'd made on that purchase. When I joined Winchell real estate and began to see other homes, I truly learned how to evaluate real estate properties. I saw our family home in a totally different light – the size of the rooms, the type of construction, and the deficiencies. It was inadequate, but it was a done deal. We were stuck. Blame it on the War and lack of housing at the time. I had to insert the above note because our house was built as an investment by Carl, our next-door neighbor. Carl built it for a young couple's first home, or for an empty-nester's final house, not for a family. Here we were, Mollie, me and our two growing boys plus Ma Hirsh and Herman – all of us squeezed into a tiny house meant for two! Luckily, we'd had years of experience in tight quarters while PenMar, in the Sinclair and even in Atlantic City. All of us had learned how to find a place to sleep, even in crowded spaces. When you're in the room-leasing business and we had been, when can make money by giving up your own space, you learn to put a cot in the dining room or the basement, even on the porch. So, we managed. It took ten years before we sold that first Miami home – at a loss, of course.

Have any of you ever counted how many different ways I've diverted your attention from my main topic in my narratives? This is supposed to be about "Jobs." And look where this is going. If you thought I was about to get back to my main topic – sorry, but I'm about to disappoint you. I have to comment about the loss when I sold that home. It may be perfectly legal on paper and tax-wise to claim a loss on the sale (I paid $16,500 for it in 1946 and sold it for $15,000 in 1956), philosophically, and in truth, it actually wasn't a "loss" in our minds. We were sick and tired of the house, we needed cash to help our son pay for college, and we had lived in the little house – regardless of its inconveniences – for ten years. What else could we expect? This is a perfect example of a truism I learned in my real estate ventures: "When people have to sell a property – no matter the reason – a buyer can take advantage of their desperation and buy it for less!" It's true today, isn't it?

Now, back to my jobs story. During my time with Winchell Real Estate, Herman had passed the exam and attained his license as a general contractor. In my prior stories I told you how Joe Weinstein, a rich guest at the Sinclair, had befriended me and lent me money to buy our guest house in Atlantic City. Joe had made a lot of money converting his air-conditioning factory to work as a subcontractor for the Armed Forces. We became close friends and even bought our homes at the same time. He and I bought three vacant lots on Flagler Street, just east of 27th Avenue, zoned for business, as an investment. When Herman got his license, Joe got the brilliant idea to form a partnership – I'd get my broker's license and handle the real estate needs; Herman would do the construction; and he'd fund the projects. It sounded like a win-win-win for each one of us. Unfortunately, as detailed in my "Real Estate" story, that venture went sour. That why, in 1949, I ended up back in the hotel business.

Incidentally, I didn't mention that I had a short position as advisor to the youth clubs of our synagogue in Miami. That job was four evenings a week, and was in between the time I left Hahn's and started to work for Becker photography. It was short-lived because, after the War broke out, they instituted a "'black-out" system. When the sirens blared, all lights had to be covered and all traffic drove with no lights. Since the youngsters couldn't drive or walk to and from synagogue meetings, all programs were cancelled. So was I. So much for another job experience.

The first building that Herman constructed was on our lot in the 2600 block of Flagler Street in Miami. It served as my real estate office as well as the office of the "Merit Construction Co.", For those who know Miami, I remind you that after one left downtown Miami in the 1940's, most of the land on both sides of Flagler was vacant. Only the main north-south streets – the 21st, 22nd, and 23rd Avenues had clusters of a few stores or a filling station on or near the corners. Thus, our little building stuck out for all the east-west traffic on Flagler. The northeast corner of Flagler and 21st, right next to our three lots, had an Esso filling station. So, North-South traffic could also see our building. The sight, especially at night, of this isolated little building on the large vacant block was a magnet that attracted a number of drivers. They stopped by to assuage their curiosity to get directions or – on occasion – to actually question a real estate transaction. One night, a distraught young man walked in to inquire if I knew where he could find someone to help him with his income tax return. Curious, I asked him what kind. He held up a large card-like page, which I recognized as the 1040A Form. It was the simplest one-page form, used by people whose income was uncomplicated. All they had to do was fill in the answers to a few basic questions, sign it, and send it in. It was such a simple job that I offered to help him fill it out. It took only a couple of minutes and I handed it back to him, telling him to mail it in – assuring him he did not have to worry about any tax. "How much do I owe you?" he asked. When I waved my hand and told him, "Nothing," he took out three dollars and insisted on paying me. "Why don't you hang out a sign on your window?" he asked. "I bet you could help a lot of people," and walked out. "Why not?" I asked myself.

As it happened, I'd been buying a popular yearly tax information book, by someone named Lasser, I believe, which had helped me fill out my own rather complicated real estate and corporation IRS tax forms. The answer was obvious. I made a large cardboard sign, "INCOME TAX RETURNS," hung it high on my big window facing Flagler Street, and started a new side business, with customers who followed me to my home on 16th street (after we dissolved our development partnerships). In fact, a couple who had what they felt were complicated forms to file continued to file with me even after I moved to an apartment in Hialeah – long after I'd given up active real estate activities. The $10 or $15, CASH, which I charged, then, was a welcome. Plus, grateful clients thanked me!

In 1949, I clerked at the last hotel on Collins Avenue as it turned a half-block west around the famous Firestone Estate – later, the site of the world-famous Fontainebleau Hotel complex. From 1949 to 1953, I worked at the Bancroft Hotel, except for the summer of 1950 which we spent at the Atlantis hotel. When the Greenberg family, who owned the Atlantis hotel complex, decided they could dispense with my services and Bert Lloyd, whom I'd brought back with me from the Atlantis, took over at less costs, I decided I wanted to be my own boss, and chose photography. Without the funds or know-how to open a studio, I became a roaming, beach-combing photographer. Although unhappy to be a picture peddler, I managed to scratch out a living for several years. Meanwhile, Mollie had decided to work as a substitute teacher and liked it so much that she started to take classes at the University of Miami – to complete her B.S. college degree requirements and get a full-time teaching job. That put us in an awkward situation. I had become a specialist in Bar Mitzvah photography. That meant that most of my work took place during the weekends. If Mollie began to teach full-time, she'd be free only on weekends. A scenario like that was not very conducive to a good family life. What to do? It was our friend and Herman's mother-in-law,

Mollie Glazer, who suggested that I join my Mollie by going back to teaching. Thus, in 1955, at the age of 45 and 44, we went back to our first love and both got jobs teaching in the Dade County Public Schools. This action was good for our family. Both of us were busy and/or free on the same days, and we could continue to live as a family again. At first I continued to do an occasional photo job, but most weekends we were together. We could socialize with our friends, go to parks or the beach, or attend operas and concerts. This lasted until we retired in June, 1973, at ages 63 and 62. Within a year after we started teaching in Miami, I had revived my interest in real estate, this time strictly as a landlord. With Ma Hirsh and Mollie Glazer as partners, and with me in control, I used Herman as contractor and built three buildings in Hialeah as income-producing properties. I became the landlord, caretaker, and janitor.

The mention of Mollie Glazer reminds me of another job I had while I was in the school system. She was an excellent salesperson with a ready smile, always easy to make new friends. During our second year of teaching, a fellow we knew had become the Florida District Manager of World Book Encyclopedia – a very popular reference set, and widely used. Somehow he enticed Mollie Glazer to join his crew of salespeople. In a short time, she became so good at it that he made her an area manager, free to find her own crew and collect an extra fee for all their sales. She invited my Mollie and me to join her. We did. During that time I was in charge of all Stanford Achievement Testing (SAT), as well as head of guidance and counseling at Filer Junior High in Hialeah. I had easy access to the files of the students. After attending a meeting one Saturday morning in which Mollie G. gave an inspiring speech to us about the value of this set of reference books for aspiring students, I decided to try and sell them to some of my 7th-graders. I drove out to four family's homes, at random. I must have learned the sales pitch that Mollie G. had taught us pretty well, because I sold a set of books to each of the four homes I visited. My commission was over $120! This was the biggest amount I had ever earned in one day. During that month, I ended up as the top salesman of the region. In addition to the commissions I earned selling encyclopedias, I won the prize of a free boat trip to the Bahamas. Although Mollie was seasick on most of that trip on the old S.S. Florida, it led to our many more cruises on larger, more stable vessels. Our sales ended rather abruptly soon after, when an edict came out that frowned on such activities by teachers. It was good extra income, while it had lasted.

Back to the real estate partnership with my brother-in-law and our family. The papers I prepared, without help from any attorney, stipulated that Ma Hirsch and Mollie Glazer were 25% partners. Mollie and I were 50% partners since we provided the cash investment. Herman would receive reasonable weekly compensation for his part in planning, working and timely finishing on budget. The partnership papers went on to say that, upon completion of the 3rd building, Herman would become a 10% owner of the project. The existing partners would lower their respective percentages proportionately. Shortly afterward, Herman and his wife Sue came to me. Sue asked that they get the value of their share in cash, since Herman was planning to go into a new business, building additions to homes. I had no idea of the value of the project and tried to sell them on my belief that – eventually – it would be worth much more. But Sue insisted they wanted and needed the cash now. We finally agreed on the sum of $3,000 as a fair net value for their share. I borrowed the money, got a release from them for further claims to their interests in the property. With the documents witnessed my Mollie Glazer and Ma Hirsch, Mollie and I became 55% partners while the others remained at 22.5% each.

It wasn't long before Mollie G. came to me and told me that she, too, wanted out. She'd decided to move to California to be closer to her son, Joe, and his family. Now I was totally lost. All the apartments were rented out, and I had no way of evaluating the property. I suggested to Mollie G. that she get a CPA of her choice to get a fair valuation of the property and I would pay her 22.5% of that valuation. She did and left for California with a hefty profit on her original investment of $2,500. When Ma Hirsch heard how much Mollie G. had received for her share of the property, she decided that she, too, might as well get her share. So, Mollie and I became sole owners of the three-building project in Hialeah.

The Cuban influx into Florida created a real estate boom in Miami. A large number of Cuban immigrants found Hialeah to be a very desirable area, and they flocked into the area.. Wealthy Hispanics from South and Central America sought out and bought any property available in Hialeah. I became an owner of a very desirable investment property, and it didn't take long for me to sell my project at a very lucrative profit. That investment proved to be the greatest source of income and the ultimate base of my retirement income. It was the main source of funds I used to later invest in stocks, and in other real estate.

When we retired from the school system we began to enjoy our leisure at The El Conquistador condominium in West Kendall. We'd moved there from The Colony Apartment complex near Dadeland in East Kendall, where we'd been living since 1968. During the five years at The Colony, I was focused on looking for real estate investments with cash I'd saved. The volunteer work I did at the El Conquistador condo helped us to win an exhausting and years-long lawsuit against the greedy builder. That's a whole other story, which led me to never again become involved in any other condo organization.

Mollie and I decided to leave Miami at that point. Our oldest son and his wife were living in Miami and raising their two boys. Our second son was living with his wife in Virginia and raising their two boys. We discovered a new community in Palm Beach County. We found a lovely place at LimeTree Court condos in Boynton Beach, where we moved in 1976. It didn't take long for me to get tired of doing nothing. I decided to look for an investment in a commercial piece of property, with the aim to take any losses as deductions from our annual income taxes.

I ended up designing, building, and operating the first mini-warehouse in Boynton Beach. Our sons had invested in the warehouse as well. My good intentions (to find a tax deduction investment from the loss) failed as the warehouses turned into a moneymaker. There I was, once again a landlord, maintenance man and janitor. And once again, I took no pay for my services. I did put Mollie on the payroll for six quarters, at the advice of a Social Security clerk, so she'd be eligible for her own S.S. funds. Funny enough, Mollie ended up with $2 more a month than I received.

By the time I sold the warehouse property in 1985, our boys got back almost 10 times their investment. Mollie and I also benefited as much. It enabled us to live in a comfortable manner in our later years, and to deed each of our sons and grandsons the money I had planned for in our wills. Mollie and I enjoyed many years in Boynton Beach before moving our final retirement community, The Forum in Deerfield Beach, where we joined the Writer's Workshop and began all of our stories.

Love, Ralphy
January 21, 2008

LANGUAGES

Languages, as I have mentioned before, have always had a peculiar fascination for me.

In my earliest days I was exposed to a variety of different languages and their nuances. I was told that the first language I spoke was the crude peasant version of Ukrainian, taught me by the peasant woman who helped care for me in Lyubar, while Mama was taking care of our family store. Yiddish was the primary language in our home. The Russian spoken by the peasants, parents, and neighbors in Lyubar was a battered guttural version of the language spoken by the educated and aristocratic or cultured people. In Cheder (the Jewish school) I learned Hebrew, as well as Yiddish.

When my sister, Chaika, (10 years older) came home from Odessa University, I listened intently as she and her friends spoke in cultured Yiddish, Russian, and – when they tried to imitate the aristocrats – in French. It was then that I learned to love and sing the French Revolutionary song, named after the city of Marseilles. Fascinated by their enthusiastic discussions and arguments – particularly in light of the fact that many of them confessed sympathetic enthusiasm for the brewing Revolutionary movement – I listened with rapt attention long after the rest of the family had gone to bed. By the time I was ready to take admissions exams to enter my first year in the Ghymnazia, I knew Russian well enough to pass. For reasons I can't explain, when I was asked to choose a foreign language during that first year, I chose German – maybe, because we were at war with Germany? In any case, by the end of my first and part of another year in Ghymnazia, I could read German in the original script. Because so many German words sounded like Yiddish I had no difficulty speaking the language, either.

The stirring Revolutionary Movement, coupled with the imminence of German troops in our area, as well as the beginning threat of pogroms, ended my formal schooling. However, my exposure to the clandestine meetings of Chaika's friends in our house, as well as the Revolutionary leaflets which abounded during those gatherings, gave me many opportunities to listen, read, and learn. At some time during these sessions, Yiddish, Russian, French words and sounds prevailed. Languages became a part of me and I devoured them as if they were my daily bread.

When the Germans invaded our town and some officers chose our house as their headquarters, I was able to converse with them with a fluency that both surprised and pleased them. Whether that had any bearing on their behavior to us is anyone's guess. I only know they never bothered us during their short stay, for which we were very grateful. The Polish troops that followed them into our home were greeted by Papa with a fluency in their language that may have affected their civil stay. I listened and learned.

When we arrived in Lemberg, Galicia, (then a Polish "country") I learned that the Yiddish – as spoken by the Galitzianer – was a strange version of the Yiddish we knew. When we came to America I learned – much later – that the people from Galicia, known as Galitzianer, were considered as a lower class of Jews. In fact, if one wanted to use insulting language toward another, it was almost a curse to call someone a Galitzianer. A good example of nuances in language. During the six months that we lived in Warsaw, waiting for passage to the New World, I had little difficulty speaking the common Polish language used in the street. By the time we arrived in Nova Scotia, in August of 1921, I felt comfortable in the use of six different tongues, at the ripe old age of eleven – Yiddish, Hebrew, Ukrainian, Russian, Polish, and German. French and English were completely foreign, figuratively and literally.

The day we arrived in Quebec City, I was greeted by the neighborly French children with the words "Muzhi Juif," which I learned to my consternation meant "Damned Jew." In spite of that, a year and a half – plus – later, I had a semblance of beginning French as taught in the public schools of Montreal. Four years after we came to Baltimore, when I had a chance to choose a foreign language in high school, I chose French. Fortunately, when I was asked to teach a beginner's class in French when I began teaching in 1931, I was able to teach very elementary French to a 9th grade class – staying one lesson ahead of them each day. I did supplement this by taking two courses in French in college.

My love and interest in languages came in quite handy much later when Mollie and I did a lot of traveling. When we were in Italy and Spain, I had no difficulty communicating when confronted by natives who spoke little or no English. I made good use of Yiddish numerous times both in our travels and when I worked in hotels on Miami Beach. At the Forum retirement community, I've used Yiddish many times. I even used my limited Hebrew to talk with an Israeli who was visiting his parents a few years ago. My very, very sparse Spanish – apparently acquired by osmosis – has also helped me. In short, other languages have been quite useful to me on many occasions, when English wasn't the best one to use.

It should be pointed out that, while languages were important in my life, school in general was always intriguing. I loved all subjects, perhaps because school came so easily to me. I'm blessed with a good memory and could easily grasp what my teachers offered me, whether oral or written. Studying and learning was actually fun for me. Most of the time I didn't even have to review my lessons in order to prepare for a test. Lucky me.

It thrilled me to see my children and grandchildren take other languages in college.

by Ralph Bartel
May 20, 2004

A LETTER ABOUT HATRED and ANTISEMITISM

The bitterness of hatred, as demonstrated by last week's murderously devastating attack on New York's World Trade Center and Pentagon (September 11, 2001), brings back painful reminders of personal encounters. The only ones who can truly understand are those who have actually experienced the humiliation and physical and mental pain caused by people against them, solely because of differences in skin color, language, religious beliefs or even political differences. It can inflict unforgettable and long-lasting suffering. Under the worst circumstances, hatred – in turn – can turn the sufferer into just as great a hater.

In my lifetime, I have been exposed to a number of these terrifying and humiliating experiences. Confined to the limits of our small *shtetl* in Lyubar – under the threat of attack from larger and stronger peasants – fear was instilled in us by our parents and neighbors to the point that we never dared to explore the countryside without the company of an adult. As a result, when the pogroms came, being scared came naturally. Papa's beating and humiliation by the pogroms was a scary, never-to-be-forgotten experience. How can one detail the constant state of the unknown and frightening thoughts going through the minds of a scared little boy, during the many days and nights of the final pogrom? How to describe the additional anxieties piled on my mind by the stories of the survivors of the ordeals, upon our return? Those indelible memories and shivers remain! I have never dared to return to my birthplace, and it's why I rarely talked about it. Who can blame me?

Fear was a constant during the few days of our stealth travels from Lyubar. All day we had to remain absolutely quiet – hiding in the deep forest – lest someone discover us. Traveling in total darkness, entirely dependent for survival upon the Ukrainian peasant Papa had bribed, we held our breaths in fear, till we reached safe terrain. In Galicia and Poland we were examined by strangers who didn't hide their animosity towards us. In Liverpool, England, everyone seemed to stare at our family. Sure, we were strangers in a strange country, but why did so many people need to stare? It was a frightening time for me, and the fears lasted for a long time. Even during our three-week ride on the ship to Canada, the crew seemed to look harshly at us and bawled us out (in a strange language) constantly. Hatred?

On our first morning in Quebec City, I heard my first two words in Canadian French from two little boys about our age: "Moujy Jief!" ("Damn Jew!") How can two little boys learn to say such words in an obviously hateful manner? In our first year of school in Montreal, I was constantly taunted, harassed, and bullied by French-Canadian boys – strangers – both in class and in recess, because I couldn't speak their language or play their games. When I struggled to say a word in their English or French, I was greeted by laughs and jeers. Can you guess how that made me feel? My constant blush at my embarrassment just added to their laughter. Hatred?

Although I was already past my thirteenth birthday when we came to Baltimore, my English was miserable. It would take four or five more years before I lost my accent, and this was the bane of my existence due to taunting by schoolmates and neighbors. The Fallbrook section of Baltimore, where our family store was located, was a predominantly Christian neighborhood. It was made up of a mixed social class, ranging from the low poor to the above-average middle class. The neighborhood children came from the low end of the strata, and behaved accordingly to us. Their dislike for anyone who was different – in any way – from them, became apparent from our first encounter. My inability to understand their language, plus my strange accent, drew out their inner animosity. When I made an error or misunderstood their intentions, the first emission was "Damn Jew." Any possible latent athletic skills I might have had or developed were quickly squelched by their unfriendly outbursts and curses. It didn't take long for me to become so discouraged and disgruntled that I quit going to the pick-up games on our street. Inadvertently, thanks to their rebuffs, I became an avid reader and soon outpaced my classmates and neighbors in my vocabulary and education.

Unfortunately, the grown-ups among our neighbors took little pain to conceal their own feelings towards us. Except for one Irish policeman I remember, who came into our store around New Year to buy pickled herring, I can't recall a single instance of a neighbor ever coming into our store. By the way, that policeman insisted the herring brought good luck if eaten before the new year began. In all fairness, maybe the neighbors did not come to our store because of the larger J.W. Crook grocery store in Baltimore that occupied the front of our Aunt's building on North Avenue. It rivaled the A&P, doing far more business than our store. Regardless, it bothered me then that our neighbors never shopped in our store, and it is still a bad memory.

When I got my work permit and quit school in February 1925 to work full time in the store, I had a few problems with some neighbors. Some kids would gang up on me and overturn the little red wagon I used for deliveries. If I tried to defend myself, I was often beaten up by an older brother of the victim. Life was a constant challenge until we bought our 1926 Chevrolet to help with deliveries.

During my first year at Maryland State Normal School, I experienced another form of hatred. In October I was asked to sing "The Three Grenadiers" in German, for Parents' Night. On my way home on the streetcar, I sat opposite a girl carrying a violin case. She complimented me on my performance and we chatted informally during the long trip to North Avenue. Eleanor McDonald, a Senior, was amazed when she found out I was Jewish. She had never seen "one" before and apologetically explained that she looked for horns on my forehead – as she had been told – in the Catholic schools she'd attended prior to going to Normal School. We became friends and saw each other at school and at the Glee Club, as we practiced singing Christmas carols. One day she asked me if I'd come to her home on Christmas Eve, at a party to sing Christmas carols. Complimented by her request, I accepted. After thanking me profusely, she added a caveat. Would I please not mention I was Jewish, since no Jew had ever been allowed in her home and she was afraid of her parents' reaction. I did go, and sang, together with her and her friends. Before graduating, Eleanor professed her love for me and begged me to marry her. She threatened to become a nun if I refused. I finally convinced her that neither her parents nor mine would ever approve such a marriage. I'd never do anything that would break my parents' hearts. I didn't think she would, either. We remained friends until she graduated.

Other than my problems with one teacher, Miss Jones, I had no other incidents of hatred in Normal School or during the thirteen years I taught in the Baltimore school system. Perhaps it had something to do with the fact that Dr. Weglein, the Superintendent of Education, a nationally recognized outstanding and esteemed educator, was Jewish-the only Jewish Superintendent of any major education system in the country. Stories of prejudice were common but none involved me, that I recall.

When we came to Florida I was amazed at the blatant public displays of hatred. We came to Miami Beach, a city where the predominant majority of residents were Jewish. Yet, a few blocks from the Sinclair Hotel – where our family first lived – a sign on a dumpy hotel on the comer of Alton Road and 15th Street read "No Jews or Dogs Allowed!" But in spite of that and other examples of prejudice we occasionally encountered or heard about, we had no dealings worthy of detailing with any of them. By far, every facet of government, business, or trade was operated or controlled by Jewish people or those willing to deal with them. Since the vast majority of people staying at the Sinclair Hotel were Jewish, the two years of living there caused no problems for any of us. We left the Sinclair mainly because it was no place in which to raise a family. With Miami Beach housing so expensive, scarce, or restricted, we bought a home in Miami.

While we were not personally affected by displays of hatred, examples of discrimination in Miami Beach were obvious. Apartment buildings that excluded Jews deployed discreet signs reading "Gentiles Only." A branch of a very well-known National 5-&-10-cent store and drug store occupied the corner of Washington Avenue and Lincoln Road. Its lunch counter served a constant flow of customers – white only – from breakfast through supper. Directly on the right side of the Washington Street entrance, the two water fountains on the wall had a sign reading "White Only" on the higher one; "Colored Only," on the lower. The maids and maintenance men we had at the hotel, all African American, had to leave early every day, to get back to their homes in Miami before the "colored curfew" hour of seven o'clock. Buses and jitneys (7-8 passenger cars that picked up riders) destined for "Colored Town" stopped running after then. The only people of color remaining after seven were provided living space on the estates or clubs of the wealthy. They were not allowed on the streets of Miami Beach at night. While it bothered me, often, I must confess that I was too busy trying to run the Sinclair to give it more than just a vague, occasional, unhappy thought.

In the fall of 1946, when we returned to Miami from our summer in Atlantic City, we moved into our new Miami home. This did not pose any problems of a discriminatory nature. Our Christian neighbors accepted us. We were friendly to them, without pushing. We had one son at Shenandoah Junior High and another at Shenandoah Elementary. I later did return to teaching, as you know, but at that time, when I looked into the possibility of returning to the classroom, I found the salaries much too low – especially compared to what I had earned as a teacher in Baltimore. I was a bit annoyed with the cool reception by the woman who was the head of the employment bureau and only learned – many years later – that she was known for her determination not to hire any Jews or Catholics.

During the nine years in Miami, following our leaving Miami Beach, I had few significant experiences of prejudice or hatred. The State of Florida had undergone major changes. The Legislature had changed from the hotbed of the "Redneck" majority and control to a more representative and liberal (call it "South Florida") body. There were now a larger number of legislators from the more heavily populated South, including Jewish members who sponsored and passed new laws that made displays of discriminations or exclusions illegal and punishable. With the boom in new construction that followed the War, Florida had a massive spurt in population growth, which included a large number of Jewish families. Drastic changes were inevitable. Cities and land deeds that had restrictive covenants suddenly faced legal challenges. The result was that Coral Gables and many heavily "restricted" subdivisions throughout Dade County gradually loosened their standards for home ownership, allowing Jews. By 1950, Coral Gables permitted a small group of residents to hire Rabbi Morris Skop as its spiritual leader and open the Coral Gables Jewish Center, the first Jewish House of Worship in the city's history. Mollie became the Principal of its Sunday School that fall. Fort Lauderdale and other cities with restricted communities soon followed suit.

Mollie decided to try substitute teaching (remember, she hadn't yet gone back to get her bachelor's degree and hadn't yet returned to full time teaching). When she applied to Coral Gables Elementary, she felt sure she'd be rejected because of her religion. Much to her surprise she was shortly called and overjoyed at her reception and satisfying results. So much so, that she then decided to go back to school at the University of Miami and complete the requirements for certification as a permanent teacher. Her struggles to complete her education were rewarded when she received a permanent job teaching third grade at Flagler Elementary School – one she held until she retired. Meanwhile, I soon decided to join her and go back to teaching, too. Then, the fun began!

The same woman who'd headed the Employment Division at the Board of Education, when I'd inquired in 1946, was still in charge. The difference in her demeanor, however, was noticeable. Unlike the last time, when I'd completed the application form, she went over it carefully and told me she thought I could fill a need in one of the schools immediately. The Board Office was located in the Lindsey Hopkins Vocational School building. She asked if I would consider teaching History in the Adult Division of the school. When I agreed, she called the school and enthusiastically explained that she had a gentleman in her office who'd fit right into their program. Should she send him over? Smiling broadly, she sent me upstairs to see the Head of Adult Education at Lindsey Hopkins.

He was a portly little man, about my own age then (45). He greeted me cordially and invited me to tell him something of my background and experience. The more I filled him in of my teaching experience and courses I'd taken, the more excited he became. He was elated with the fact that I had graduated from the University of Maryland with a major in Vocational Education and a minor in History. Plus, I had my 18 graduate hours in Guidance and Placement, so he felt I could fill a void in both their History and Guidance departments. He wanted me to meet the heads of both these departments, if they were in the building. "Yes? Fine!" A couple of phone calls later, he could only find the Guidance Chairman. Could I please wait about ten minutes, till his meeting ended? "Splendid! Oh, while you're waiting for him to come down, would you mind filling out our application form? It's exactly like the one you filled out at the Employment Office, downstairs." I took the form and proceeded to fill it out. Just as I finished, the Guidance Chairman entered the office. After the introductions, I submitted my application form and left with the Guidance Chairman for a tour of the school and the classrooms, upstairs.

After a few questions, my guide took me through several of the upper floors to show me the offices of the faculty, the number of shop facilities, and the classrooms for the Related Subjects that were taught in the Adult Division. His chatter made me feel as if I were already a member of the faculty. He looked forward to using me in his department. We took the elevator down together as he escorted me back to the office.

When I entered the office, I could see on the administrator's face that something was wrong! This did not seem like the same man whom I'd left a short time ago. When the department chairman told him of our successful tour, his answer was surprisingly noncommittal. He scowled and mumbled something inaudible in reply, then an awkward silence followed. I decided I'd better leave. "When do you want me to call you?" I asked. "I'm not sure when we'll decide," he answered, "We'll call you." The tone he used and the expression on his face told me that I probably would never hear from him again. Something had happened. What? What did I do? How could a man who'd been so cordial and enthusiastic about my future in his faculty suddenly become so cold and taciturn?

On my way home I went over everything I'd said or did while I'd been in that office. The last thing I'd done was hand him my completed Employment Application Form. When I left he was looking it over. What had I written on it that could have upset him so? Fortunately, I have a good memory and I could visualize every question and every answer I'd given. Finally, it dawned on me. The last question asked for memberships in organizations or affiliations. I proudly listed myself as Vice President of Coral Gables B'nai B'rith, member of the Education Committee of Beth David Hebrew School; and, members of each of their respective bowling leagues. It seemed obvious that these items had upset him. I'd wait a few days and see if I'm right.

There followed several days of agony as I waited – in vain – for a call from my interview. The more I waited the more I grew nervous and upset. A week passed before I decided to call him. His secretary kept putting me off. I called and explained that all I wanted to know was if the job was still open. Finally, she said that they'd "found a more qualified" person for the job. I burned up! I was sure that my religion had caused me to become "less qualified."

With the start of school less than two weeks away I had to do something about this. Who can I ask for help? I called Harold Turk, a former Mayor of Miami Beach, whom I'd helped elect, and told him my problem and suspicions. He advised me to call Anna Brenner Myers, the only Jewish member of the Dade County Board of Education. I called her office. She was traveling in Europe and would be back at the end of August. After calling her brother, Bob Brenner, a friend, and Rabbi Skop, with whom I was also close, for advice, and getting no satisfying solutions, I decided to go back to the School Board Office and raise hell. I was determined to tell that woman what I thought of her and the whole school system!

Unshaven and wearing a sport shirt, I drove to the School Board Office. I stormed into the room and loudly told the receptionist that I wanted to see the Head of Employment RIGHT NOW! Apparently afraid of the scene I'd created, she quickly dashed back to relay my demand. She returned to tell me that Mr. Westfall was waiting to see me. The woman I'd expected was on vacation and Mr. Westfall (a District Superintendent) was taking her place. The first thing he did was to calm me down. In a still voice he told me that – whatever my problem was – we'd make much more progress if I cooled off and discussed it in a quiet manner. "Take a minute to catch your breath," he suggested, "you look exhausted." In the few seconds it took for me to calm down I decided to ask if the position I'd applied for had been filled. He looked at his stack of file cards and said, "No." Then, I exploded.

Without a change of expression on his face he listened to my detailed report of what had happened from the time I'd last been in this office. Calmly and deliberately he explained that every principal of every school had the right to select his or her own staff. While he certainly didn't agree with what had happened to me, he'd look into that and do whatever was best to correct the situation. Meantime, if I would just wait in the reception room, the Principal of Hialeah High School was due in within the hour and was looking for someone with my credentials to fill his staff. As I reflect back at this scene I marvel at his ability to make me eventually calm down and accept his invitation to wait for the Hialeah High School Principal.

Ever since we'd come to Florida, all I knew about Hialeah was – at the time – it had a reputation as the home of the Ku Klux Klan and had saloons and/or churches on each corner. How could I – a Jew – dare to work in such an environment? How would a Principal of a Hialeah School consider me as a prospective teacher? All such thoughts were going through my mind as I sat and waited for this mysterious man to come.

Surprise! Surprise! Mr. Pease finally came; introduced himself to me; and, after a short conversation, invited me to come to teach in the Junior High section of Hialeah High School, which was temporarily housing 7th and 8th grade classes in its buildings. The school year 1955-56 was one of my most rewarding experiences in the profession of teaching.

Mr. Pease was a gentleman and an excellent principal who treated me and everybody else with the utmost respect. If more of us were like him, there would be more room for love in our hearts than for hatred.

Love, Ralphy

LYUBAR

I t was 1920 and a typically cold October morning in Lyubar. A sense of quiet sorrow filled the air. The snow was tightly packed on the ground. The dark clouds looming overhead seemed to predict the certainty of more snow. The quiet whispering of the neighbors, watching our wagon being packed with the leftover worldly goods of the family, heightened the tension of our departure. Everyone wondered – would we be able to overcome the dangers facing us as we fled Lyubar for America?

This was the scene that faced me, Rachmiel, as I came out of the house where I was born more than 10 years ago. I knew I was going to America. Never again would we have to fear the pogroms we'd lived through. No more hiding in the cornfields during the days, lying quietly all the time, for fear of being heard and captured by the roving soldiers. No more trying to sleep on the narrow boards of the farmer's bathhouse, shivering all night from the cold and from fear of capture. No more waiting for the farmer to bring out the warm boiled potatoes and warm, fresh milk that was to be our only daily meal. Best of all, I would never have to watch Papa being beaten with swords and rifles, as the brutal peasants-turned-soldiers had done last month. They had been trying to find hidden gold, that they insisted all Jews had. Time to forget all of that, if we could. Now, a new adventure was facing the family as we left for that faraway golden land of America.

Mama and Papa had sold – given away would be a more truthful term – our family home. They had sold and bartered as much of the beautiful dishes, linens and furniture as the *Goyim* (Gentiles) wanted. They had given away as many other of our family's treasured goods as were left, taking only a few of the goose-feather pillows and a "perena," plus all the warm clothing needed for their perilous voyage. Also along, one of the *samovars* (a heated metal container used to heat and boil water). Everything was loaded to the top in a wagon and we were ready

This portrait of Lyubar citizens includes members of the Bargteil family, as well as Chaika's husband, Muni Alter.

to leave Lyubar for good.

As the goodbyes were being said, Mama noticed that my face seemed unusually flushed. Touching my forehead with her lips, Mama realized her worst fears. I had finally contracted the dreaded Typhus fever which had devastated Lyubar during the past six months. With fear in her heart, she whispered the dreaded news to Papa. They looked at each other, at my two brothers, then at the fully-loaded wagon and over at the reluctant peasant who had been heavily bribed to lead us through the treacherous escape to Poland. They decided we had to go on. With me on top of the wagon, final goodbyes were said and our journey began.

The ensuing 75 years are filled with many, many stories of our family's journeys. The joys and sorrows, the struggles and accomplishments all left memories for each us in our family and could fill many chapters of many books. But a new chapter is about to begin that needs telling.

Soon, I – Rachmiel (now anglicized to Ralph) – will have a chance to relive memories of those early years through the eyes of my oldest grandson, Gary Bartel. Gary is 31 now, a young entrepreneur who decided to go into the import/export business that include Eastern European countries. He is leaving for a two-week visit to Russia and the Ukraine. Among the things he's packed in his suitcase are a map of Southwestern Ukraine. He's hoping I can help him find the correct route to take from Kiev to my birthplace, Lyubar. Gary plans to drive to Lyubar and take pictures of the places I have only recently begun to talk about. Despite all the hardships we endured there when I was little, I am looking forward to this "return to Lyubar" through the eyes of my grandson. (Gary's "Return to Lyubar" begins on page 192.)

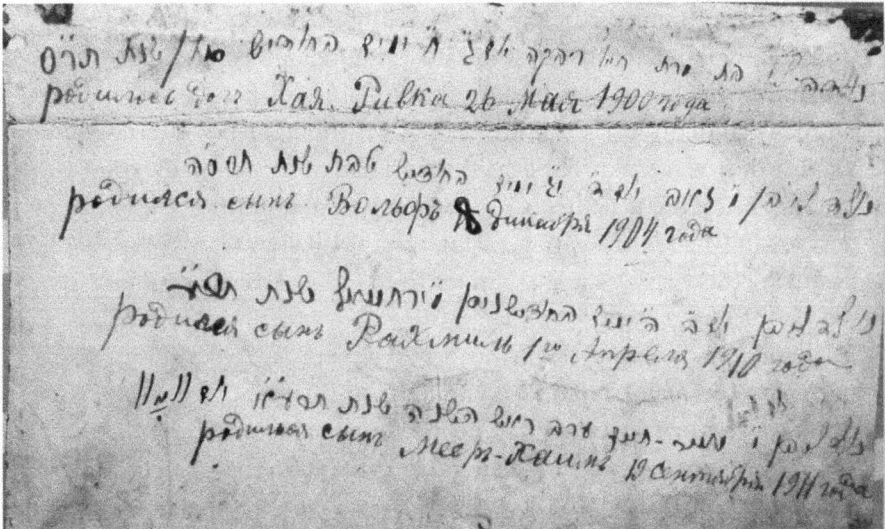

Russian document regarding Gdalya Bargteil, the father of Rachmiel (Ralph).

MIGHTY MIKE

One of my stories about my younger brother, especially his devotion to the Chalutz Movement and Zionism, makes me realize how little is known about Mike. Perhaps my recollections of him should be recorded and added to the readers' memories. A disclaimer must be included: What follows are my own best remembrances.

Of course it took many years for me to realize the extent to which Mayer (Mike) differed from the rest of our family and from so many others. No one could ever call Mike an "average guy." From his earliest years, he worked harder than anyone around him. No matter what, he avoided mediocrity. He had a passion to do everything, be everything, better, faster, funnier, or more hardworking than anyone else. If he saw someone do something that interested him, he immediately decided to learn. Mostly, he succeeded. On a personal basis, he often bested me in many ways. I don't recall feeling jealous, though I was aware – quite often – that he not only duplicated what I had done, but many times, did it faster or better. Whether it was learning *Chumosh* (the Five Books of Moses) in Cheder as a youngster, playing baseball or tennis as an adult, *trabering* (de-veining meat and poultry to follow kosher requirements), delivering orders or driving a car, raising money for a worthy cause, even accumulating money – the list could go on and on. Mike always drove himself to do his best and to do better than his peers. The results were mostly a series of successes that defied circumstances.

Long before he was old enough to drive, Mike had taught himself so well that he became the scourge of the neighborhood police with his wild escapades, as he zoomed down North Avenue in Baltimore, in borrowed Fords or Chevrolets. In spite of his constant speeding, he somehow charmed the police over and over again, so that they let him off with a warning. When I took my younger brother to get his real driver's license, Mike actually failed twice because he "drove too carelessly and dangerously." Both examiners who refused to approve his license told me to "take him home and teach him to slow down." I warned him that if he failed again, I'd refuse to take him. He finally passed and got his license, on his third try. But it never slowed him down. He burnt out the clutch on our 1926 car. Then our 1929 Chevy was totaled, when Mike rolled over three times in an accident in which he was speeding. Miraculously, he walked away from this with just a tiny scratch on one finger. That was Mike!

In our store he always delivered orders faster than I could. He became a better butcher than Pop or me. He found ways to charm and/ or please every customer in spite of his often rash behavior. His quick wit and jovial manner quickly brought smiles to the same people who'd just found some reason to complain. In the end, he won them over. To the best of my knowledge, no customer ever complained of his behavior. That, too, was Mike!

Mike couldn't resist his constant drive to question or challenge everyone's way of doing or saying something. This often resulted in controversies and sometimes unpleasant experiences. Our family was regularly informed of Mike causing an argument with someone (though not with a customer). When he thought he was right about something, no one could make Mike change his mind. Even in our *Gordonia* (Lions) Club, Mike aroused the ire of other members by arguing over just about any assertion. He always had an opinion and didn't mind letting you know, especially if he differed from you. Once he gave that to you, that was it! Period! Never wrong!

After Mike married Hannah Stone, they moved into his in-laws' house – customary in those days. The Stones had a well-established grocery business in an upper middle-class white neighborhood (Baltimore had a very solid segregation policy, carefully dividing "colored" and whites). Their store had a steady clientele providing a nice income. With his background, Mike was invited to work in their store, and it didn't take him long to find that there were a number of things in the operation of the business that needed his "fixing." Naturally, there was no way Mr. or Mrs. Stone, successful for so many years, could be told by this young upstart that their tried-and-true methods of running their business could be improved. The nerve of him! When he saw that his suggestions were not accepted, Mike convinced Hannah that they should find someplace to live on their own, that he'd get another job somewhere else. They found an inexpensive, tiny three room apartment in a converted row house, bought some inexpensive furniture ($1.00 down, and $1.00 a week, on the balance). Within a week, Mike was working, He'd walked into the biggest dairy in Baltimore at two o'clock in the morning, cornered the foreman, and convinced him that he, Mike, was the best salesman in the city. "I can improve any route. Give me three months and I'll show you at least a 25% improvement in business," Mike said. As it happened, one of the milkmen had called in sick and the foreman offered Mike one night's work, with no promises.

He then worked for that dairy for several years, without missing a day, often filling in for others as well. In due time, he proved to be their most productive milkman on several different routes. This was back in the horse-and-wagon days, where the horse knew the routes so well and would automatically stop at each house or store – until the delivery man returned and ordered the animal on.

Hannah's and Mike's marriage bonds were very strong, While he was working very hard and long hours, his job required him to report for work at 2 a.m. and work till 10 or 11 p.m. or later. Hannah didn't like the idea of their paying rent, so she soon found a row house for sale. Copying the style of their own rental apartment, they bought the row house and converted it into two tiny units. They lived in the downstairs part and rented out the upstairs. By the time their first son was born, they'd bought another house for themselves and had rented their former apartment out, become "real" landlords.

Neither Mike nor Hannah ever asked for any help or advice from their parents, siblings, or friends. We only found out of any event or changes when they offered to tell us. Somehow, they managed to scrounge up enough money to buy a car or house when they felt they wanted or needed it. Mike was an inveterate gambler and often was involved in any kinds of games of chance – either at work or after. I have no idea how this may have affected their lives. In any case, they'd surprise us often with an announcement of a change in their lives.

With the birth of Mischa, their first son, Mike assumed the added burden of providing extra income in his usual stride. One day, he informed us he would become a taxi driver, in addition to his milkman's route. How he managed or when he slept, we weren't told. Somehow, he'd found out when were the best hours – with the most income – for taxi drivers. He'd finagled to get a cab to drive at that time. During those years, driving a cab was not considered as dangerous as it is today. As usual, Mike was able to "milk" (no pun intended) that business so well that he always made more money than his fellow drivers. Also, as usual, he never complained of his hard work or long hours. To him, it wasn't at all unusual to end a night of driving a cab and reporting to work as a milkman, directly afterward. That was Mike!

The birth of two more sons, Morty and Michael, did not add any significant burdens on Mike or Hannah. They adjusted their lives and continued to work hard. Somehow Mike decided that a new wholesale produce store was needed in the very busy morning hours of the downtown market, where all retail store-owners went. In no time at all, he'd built it up to one of the busiest places for store owner-shoppers. It meant nothing for him to work many hours/days, to keep if open. He also did nothing to dispel rumors that there was gambling going on in the back room of his store. We know only that he apparently did well and supported his family well, When asked, he always smiled and said he was happy to work hard and make a good living.

Tragedy struck suddenly when they discovered that Morty – their brilliant little second son – was born with a terrible birth defect. He had a rare kidney disease that was incurable and life-threatening. They took Morty to the best specialists on both coasts, only to find that after he lost one kidney, he was condemned to a life of constantly wearing a catheter and unable to live a normal life. Worst of all, he was in constant danger of dying if his catheter became clogged or infected. It became almost routine for him to be rushed to "Emergency," for immediate attempts to save his life. Somehow, as Hannah said, they "coped."

As if that wasn't enough, they were hit with another catastrophe. Their oldest son, Mischa, their lovable, good-looking, laughing, perfectly healthy boy, drowned in the swimming pool of the Hebrew "Y" while attending summer day camp! It was a devastating shock to all of us. The effect on Mike was greater than on anyone else. He was a total wreck after Mischa's passing, unwilling and uncaring to function in the world that faced him, doing the bare minimum work to provide for his remaining family.

I had insisted that Mike and his family move into our house after the death of my nephew, Mischa. They spent several weeks with us, during which time Mike was so distraught that we feared he'd become suicidal. He told me he spent sleepless nights, trying to figure out reasons why he and Hannah were being punished with these tragic happenings. It was then that he decided to enlist in the Army, to serve in the infantry. He later confessed that he hoped to be killed, since life no longer mattered to him. Enlisting was not so easily done, then. First of all, he was a married man with children, someone who'd normally be deferred. Secondly, he was already 30 years old. The Army wanted only young and unattached men. But, stubborn Mike told them he was aware of all that and still insisted on his right to volunteer. After much wrangling, he filled out the proper forms, passed the physical test, and was told he'd have to take a written test to see if he were mentally and educationally competent – especially since he had not finished high school. Even under his circumstances at the time, the Mike we had all known could not resist any challenge that confronted him.

After taking the exam, his sergeant took him to see the base commander. The captain started asking all kinds of questions. "Who had helped him study for the exam?" "Where did he get his copy of the exam?" Of course, Mike indignantly denied and protested these questions. Finally, they told him he'd scored the highest grade on this exam, ever, on this base, and they wanted to know how he had done this. In fact, the captain told him, anyone who scored in the upper ten per cent of that exam was invited to attend Officer Candidate School. "In that case," Mike retorted, "I'm eligible and want to attend O.C.S.!" "That's impossible!" yelled the commanding officer. "You're much too old and you'll never be able to pass the physical training required to finish." "Try me!" Mike yelled back. The facts are that Mike did go to the O.C.S. He completed all the tests required, including the physical, and became the oldest lieutenant in the graduating group. Not only that, he'd done so well that they immediately assigned him to form a cadre to teach incoming candidates to O.C.S. He never was considered for overseas duty and remained on base until his enlistment time was up.

Thanks to that penchant for gambling, Mike made enough money to support his family while serving his country. It was while Mike was in the Army, reflecting on the tragedies he endured, that decided that G-d had been punished him for rejecting his Jewish upbringing. He began to attend Friday night services, held on his base for the Jewish servicemen. Because of his strong early background in religious services, Mike was usually the best qualified person to lead the service. His strengths became well known and, when the High Holidays approached, he was invited to conduct services at joint bases. Soon, he found that he enjoyed doing that and decided to make Judaism a very important part of his life. His return to practicing the religious tenets of his youth brought a great deal of pleasure to our parents in their later years.

Mr. Posin, the owner of the largest and most successful kosher supermarket in Washington, who had employed Pop as a Kosher butcher for many years and had become very friendly with our family, invited Mike to work for them when he came out of the service. It didn't take long for Mike to, once again, show his innate superiority. He became the best worker of the very busy delicatessen department. Mike arranged for our older brother, Willie, to get a job in the produce department. Mike became so popular that Posin's sons – who hoped to inherit the business when their father retired – felt threatened and started to complain.

The story of Mike's numerous endeavors requires much more detail than can be covered in a few pages. Suffice it to say that his many ventures and adventures in a number of varied fields were predominantly successful. This is not to say that things came easily to him. In fact, in most cases, he did struggle to overcome serious obstacles. But, his determination and drive knew no bounds. Whatever he decided to do, he strove to be the best and drove himself (and Hannah, too, incidentally) until he proved himself superior. In the few cases where he failed, his stubborn will kept him at his task long after the average person would have given up. A perfect example is the story of their motel adventure. After leaving Posin, Hannah and Mike acquired a dumpy, run down, eight-unit motel on U.S. 1, then the main highway from Baltimore to Washington. Although neither Mike nor Hannah had any experience or idea of how to operate such an enterprise, they had somehow determined that this was going to be their means of becoming successful and wealthy operators. The Hillcrest Motel was such a mess that they spent several weeks cleaning and painting the inside and outside of the units, clearing the grounds and installing plants, just to give it a semblance of a desirable place to spend a night on the way to our nation's capitol. Their neon "Vacancy" sign was lit every night. Even though they had worked nonstop all day, cleaning and painting, Hannah would sit in their tiny cubicle of an "office" till two or three in the morning, waiting, until all units were rented for the night. Most nights she was successful. In the meantime, they'd read every book and magazine they could get their hands on that dealt with motel operation. Soon, they decided to enlarge the place by building an addition, built to include suggestions from successful motel operators. Then they renovated the old units to conform to their newest ideas. In sum, by the time they were ready to sell The Hillcrest, it was a very up-to-date, verifiably good income-producing enterprise on a top location along U.S. 1. Mike was then so well-versed in the motel business that he claimed he could build the finest and most up-to-date successful motel in the area. And he proceeded to prove that claim, not by words but deeds!

This story requires an explanation of my brother and my sister-in-law's involvement with their Synagogue throughout their lives. One of the first things Mike looked for when he began working for Posin (after the Army) was a place to worship and practice his newly-found enjoyment of participating in the services. Although we'd been brought up in an Orthodox atmosphere, he chose at that time to join a Conservative congregation, not far from his new home in the Maryland suburbs. As usual, when he decided to join, he did so in full force. It didn't take long before Mike was recognized as a valuable and active member. Next thing we knew, Mike was not only a board member of his Synagogue but was being sent to the National Board of Conservative Synagogues as his Board's representative. Meanwhile, Hannah, who'd been raised in a non-religious household, attended services with Mike and soon found a need for her skills in the Temple library. Before long, she'd catalogued and reorganized the library so well that it became a very popular place for members and their children to visit and use. Her enthusiasm and skills led many members to dedicate new books as their contributions to the enlarged library. "Her" library became a model for other Synagogues.

As an active board member, Mike soon made friends with the richest and most influential men of the Synagogue. Among these were several successful developers and builders in the Washington community. When talk centered on motels, Mike soon convinced them that he not only had firsthand experience in owning and operating a motel but could also build the finest and best-run facility in the area. All he lacked was the financing. In sum, he ended up building a multi-story hotel not far from a Marriott – all under his supervision, from blueprints and plans that he designed. Upon completion, he hired every employee. He even demonstrated to the maids exactly how they were to clean the bathrooms and make up the beds in their allotted time for the eight rooms they were each responsible for daily. It was a successful enterprise. Unfortunately, the people responsible for successful endeavors don't

Mike on his birthday, in Israel.

always reap the benefits for long. Mike, as usual, made sure that he hired only top-notch employees. After a couple of years of success, the owners realized that their building was operating so smoothly that they could do without Mike's personal involvement and large salary. They thanked him profusely and gave him their best wishes for his next endeavor. Suddenly, he was free to tackle another experience.

Next thing we knew Mike was operating a men's store in the "colored section" of Washington. Again, in typical Mike fashion, his new challenge was turned into a success. While we couldn't understand why he chose to run a business in that neighborhood, Mike assured us that he'd taken precautions to protect himself and the business. He'd hired only black employees to run the shop and even had an armed guard to conspicuously stand near the entrance and watch all shoppers. Apparently, it worked. When the famous riots took place in Washington and fires gutted many businesses, his store was the only one in his block that was not looted or burned down. His manager and loyal employees saw to it that "their store" was left alone! We know only that he said he was making out well there. He did so well in the men's retail store, selling only high quality merchandise. Mike made such good connections with suppliers that he decided to open another store in a small town in the suburbs that catered to an upscale middle class white clientele. This, too, was soon a success.

Hannah and Mike soon desired to make Aliyah and move to Israel, even with their two sons' challenges. In spite of their son Morty's physical challenges and need for medical/hospital aid, he was a very bright young man and was determined to live an independent life, alone. He took courses in bookkeeping and accounting and became so proficient that he soon found work. His skills brought him enough income to enable him to move into his own apartment and remove himself from his parents' constant control and supervision. A remarkable achievement!

Michael, Mike's youngest, was not so lucky. A good college student, he early expressed his ambition to go to Law School as soon as he finished his courses. Unfortunately, his parents determined that they knew what was best for him. He was put in charge of the men's stores while they went to Israel to prepare to make *Aliyah* (immigrate) to the "Promised Land." The fact that Michael hated the work and was miserable made no difference to them. By taking over his father's job, Michael would make a good living and be able to support his family quite well. At the same time, Mike and Hannah could live in their beautiful new home in Jerusalem, furnished with the newest and best appliances money could buy, duty-free. The extra income from the men's stores would help them live in luxury in that new home. Ah, the dreams of man! We plan so carefully and diligently, look at every angle, to achieve our most ambitious plans – to no avail.

I'm certain that Mike and Hannah felt they were doing their best to establish Michael in a successful enterprise that would benefit them all. Sadly, it didn't work out that way. Michael tried, but his heart was not in the clothing store business. His distress led to neglect of not only the business but his own family, too. It is my firm belief that poor Michael just didn't have the strength and courage necessary to deal with the stresses of running a business he hated, let alone one so dangerous to supervise in the post-riot days in Washington. The end result was a substantial financial loss for Mike and Hannah, and the ruination of a life and career of a fine young man. Michael had always had a wonderful sense of humor and a delightful, witty personality. What a waste! As much as I admired Mike and Hannah for all their wonderful deeds and achievements, and for making Aliyah, the traumatic events in the life of their youngest son were seen by many as a direct result of their determination to run their son's life.

April 2, 2001

MORE CHARITY

In my earlier story on charity, I said I would not go into too many details about my experiences in that area. A visit last weekend by my grandson, Jeff, prompted a request for more.

I can't be sure about the order of Maimonides' degrees of charitable contributions (Maimonides is a medieval Sephardic Jewish philosopher who became one of the most prolific and influential Torah scholars) – though I feel certain that the following is among the lowest on his list. Excuse my explanations. As I have related, the Jewish population of the Fallbrook neighborhood in Baltimore was scattered over a wide area. We would walk over a mile to the Har Zion Congregation. Before the High Holidays approached in 1923, Papa – worried about the walk, the cost of tickets and the possibility of bad weather – talked to some of the customers in his store about finding a way to conduct services closer to home. A committee formed and they found a vacant, unfurnished house just a long block from our store. The group leased it. Volunteers put a coat of whitewash on the inner walls, rented folding wooden chairs, prayer books and a Torah. They made it suitable for Holiday Services at a very low cost. Tickets for Services were offered at a fraction of going rates at Baltimore synagogues, a sizable number of families joined. Several people volunteered, including Papa, all capable of conducting various parts of the Services. Thus, a temporary Orthodox Synagogue was born in Fallbrook. It is the practice, in Orthodox and in many Conservative Synagogues, to raise funds to cover its considerable costs by auctioning off the many parts of carrying out High Holiday Services. For examples: Opening or closing the Ark containing the Torah during certain prayers or when taking out the Torah; being called up for a portion of the Torah. Being part of the many rituals of the Prayer Service, is considered – by a pious Jew – to be a great honor, especially during a High Holiday. So, they are willing to pay for that privilege. By taking donations for these many honors, the Congregation always raises considerable sums to offset its costs.

Thus, during our very first day of Services, they were interrupted to allow our auctioneer to make his pitch. Before he began his offerings, he paused to introduce our acting president, Mr. Joseph Shugger. Mr. Shugger was the founder and president of the Baltimore Paint Co. and wished to say a few words. Presidents are always ready to "say a few words" – words that often boring the captive listeners. Anyway, Mr. Shugger welcomed his fellow worshipers and pointed out the burdens facing us to form a permanent House of Prayer. In effect, his comparatively short remarks urged everyone to open their hearts and pocketbooks for our most worthy cause by bidding as high as possible for each honor in this holiest of Holidays. Our needs were great.

To emphasize his own commitment, he himself hereby pledged to add 15% to every dollar raised during these holiday auctions! Think of that, he said, if you pledge $100, he will add $15; if we can raise $1,000, he would add another $150! No limit! In an Orthodox Congregation there is no applause to a speech during the holidays. Still, the murmur of subdued voices – even from the curtained-off women's section – was indicative at the surprise and welcomed announcements. True to his words, at the end of the auctions, Mr. Shugger reiterated his 15% additional pledge as he thanked all bidders. From that day on, whenever there was an attempt to raise any funds, he always rose to remind his audience that he would add his 15% to the total raised. Needless to say, I joined everyone else in holding him in very high esteem for his charitable acts. And, he was reelected president yearly, without opposition.

Several years later, while I was an active member of the Gordonia Club – a young adult division of the "Zeire Zion" Club. The club was dedicated to helping the development of Palestine. We decided to start a magazine devoted to educating the public about the movement, and I was elected the business manager. My job was to raise the money needed to publish the *Yardena* (The Garden), the name of our endeavor. Getting people to place ads, both as individuals and as businesses, was a critical part of that job, I immediately thought of Mr. Shugger as a surefire person who'd help us in our worthy cause. The cost ranged from $20 for a full page, to $3.00 for an eighth page. At my first opportunity – not on a Sabbath – I approached him and enthusiastically explained our purpose while assuring him that I'd be glad to display his full-page ad in any part of his choosing. Since I knew of his largesse in supporting our Synagogue, I had come to him as my very first and most important advertiser of the famous Baltimore Paint Co. Imagine my surprise and my dismay when he shook his head and rudely told me that he wouldn't consider it. "Son," he said, "I wouldn't give two cents for one of your ads. I'd rather pay $600 for a color ad in the Saturday Evening Post than to waste any money on yours. More people throughout the country will read my ad in the Post than in your measly magazine." My pleas to take any smaller portion of a page, even a $3.00 one, fell on deaf ears. My chagrin at my initial failure was a bitter blow to my ego. Even worse was my disappointment when I realized that this man whom I had idolized as an example of a most worthy charitable man did not seem to deserve that recognition.

Thinking back to Lyubar, our house there was constantly besieged by every itinerant beggar who passed through. No matter how scrawny looking the individual, our parents always provided a coin or a meal. It was natural, therefore, for me to follow suit whenever I was approached, even in my newly adopted country. During one of my early morning stints working for Papa in Baltimore, when I was driving him to market in those dark pre-dawn hours, I remember sitting in the car while waiting for Papa. A bedraggled man approached and asked if I spoke Yiddish. "Yes," I said. In a whining voice he told me that he was broke and desperate. He'd come to Baltimore to get a job, only to find it had been filled. He needed to get back to Philadelphia to his family and lacked the fare. Could I spare a coin? Anything would do, please. Understand that a man, speaking Yiddish in a Gentile marketplace, asking for help, is a pitiful subject to a tired, half-asleep young man – even one like me who was in the habit of helping beggars. Without thinking I put my hand in the watch pocket of my trousers (pants then had a little pocket directly under the belt, on the right hand side), took out my only two quarters, and I gave them to the poor man. When Papa returned we took off to go home. Imagine my humiliation, hurrying to anger, when – as we turned a corner – I saw my erstwhile beggar come out of an open saloon door. I must have made some sound because Papa asked me what was wrong. I pointed to the swaying drunk and told him what had happened. Without a word he took out his little beitel (purse) and gave me the two quarters. "It's not for us to pass judgment on our fellow man," he said. A lesson.

A different kind of charity experience comes to mind. In 1944, shortly after our arrival to Miami Beach, I was standing in an empty Sinclair Hotel lobby, worrying about how I was going to pay the upcoming rent due the owners. This was during that terrible first year of operation. All animal racing had been closed, people were warned not to come to Florida because there would be no Ration Coupons, and I had a bunch of cancellations from people who had reserved rooms. Two men walked in. After ascertaining that I was Ralph Bartel, they informed me that they were volunteers from the Combined Jewish Appeal of Greater Miami. They presented me with a card that had my name on it and told me they had decided that I should contribute $360 (ten times Chai). I became so upset at the nerve of strangers determining what I should contribute that I was afraid I'd physically attack them. Fortunately, the lobby was empty, for I berated them in a loud and threatening manner and shouted them out of the Sinclair. It wasn't enough that I was worried sick about meeting my obligations for the month, and that I was indebted to so many of my family and friends, and could see no way that I could even repay them – here were two strangers coming to tell me not only to contribute money to a charity I'd never heard of – but they also had the Chutzpah to tell me how much to give! It would me quite awhile before I cooled off.

Believe it or not, a couple of years after that tirade, the president of Ralph Realty Co. (yes me, the very same Ralph Bartel) was busy visiting some 20 Jewish strangers in Southwest Miami, to solicit contributions for the Combined Jewish Appeal of Greater Miami. I can't remember who got me to volunteer. But I distinctly remember how hurt I felt when my pleas were rudely turned down. You bet I was disappointed, as had been sure I'd raise more than my quota.

From the time when I was a new immigrant, hardly able to communicate, in a strange country, in a strange, mixed neighborhood, I seem to have been actively involved in trying to raise funds for a variety of causes. On Sunday mornings I carried a Pushke (a green can) in which I asked total strangers – Jewish or not – to drop in any spare coins, towards the Jewish National Fund's attempt to plant trees in what was then called Palestine. As an aside, when Mollie and I visited Israel many years later, we went to see the forest built with those tiny donations and thanks to the many larger contributions by the Kennedy family and others. Of course, some of them were because we were personally or directly involved. After our son, Alan, recovered from his polio attack, we set out to raise funds for the March of Dimes. Mollie and I worked endless hours to plan and execute a March of Dimes Ball, to raise funds to fight polio. It was a most successful one-year effort. Years later, when I learned that B'nai B'rith sponsored a hospital in Denver that helped tuberculosis and other lung disease victims – without questioning ability to pay – I gladly contributed and sent annual contributions. I may not have mentioned that my father-in-law, Alexander Hirsh, had lung problems that contributed to his death. When Israel was attacked during the 1973 War, Mike and Hannah were already living there. I didn't need any incentive to try to help. The day I learned of the attack I drove to the bureau's offices on Biscayne Boulevard. My check was the largest I had ever drawn for any charitable organization. Even my start in stamp collecting of Israeli issues sprang from my interest in helping the State of Israel.

Love, Ralphy
January 17, 2005

Ralph Bartel in 1963, from a U.S.
citizenship document.

MY FATHER

My father was the kind of person who'd be ignored in a crowd. He had no outstanding features or marks to distinguish him from anyone else. He was just the typical "average" man in height, weight, voice, manner, achievement, or any measure of a man's accomplishments or characteristics. Yet, if one were to try to find an example of what defines courage, he meets every criteria.

The following details of events in his life illustrate how fitting the dictionary's description of "courage" relate to the gentle and unassuming man who was my father. I called him "Papa," then later in life "Pop." *G'dalia* (Gedaliah) *Bargtale* (Bargteil) was born in 1870, in the little village of Lyubar where I was also born. By the age of thirteen he'd become fatherless. Apprenticed to a butcher, he learned the trade and helped support his widowed mother and younger sister and brother. For 16 years he worked at various endeavors in Kiev and in Lyubar before he married *Pessel* (Bessie) Kashtaluke. Mama was the daughter of Mayer for whom my younger brother was named. Mayer Kashtaluke was a respected and learned scholar from Odessa. With very little formal schooling, Papa became fluent in Russian, Ukrainian and Polish, as well as Yiddish and Hebrew. He could read and write and was often asked to read a message or letter addressed to one of the illiterate neighbors or a peasant customers in our family store. In Shul, many would come to him for help in locating the passage being read or prayed. Although not a rich man or formal scholar, he was held in high esteem by the townspeople and was elected *Gabbai* or board member in the town's big Shul, "Bes Hamigdash Hagodol." It was a very high honor for a very ordinary person.

This quiet man was not only respected by his peers in the predominantly Jewish population of the village but also by the *Puritz* – the town's wealthy landowner – as well as all the farmers and workers in the entire area. The army recruitments, the constabulary, the operation of all businesses both in and outside of Lyubar were all in the Puritz's jurisdiction. Since this man was judge and jury over all disputes and meted out his favors as he pleased, it always required his permission to start or carry out any new or different enterprise. Papa often acted as negotiator for the Puritz. The constable came to our house or store to tell of impending news or action, both in good times and bad. Thus, Papa knew of coming proclamations (even possible pogroms) affecting townspeople; he could inform the Rabbi and other leaders to plot actions or preparations.

With World War I, many of the teachers in Lyubar left the Ghymnazia for service, while a few farmers and sons were called for duty. Residents became aware of difficulties only when shortages appeared. Our store catered to the needs of all citizens with basic household necessities – sugar, salt, tea, flour, spices, dried fruits, peas, several kinds of beans and nuts – all the daily requirements. When supplies of an item became low, Papa would take a wagon to Berditchev or another town or even go to Galicia or Poland for replenishments.

Gdalia Bargteil

The War changed all that. All commodities became hard to get and much more costly. The muddy rutted trails that served as roads in or near us became dangerous places to travel. Hooligans and thieves found a ready market for any goods they could pilfer. If anyone tried to prevent them from robbing, he would invite a terrible beating or even death. In spite of all those hindrances, Papa somehow managed to find the goods Lyubar needed, and return safely with them, time after time. In spite of my immaturity, I was aware of the dangers and spent many sleepless hours imagining all the possible things that were happening to him while he was gone.

The oncoming Revolution was a constant topic of conversation in town, amplified as conditions worsened and shortages grew more severe. The poor peasants suffered even more because their very lives depended on their abilities to obtain goods on credit until their crops were harvested. In effect, they were serfs whose primary and greatest obligations were to the Puritz. After that, they were free to pay off any other debts and use any leftovers for barter or sale. Thanks to people like my parents, they were supplied with all their needs on credit with the proviso that they'd later reimburse us. As conditions worsened and goods became harder and costlier to get, some merchants found it difficult to extend credit because they, too, were suffering. But, not Papa. They could depend on him. Sometimes, there would be disagreements and arguments. Most peasants and their families were illiterate. The few younger ones, who'd had some education, became soldiers and/or Revolutionaries. Everywhere people went, their plight was emphasized by speakers opposed to the Tsar and his followers. The obvious oppressors were the monarchists. Closer to home, the Jews – who all owned the stores where supplies were denied – were held responsible for the struggles of the hardworking slaving farmers. On a given Saturday night, after enough vodka had been drunk to dull their senses, a few whispers among the farmers soon led to the conclusion that it was the local merchants who were to blame for their problems. "Look, there goes a Jew! He refused to let me charge anything at the store. Because of him, my family is starving!" Confrontations were inevitable and incidents took place that led to beatings and bloodshed.

Our only true contact with the war came when troops happened to pass by our village and made camp close by. If they stayed for any length of time, the officers looked for homes for accommodations. Our house served as one of those chosen. Although they disturbed our sleeping and eating plans, we never had any problems with either German or Polish occupants, both of whom were our "guests" at different times. We heard that, in some other places, there were "happenings." Papa was kept informed by the local constable and warned of potential dangers.

Before the Revolution was firmly established, things changed for the worst for us. First, the "White Army" or "Cossacks" who represented the old regime, would come by and camp in or near Lyubar. They'd stay for a couple of weeks or longer until the ragtag "Red Army," representing the Revolutionaries, would chase them away. Each of these troops would demand food and supplies from us and sometimes shelter too. It was a very unstable time and caused a lot of problems. Life as we'd experienced it was completely disrupted. No one knew what to expect each day. Everybody was nervously aware of the "soldiers'" presence and alert to prevent any incidents. The Ghymnazia closed. Hebrew school or Cheder was conducted in secret and with constant lookouts for soldiers approaching. Studying was conducted quietly lest attraction brought inquiries and possible beatings.

The ragtag "Red armies" were composed of predominantly uneducated, hungry and ill-bred peasants. They suddenly became important because they carried a rifle and could lord it over the hated Jews. Compared to them, every Jew was rich and therefore responsible for their own miserable conditions. Without leaders' restraint, the bullies taunted and badgered the helpless Jews, who were cautioned not to resist or fight back They believed every Jew had money "hidden" in his home, and would harass or beat the Jews until the money was given up. *Pogroms* (organized massacres) followed. Probably because Lyubar was such a comparatively small village, we were not subject to as many disruptions as other places. Thanks to being forewarned, Papa was one of the first to close his store when trouble was coming, and he would warn others to go home or hide. Even when one of the marauding gangs came through, our own family was not actually bothered much. With the shutters closed and everything boarded up, our house looked deserted. All of us huddled quietly in a corner of our large living room, and I shivered with fear, ignoring the banging on the front door till they gave up and went away. Mama had baked the usual large round loaves of black bread that was our staple, and we ate cold food. When conditions quieted and word came that the invaders had left, doors reopened and life was cautiously resumed. It was a very stressful period of our lives. Papa, in his quiet manner, calmly guided us through the days and nights. It didn't last too long.

It was inevitable that the Pogroms would find their way to us. Even though our village was on a little used excuse for a road, some of the passersby decided to see what they could find. The first excursion brought harassment and looting from any stores still open. Then, a young 16-year-old girl was accosted in the street. We later learned that she was subjected to pushing and shoving until one of the gang pulled her into a wooded area, where she was repeatedly raped and tortured until she died. It was the first casualty in Lyubar and brought a terrible cloud on our comparatively peaceful existence. Unfortunately, it was not the last.

As I tried to focus on our last years in the place where I was born, it dawned on me that – even though I didn't realize it at the time – Papa courageously made it possible for all of us to both survive and escape.

Our house was broken into several times. Each time, Papa was ordered to hand over the money he had, or they thought he had. He led the robbers into every room in our house where they searched for any additional loot. Always, he was threatened when they weren't satisfied. Quietly and steadfastly, he explained that – because of the bad conditions caused by the War and upheaval – we were unable to earn as much and therefore had no more money than they had found. Unfortunately, it was the truth! Our source of income had dried up and we, too, had lost most of our wealth.

Shortly after that another marauding group of "soldiers" passed through. They methodically selected the largest houses and forced their way into ours. There followed one of the most harrowing experiences of our lives. It started with their demand for all our gold. When told we had none, they began to beat Papa right in front of our eyes. We had been forewarned not to make a sound, no matter what happened. Through the blur of tears I watched as first one, then another swung his rifle butt to whack Papa's shoulders and back. The sound of each blow caused me to jerk and shudder, as if I were being hit myself. Not content with their results, one of them put a revolver against Papa's head and threatened to kill him if he didn't give them his gold. Protesting, he quietly told them that even if they did kill him, there was none in the house. Unbelieving, they then decided to drag him into one of the bedrooms and continue torturing him. We could hear them continue to hit him. The muffled sounds were followed by a quiet moaning from Papa as the beatings apparently ended.

When the harassment stopped at last, we didn't know whether Papa was still alive. Finally, he dragged himself into the living room. His appearance was so bad that some of us became hysterical. The coat on his back was torn, disheveled, and full of blood. His upper lip and nose were black and blood was running down his face and beard. Mama and I became hysterical.

After Papa had been tended to and some calm had been restored, he filled us in on the terrible tortures he had survived. They had taken turns beating him with their rifles, although he'd continued to beg them to take anything we had – we had no gold – and beatings would not bring any. Then, one of them took his sword and used that as a weapon, with no better results. Finally, their leader took one of the candles, lit it, and started burning Papa's nose, to try to get him to tell where gold was hidden. Frustrated at their lack of success, one of them punched his nose so hard it started bleeding. At last, their leader decided they'd wasted enough time on our house and it was time to move on.

Papa finished the gory tale by telling us that he thanked G-d for sparing his life, and that he'd decided we could no longer go on living in Lyubar. He planned to send a telegram to Mimeh Billich in America, to help us escape. Although I had only a vague idea what a telegram was and forgot we had a *mimeh* (aunt) in America, the looks on our parents' faces showed how terribly serious and important this action was. Fortunately, he added, their premonition of danger had been right—my sister Chaika had been spared our experiences when he'd sent her in hiding to one of their peasant friends a few days ago. Furthermore, he promised, we'd never have such an experience again. He'd arrange for all of us to find some place to hide the next time they were threatened.

A period of calm and peace followed. Life began to reawaken. Chaika came home, friends began to visit again, discussions and plotting and planning resumed. Muni, who'd been a steady visitor (and

Chaika Bargteil and her betrothed, Muni Alter.

whispered among us as Chaika's suitor) became a regular guest in our house. Rumors of troubles elsewhere brought little comfort to us. When Papa heard that, he instructed Mama to take extra loaves of bread each time she baked and made plans for us to leave immediately if necessary. The very next day, he came home and herded all of us, including Chaika and Muni, to get our prepared bundles of clothing and food and get ready to leave. Each one of us had been given a bundle containing a change of clothing, a blanket and instructions of what to do if accosted or – for any reason – we could not meet with the rest. He divided us into three groups, each going by a different route and told us to meet at the arranged farm of the peasant that was going to hide us. If the man would not accept us, we were given an alternate place to meet.

The reader should understand the danger this peasant family faced.

During the previous pogrom a farmer who had been caught hiding Jews had been brought to the market place in the center of our village and had been publicly burned alive, as people were forced to watch. Others had been severely beaten. Their leader had warned that anyone caught harboring or hiding Jews would be treated harshly. There followed the most tormenting experiences in our lives. Seventeen of us, from three different families, were hidden for a total of eighteen days by the farmer who volunteered to help us. When we joined the rest of our family, he led us into a barn to hide in a hayloft till dark. He instructed us to keep hidden and speak in whispers only. No one was to leave our hiding place for any reason. Only my brother Velvel (later Willy) – thin and small and when dressed in farmer clothes looked just like any peasant – was allowed to walk around the farm with a pitchfork and act as our lookout. When it became quite dark, the farmer led us very quietly to his dilapidated and unused steam bath house, located near a creek behind the barn. Using a coal oil lantern, he pointed out the shelves along the walls and benches on the dirt floor and told us that all seventeen of us would spend the nights here – as long as it was safe. Papa was immediately chosen by the other families to act as our spokesman and leader. He assigned the shelves and benches for each group, saw that everyone had food to eat and some cover or shelter, then gave instructions for each family to use a section of the nearby woods for their bodily needs. There was no outhouse around. In the dim light of that shelter that smelled from disuse and mold, each of us finally found our place and settled down for sleep. Exhaustion overcame fear and somehow, we all slept. Before dawn, the farmer awakened us. He and one of his sons brought a pot of boiled potatoes and two buckets of fresh milk. That would be the only visit and food he could offer us that day. Alongside the bathhouse, a large field of corn would serve as our hiding places, if necessary. Then, we were to break up into small groups of two or three and scatter among the very large field, in absolute quiet! Our – and the farm family's – very lives depended on our not being found!

Hungry, scared and worried, we remained in hidden solitude for over two weeks on the farm. None of us dared to venture out of our designated hiding places except to use the wood facilities when absolutely necessary. After about a week, Velvel, well disguised as a peasant, sneaked into town and stealthily entered our house. He'd brought a filthy looking potato sack full of our dirty clothes back with him. Using the same sack, he brought back some clean things for us and hidden among them he also sneaked in three large loaves of black bread that Mama had left in the oven when we fled. It's difficult to describe the unbelievably wonderful taste of plain slightly stale black bread when you haven't had a decent meal of any kind for several days. Papa wisely doled it out in small portions for three days.

News was limited to what little the farmer shared with us. Muni and several others had family that had remained when we fled. We were all concerned for their health and safety. We relied entirely on the farmer for our daily meager helpings of food, which did not vary. He had nothing else to offer us, since none of us would eat anything that was not kosher. Good water to drink was available from the spring nearby. Finally, after two weeks had passed by, the farmer told us things seemed to have quieted down and – if we dared – we could go back with one of the other families. We decided to leave the next day. Eleven of us remained until we were sure it was safe. After tearful hugs, kisses and many thanks to the farmer family, we returned to find, joyfully, that our home had not been disturbed while we were away.

Unfortunately, many horrible tales soon revealed what had happened while we hid. A number of our friends and acquaintances had suffered casualties, including deaths. The worst news closest to home greeted Muni. His young sister, a beautiful innocent girl, had been killed when she fought the soldiers who tried to take her with them. Our neighbor, across the street tearfully welcomed us home. We all stared at her in disbelief. Her lovely long brown hair had turned snow white! The invaders had tortured them and taken many of that family's precious belongings. Similar stories were repeated by practically every survivor. Amidst all the grief and tears Papa's determination to leave Lyubar grew stronger each day.

The primary goal now was to arrange for all of us to leave as soon as possible, The first priority was for Chaika and Muni to get married and send them safely out of possible harm's way. The announcement of their engagement was hurriedly made, with the marriage to take place shortly thereafter. Shortly after the engagement took place a new problem caused an unexpected delay of the wedding. An epidemic of Typhus Fever broke out in Lyubar. Typhus was a very debilitating, highly contagious disease. The patient had to be kept very quiet, with constant applications of cool cloths to try to reduce the fever. The crisis came after three or four days.

If the fever broke and the body's temperature came down, the patient gradually began to recuperate. Meanwhile, the person(s) tending the sick had to be careful – first, not to catch the disease then, not to pass on the germs to anyone else or touch anything that might cause contamination. All the clothing and dishes worn or handled by the "nurse" were washed in boiling tubs of water.

Although we had taken all known precautions to avoid contact with any victims of this dread illness, Muni came down with Typhus while in our home. He was put on a cot in our living room where Chaika tended to him. The next ten days were excruciating. We all avoided going near him or touching anything that might be contaminated. A constant supply of hot water washed our hands and all our clothing. Boiled water was used for drinking and cooking. Luckily, we avoided catching the fever.

While Muni was still in the critical stages of his illness, Papa was making preparations for the disposal of the store and whatever merchandise remained. The continuous shortages of all things made bidding for his wares intense and much bargaining took place between him and the many and frequent visitors. The value of the paper Ruble changed constantly so that most transactions were finalized by the exchange of silver or copper coins. All our beloved furniture, dishes, crockery, clothing and glassware were either sold or given away during the short weeks that followed. The farmers and peasants who had helped shelter us were amply rewarded. Reliable draymen were hired to move and dispose of everything.

Papa frequently disappeared for several days at a time and held many secret meetings with strangers; meetings that lasted for hours. We later learned that these were the plans that enabled us to leave and travel safely and have accommodations waiting for us when we finally arrived in Lemberg, Galicia, the nearest safe city of escape. Noticeably, everybody constantly treated Papa and Mama with the greatest affection and respect.

Shortly after Muni's recovery, harried plans were finalized for he and Chaika's hurried wedding. It was decided that they must leave immediately afterwards, since conditions still were very unstable. Frantic attempts went on to find a way for them to leave Lyubar safely. Travel was dangerous. With the continuous changes in occupants of the regime, passports and permission to travel were difficult to obtain and consummate. A fortuitous change in occupants took place during the early fall, to help solve the problems.

Muni had a brother, Shameh, who was an ardent believer and follower of the new Revolutionary movement. A bright and garrulous young man, his leadership qualities propelled his quick rise in the ranks. When his squadron came by Lyubar he learned of the predicament and quickly came to our aid. With the help of a friend who was a very gifted artist – false passports were formulated, along with orders to let the bearers pass peacefully. Muni and Chaika received their papers even before their marriage. Another set was prepared for our family, all with the "official seals" of the new regime. Chaika and Muni were married in a solemn ceremony outside our house on a balmy day, before a quickly gathered, quiet and saddened small group of family and friends. That same night they quietly left, with fear and trepidation in all our hearts. It was more than a week before we learned they had arrived safely. Plans for the departure of the rest of us were expedited and, we, too, left Lyubar forever.

The tale of our escape to Lemberg is told in more detail in another story which I wrote in 1995. Both our parents and my two brothers came down with Typhus. I had barely recovered from having the dreaded disease, yet I became their caretaker in our temporary safe house. Even while still weak from their ordeal, Papa tried to find Chaika and Muni and soon reached them. Our reunion brought happy tears of joy. We joined them in larger quarters and were reunited with the large group of Lyubar refugees who had also settled there in Lemberg. Papa was immediately elected an active advisor to the group.

Correspondence with America resulted in our next moving to Warsaw to await word of possible immigration. Meanwhile Mimeh Bilich sent us enough money to live on, temporarily. Winter passed, then spring, and still nothing. The quotas were closed to the United States. We could go to Argentina, where Mama's younger sister had emigrated. Papa did not want to go there. Finally, after nine months of frustration, we learned that we could go to Canada, which was not too far from where Mimeh lived in Baltimore. We accepted. Arrangements were made for us to be met upon our arrival. We would then be sent to Montreal.

The two-week voyage in the "third class" steerage section of the *Megantic* was another terrifying experience. Accommodations consisted of two hot inside cabins, across a narrow passageway from each other. Our parents had one, alone, because Mama was sick during the entire voyage. (I'm not sure if Papa paid extra for this.)

My brothers and I shared the other with a young boy of about 12. Each cabin had four bunk beds, divided by just enough room for a thin person or child to squeeze through. The airless place reeked of the accumulated stale sweat and body odors. Meals were served twice a day in an airless large space, on rough wooden tables and benches. Every meal consisted of a watery soup and black slabs of bread. Since we were observant Jews, we limited our meals to the bread. Papa bought some apples and gave the cook some coins for hot boiled potatoes, unpeeled. After our first meal, all of us became seasick. Mama never left her cabin after that, using a pail, always by her side, as she threw up constantly. Mayer and I held on to the railing of the ship the first couple of days, to rid ourselves of our food. Gradually, as we got used to the swaying and noise of the ship, we adjusted and walked outside – in our limited allotted area – whenever the weather permitted.

About a week after we left Liverpool, icebergs appeared in the ocean. The ship was forced to crawl along at a slow pace. All of us had another nightmarish cause to worry. Finally, on August 9, 1921, we anchored in Halifax, Nova Scotia, safe but not very sound.

The Immigration Terminal in Halifax consisted of a large brick building into which all new arrivals were shunted, to clear customs. The entry level showed a very high-ceilinged warehouse with baggage stacked along two walls and lines leading to glass booths, behind which uniformed men sat. Those with passports and visas went to the booths for examination and clearance. The rest, consisting of immigrants like ourselves, wearing identification tags, were herded into big holding rooms on the higher floors. Wooden benches lined the walls and filled the areas in between. We followed the others and chose one of the benches along a wall and dropped our cardboard valises and pillowcases, holding all our worldly possessions on the floor beside us. The windows behind us overlooked the harbor, while those towards the front of the room looked down on a cobblestone street and sidewalks. All the windows, although open, had strong iron bars across.

The uniformed guards spoke to us in French and English and motioned for everyone to take seats. After a while one of the guards clapped and waved his hands for quiet. We were shushed to silence while he explained the procedure. As he spoke a couple of men and a woman alongside him translated his remarks into several languages, including

Russian and Yiddish. They told us that all immigrants had to have a sponsor to guarantee that we wouldn't be dependent on the Canadian Government for help. We would remain in this place until our names were called or until we could identify our sponsor and knew he was waiting for us. Needless to say they were barraged with a harangue of questions by a bewildered crowd of exhausted, frightened, and confused people.

Like many others, we couldn't identify who was supposed to meet us or what arrangements had been made for us. Patiently, the guards informed us that we'd just have to wait until we heard our name called. Meanwhile, we boys had looked down into the street below us, where crowds of people were coming in and out of the terminal. Several men were milling about below, gazing at our open windows and calling out names as they walked. Suddenly, Velvel called out, "Papa! Papa! Come here! It sounds like someone is calling Gedalia Bargtale!" Papa hurried over and shouted, in Yiddish, "Yes. I'm Gedalia Bargtale! Who are you?" The man tried to shout his name but there was so much noise and confusion they couldn't hear each other. Finally, he took out a piece of paper, wrote something on it, and tried to throw it up to the window. After a few futile attempts, someone spoke to him and pointed to the street and made throwing motions. We watched as he bent down, pick up a stone, wrapped his note around it, and tried again. He'd attracted quite an audience by this time. None of his tries came anywhere near high enough to reach a window. After several failures, one young man took over; and, after a few tries, succeeded in throwing the stoned note through. Our sponsor had come.

Our guarantor had been hired by someone known to the Bilich family to meet us and see that we arrived safely in Montreal. My memory of our travel to his home in Quebec City is very hazy. I remember only that he lived in a gray stone house, not far from a synagogue. We went to services, where I met a little boy my age, and when told my name was Rachmiel, he said that was his name, too. Excited, I asked what he was called in English. He told me, "Joseph or Joe, for short." (When I registered in school in Montreal, I gave my first name as Joseph, and only changed it when we came to the U.S. after I'd learned that Rachmiel, in English, would be Ralph.) Unfortunately, the French registrar at Immigration, spelled our last name of Bargtale as "Bargteil" and we were stuck with that until I changed our name to "Bartel," in 1956. Sunday

No 319

Важний лише на оден рік.
Good only for one year from date.

ПАСПОРТ

PASSPORT

В ІМЕНИ УКРАЇНСЬКОЇ НАРОДНОЇ РЕПУБЛИКИ

проситься отсим всі цивільні та військові власти дозволити горожанинови Української Народної Республики

GDAEL BARGTEIL

який їде   ETATS UNIS D'AMERIQUE

переїхати безпечно і свобідно і в разі потреби дати йому (їй) всяку законну поміч і охорону.

Властитель паспорта їде в товаристві
SA FEMME PASIA CASHTALUKE BARGTEIL
42 ans and deux enfants Rachmiel
11ans and Meyer 10 ans.

IN THE NAME OF THE UKRAINI-AN PEOPLE'S REPUBLIC

all civil and military authorities are hereby requested to permit the citizen of the Ukrainian People's Republic,

BDAEL Bargteil

going to   UNITED STATES OF AMERICA

to pass safely and freely and in case of need to give him (her) all lawful aid and protection.

The bearer is accompanied by
HIS WIFE PESIA CASHTALIKE BARGTIEL
AND TWO CHILDREN. Rachmiel 11 years
and Meyer 10 years.

Montreal, Can.
дня 22 janvier,   192 3 року.

Montreal, Can.
this 22 day of   January   1923

НАДЗВИЧАЙНА ДИПЛЬОМАТИЧНА МІСІЯ УКРАЇНСЬКОЇ НАРОДНОЇ РЕПУБЛИКИ ДО УРЯДУ ЗЛУЧЕНИХ ДЕРЖАВ АМЕРИКИ.

EXTRAORDINARY DIPLOMATIC MISSION OF THE UKRAINIAN PEOPLES REPUBLIC TO THE GOVERNMENT OF THE UNITED STATES OF AMERICA.

Голова Місії
For Head of the Mission

**ОПИС ОСОБИ
PERSONAL DESCRIPTION**

Вік 51 ans
Age

Краска лиця frais
Complexion fair

Ріст 5'4"
Height

Очи bruns
Eyes brown

Вага 130 lbs.
Weight

Волося bruns presque gris
Hair brown almost grey.

Особливші знаки   Nil
Distinguishing Marks

The Bargteil family's passport, 1923.

morning he put us on a train to Montreal and bid us goodbye.

Whenever I see a scene or picture of immigrants trudging wearily in the streets of their new land, I become very emotional. It brings back the bitter recollection of our arrival in Montreal. Nobody at the station could tell us what to do or where to go for help. After what seemed a very long fruitless time, Papa led us out of the station and started to walk down one of the long practically deserted streets. He assured us that sooner or later we'd find someone to help us. We didn't know that on Sunday, most of Montreal stores were closed. The Gentiles were either in church or having a holiday at home. The Jews were busy in their own neighborhoods.

In spite of the warm day, all of us wore heavy coats on top of our threadbare clothes, carrying and dragging our cardboard valises and large pillowcases. We stopped only when Papa accosted someone who looked Jewish and asked for help. Time after time, we were disappointed. Either they didn't speak Yiddish, Russian, or didn't want to get involved, Perhaps the sight of our disheveled, emaciated appearance caused their discomfort or fear. The further we shuffled, encumbered with our loads, the more discouraged we felt. Hungry and exhausted from the endless efforts, Papa called a halt at a closed shaded store entrance. Wearily, we put our bundles down, as we saw a large wagon pull alongside the curb and stop. The driver was a strong looking, plainly dressed man with a brown beard, who examined us very carefully. In Yiddish, he addressed Papa, "Where are you going?" Surprised and a little scared, Papa shrugged his shoulders and said, "I don't know!" "What do you mean, you don't know?" he countered. "Where did you come from? Tell me. Perhaps I can help." Hesitantly, Papa told him our plight. He jumped down from the wagon, introduced himself, and assured us that he would help us. Putting our parents up on the seat with him, he told us three boys to climb into the empty back of the wagon, together with all our belongings.

No gifted author, playwright, or movie director could have picked a more poignant or moving scenario than took place that Sunday in mid-August of 1921, on the empty streets of Montreal. Out of the million inhabitants of this metropolitan city the one man who had the compassion and desire to help his less fortunate man just happened to drive by that street and see this straggling family in need. It is an event that firmly strengthens a person's belief that true faith and prayer is rewarded by G-d. Certainly, in my father's case, he fervently believed that this miracle was the work of G-d, repaying him for his unalterable faith and daily devotion – no matter the place or circumstance. Who can argue with him?

I remember only that our savior's name was Yacov (Jacob). Thanks to our dear niece Rosie (my sister Chaika's daughter), I learned some other details. Yacov Avrevtik, as kind a man as ever graced this earth, took us into his already crowded modest apartment. His devoted wife, busy with what seemed a houseful of little children, immediately started to prepare a meal for their starved guests. Somehow, room for us to sleep became available. We became part of this generous family, who fed and gave us shelter.

The very next day, Yacov found a job for Papa as a butcher. Within a week we were moved into a furnished three-room, third-floor, walk-up cold water flat, above a stable. For the next nineteen months we lived in Montreal, at some time on Demontigny, Casgrain, and/or Cadieux Streets. While life in that slum area was hard, we managed to survive – with never a complaint. In less than a year, Papa had saved enough money to send for Chaika and Muni, to join us in what was to become their permanent home (they did not join us when we moved to Baltimore). Mayer and I enrolled in school, where we were shunted into a succession of lower grades, while we attempted to learn English and French, both of which were a part of the daily curriculum. The usual struggles of immigrant life were both a constant challenge and a character builder. The strong survived and became the better citizens.

In those days, an immigrant who filed an application could apply for full Canadian citizenship at the end of a year. Papa registered as soon as he was told and became a citizen shortly after our year's residence, both for himself and his dependent family. A Canadian citizen could come to America and apply for U. S. citizenship, without quotas or restrictions. Meantime, we continued our correspondence with Mimeh Bilich and her family in Baltimore. *Feter* (Uncle) Bilich, who had experience as a grocer and butcher – although not as a Kosher butcher – agreed to convert the garage back of their home. Together with Papa, they would open a kosher meat and grocery store as equal partners. In early March of 1923 Papa left Montreal to establish the new venture. If it was successful, he'd send for us to join him, finally, in the United States.

In Papa's absence, my brother-in-law Muni took me one Thursday morning to a synagogue nearby, where I was initiated into Jewish manhood as a Bar Mitzvah boy. I was called to a brief Torah reading, chanted the blessings over the Torah, and was congratulated by the elderly gathering of the daily *Minyan* (prayer group) over their glasses of "Schnapps" and cake – the food courtesy of our family. A couple of weeks later, Papa sent us our visas and railroad tickets to Baltimore. Our family's journey to America, begun on that miserably cold day of October, 1920 in Lyubar had finally ended, successfully, thirty difficult months later during the month of April, 1923.

Life in Baltimore was another bittersweet experience and a challenge for Papa. His share of the partnership was a draw of eight dollars ($8.00) a week plus the meat needed to feed us. The space above the 9'x18' garage had been divided into two small rooms. The smaller one had an iron sink with a cold-water faucet, for our daily washing and drinking. It also contained a two-burner gas stove where we could boil water or make tea. The second room had enough space for one steel double bed, with iron spring and straw mattress, a small wardrobe plus an army folding cot. Mayer (or Mike, anglicized now) and I shared the bed, while "Willie" slept on the cot when he came home from work. He quickly got a job as a helper in a grocery store for $4.00 a week. Mama and Papa were allowed to use a bedroom in the large house, owned by our Aunt and Uncle. Our toilet was located in the alley that led from the main house to the garage. Once a week on Friday afternoons, we were allowed upstairs to take a hot bath, with a warning to be sure to clean up the ring around the tub after we finished.

At first, on Friday nights and Saturdays, we were invited for dinner at our Aunt's spacious dining room. Uncle, who was the most miserly man I ever knew, doled out everyone's food. The portions were so small that we all came away from the table hungry. Too embarrassed to ask for larger or more servings, we thanked them for our meals and left. Most times Mama would find something to serve us when we went up to our wretched apartment. Finally, Mama suggested that it put too much burden on Mimeh to have us for the weekly dinners. We were grateful for all they had done for us and felt we should now take care of ourselves, upstairs. With the bare facilities and no heat, our tiny space would be very inadequate during the coming winter, so we soon found a small house for rent four blocks from the store. Although the rooms were very narrow, the house had the typical Baltimore layout of a miniature "parlor", dining room and kitchen on the ground floor; then three very small but individual bedrooms and bath on the second floor. It also had a gas stove with an oven and four burners, plus a gas hot water boiler in the kitchen, to heat water for washing and baths. And, steam heat. It was the finest house we'd ever lived in. Best of all, we were independent of Uncle's influence.

Our Uncle made it hard for us to adjust and have a peaceful life. He could not get along with anyone. No matter what Papa did at the store, Uncle found fault: "Gdalya gave too many free soup bones to customers" – a common practice in butcher shops, Gdalya "was too generous in cutting the meat." He "delivers special orders without charging extra." A constant array of complaints permeated the day's work. Worst of all, Uncle not only criticized Papa in front of the customers, but he also quite frequently scolded and argued with these very same people. Some threatened to leave. Frustrated, our parents spent many hours discussing our plight – Mama went to Mimeh and begged her to talk to Uncle, to no avail. Papa, resolved to end this misery, finally delivered an ultimatum. He could either pay us out and take over the store, or arrange terms for us to buy him out. A sick and old man, Uncle had no alternative and reluctantly gave up his direct interest in the running of the business. Our parents took over and with their 14- and 12-year-old sons, and together we put in unbelievably long and difficult hours to run their store for the next eight and a half years. Business grew slowly.

For those of us who have become accustomed to get into our cars whenever we need something in the supermarket, it's difficult to envision the handicaps attached to running a meat and grocery business in the mid-1920s. In that cramped 9'x18' cement-floored space, fresh Kosher meats, lying on chopped ice, were arranged in a glass display case. Canned goods especially made to attract Jewish customers filled some shelves, Breads and rolls – delivered fresh daily – together with wooden boxes containing dried fruits, used up the rest of the shelves. Bushel baskets of fresh vegetables, 100 lb. bags of sugar, tubs of salted butter, lox, sour cream, and any other food expected to be found in such a shop, fought for a place to be stored or shown. A large walk-in icebox (cooled by two 300-lb. blocks of ice on top) stored all the excess meats, chickens, and perishable dairy products. If three people came into the store at one time, it became crowded.

To complicate things a bit more, ours was a STRICTLY KOSHER

market! Pop's strict observance and strong ethics dictated that nothing would ever be done, by any of us, to mix or handle meat and dairy foods in any but the proper way. All knives and utensils as well as the foods were kept in separate parts of the ice box and store. Separate papers and bags, too.

As I've mentioned, our store was located in the Fallbrook section of Baltimore, a predominantly Christian middle-class neighborhood. While not a restricted area, the Jewish families were either in small stores or otherwise scattered. Thus, most of our business depended on delivery. Enter Mike and me. Before we left for school each morning, we both took a basket filled with orders needing early delivery, either by streetcar or foot, near or on the way. It kept us hopping.

By far the greatest burden fell on Pop. Before dissolving their partnership, Uncle, who spoke English well, used to take orders on the telephone. Pop could not speak or read English yet so when the partnership split, he had difficulty understanding and answering customers on the phone. Again, Mike and I helped. As I reflect on his life, I'm still amazed at the numbers of hours he toiled. On Tuesdays and Thursdays Papa arose at 2 or 3 o'clock in the morning, went to the store and cut up the side of beef (250 lb. or more) into smaller sections – steaks, flanken, soup meat, breast, etc. – and then subdivided those sections into even smaller parts, ready for individual sales. Next, he would take two streetcars downtown to the wholesale markets, for chickens, fish, and vegetables. Since the chickens had to be taken to a Schochet (official Kosher butcher) first, and then plucked, he'd spend more than an hour gathering all his purchases before lugging them in two large straw baskets on two streetcars, to get home as near 7 a.m. as possible. Finally, he'd cut the meats on the early orders to be delivered.

Mike and I would help make up the early deliveries before 8 a.m., when the store would open for business. Mom would join Pop and the two of them would carry on till we came back from school. Pop had registered his application for citizenship in the middle of 1923, so he had to attend night school two evenings a week for a two-hour session, to learn enough American History and English so he could learn to speak and write and pass the citizenship test. It was a prodigious task carried out day by day without ever a complaint. The "Open" hours of our store were 8 a.m. to 3 p.m. Sunday; 8 to 6 Monday to Thursday; 7:30 to 2 Friday; and from dark till 11 p.m. on Saturday nights – about 60+ hours a week

– every week! The horrendous schedule and pressures took a terrible toll on Mom's health. Standing on the cold cement floor made her legs swell. By the time she came home to fix dinner, she couldn't tolerate the pain. Pop sent her home as often as possible. In cold weather – with only a little coal stove – her hands swelled to twice their size. The burden on both of them became more than they could handle alone. To hire someone to help, on the store's meager income, was impossible. Thus, the ultimate solution was for me to stop school, get a work permit, and help out full time. Even though I was a good student and loved school, I left school and became a full time worker at the age of 15. After accompanying Pop to the markets, I eased his load considerably. Later, I went on my own, most days, to do the marketing.

Business in 1926 increased considerably, since I took care of all telephone calls, delivered the orders (Mike still took those near school, on his way), and relieved Mom from most of her duties. However, with an increased business, new problems arose. It soon became too hard to please everybody, every time. Pop decided that we'd have to buy a car.

In 1926, when one bought a car, the salesman was obligated to teach the new owner how to drive and help him (the vast majority of drivers were male) get his license. The salesman tried to teach Pop. After two weeks of trying he told Pop to let me try to learn. Reluctantly, Pop let me. I received my license and, eventually, taught all our family and many friends how to drive – except Pop. He never could figure out the intricacies of shifting gears, steering, parking and stopping.

The next year Mike decided that he'd had enough school (he was too bright and couldn't tolerate the mediocrity of the average classroom), so he offered to let me go back to school and replace me at the store. By then, he was as tall as I, and heavier, too. We faked his age as 16, got him his driver's license (he'd already learned how to drive – without a license) and he took over in June of 1927. Although I continued to help daily – both before and after school – Mike was the mainstay of the business for more than five years, till he got married to Hannah in August 1932.

Before long, we rented a nicer house just a half block from the store and life became a bit easier. Pop opened a small account in a Building and Loan Association (savings and loan) near us and regularly put a few dollars away. Many people were affected by the 1929 stock market crash and lost their homes when they could not pay their mortgage loans. The B&Ls foreclosed on them and soon there was a glut of homes on their books. Pop was offered one of these homes, across the street from the store, for $2,800, just $100 down, with monthly payments of just a few dollars more than we paid in rent. Our new house was a good home to us and become a source of income during World War II, as well as bringing quite a substantial profit to our parents when they finally sold it.

The Great Depression that began in the late '20s followed a succession of bank failures and closings. The ordinary worker, who knew nothing about stocks, soon joined the former well-to-do in competition for every job. The bad conditions affected everybody. Small storekeepers like Pop had less and less business. Debts piled up so much that, when I started teaching, in September of 1931, I gave Pop $90 – out of my monthly $120 – to pay his accumulated monthly bills. At the end of the school year I returned to my summer job, as a waiter at PenMar Park. The marriage of Mike and Hannah at the end of August brought me back to Baltimore early from PenMar, to help out in the store. Somehow, even now with me teaching full time, Mom and Pop managed to keep the store open and satisfy their dwindling number of customers. In addition to teaching, I still did the marketing and delivered orders on my way to work and upon my return. Those were not the best of times – for them or for me.

My second year of teaching saw my salary cut by 10%. I was assigned to a school closer to home, thus making it easier for me to help out. Unfortunately, by January, all new teachers were reclassified as "Permanent Substitutes" and paid $3.00 per day for the number of days taught per month. Thus, for February, my pay was $57, instead of the $108 reduced monthly rate I'd been receiving. Since there were no other jobs available, we remained stuck. Mollie, one of the lucky newly-placed teachers, became a "regular substitute" at $2.50 a day, while working full time as a teacher. Even without my personal needs, there was very little money left to lend Pop.

Conditions worsened. The store's gross income had deteriorated so much that Pop had used up all his savings and was in danger of losing our home. By now, my help was needed in PenMar too. Mollie's brother Herman had left for a job on his own and the Hirsh's couldn't afford another waiter. Mr. Hirsh's health had not improved, and without me, their summer business looked hopeless. After three years of "going steady" with Mollie, I still couldn't consider marrying her because Pop depended on my help so much. Something had to be done.

By the end of summer, 1933, all of us were convinced that Pop's chances of making a living from his little store were now hopeless. Upon my returning to teach in the fall, Pop and I had several long talks, culminating in his agreement to close the store right after the Jewish Holidays. Meantime, he visited all the butchers in town and offered to work full time for as little as $10 a week Although most of them knew him and respected him both as a worker and person, not one could afford to hire anyone else. Sadly and dispiritedly we told our loyal customers of the store's closing. Most of them were friends as well as customers for many years and joined in expressing their regret at the circumstances.

The affection and respect that they had for Pop was revealed shortly afterward. One of them, a painter and paperhanger, mentioned that he had a big job in Washington and offered to make some inquiries when he went back. A few days later he called Pop to tell him of a possible job opening there. He even offered to drive him to Washington for the interview and bring him back. At the age of 63, considered an "old man" in those days, Pop got a new job at the unbelievably high pay of $35 a week, plus all his personal meat needs. It marked the beginning of what were to become his happiest years of work till he retired – at the "very old" age of 72 – at my insistence. I finally convinced him to retire, to return to his home in Baltimore, and to rent out the second floor of his house. The War had created a need for housing for the many workers in war industries in Baltimore. We converted the large pantry into a bathroom and they rented the upstairs for the duration.

During the War, with the rent from their tenant and their combined Social Security income of $59 a month, my folks were able to live fairly comfortably. Their needs were few. Their children and grandsons lived nearby. They should have been reasonably happy and content.

Tragedies are also part of life. My oldest brother, Willie, was having serious problems. He worked very long hours in a store that was open till late at night seven days a week. His livelihood depended on his getting these desperately poor people to buy on credit. Often, they only had a dollar or two, if any – to pay down on their weekly bills. He'd been robbed and beaten.

In spite of all these hardships, his wife, Pauline – who did not help him in the store – was not happy to be confined to this kind of life. Her complaints and nagging added to the pressures of the work, and caused

Willie to become an alcoholic. We eventually induced him to close up his store. My brother Mike got him a job in Washington, working at Posin's Supermarket, run by the same family that had employed Pop for so long.

Mike's oldest of three sons, Mischa, was a wholesome child, full of life. In the summer of his tenth year, while attending camp at the Jewish Y, he somehow fell into the swimming pool right after lunch and drowned. The terrible effect this wrought on Mike, especially, brought great sorrow to our parents and to all of us. Unhappy times were interspersed with a number of enjoyable occasions.

When Pop passed away, in February 1956 at age 86, he had lived longer than anyone in our family. Physically, he had overcome the tortures of the Pogroms; the welts and scars of his beatings were still visible on his back in Canada, over a year later. The burden of a double hernia – for which he refused medical treatment – and of having to wear a cumbersome truss all his adult life; a serious case of obtrusive hemorrhoids; the strength needed to lift and carry sides of beef weighing almost twice as much as he; the power to ignore the weight of the many tortuous hours of hard labor; and, even the loss of all but three of his teeth. Although he could've gotten relief, medically, for most of these ailments, he chose to live with them, in spite of my many attempts to get help for him.

That's why I chose the word courage. It exemplifies Papa's/Pop's life better than any word I can think of. Truly, he was possessed with the mental or moral strength to venture, preserve, and withstand danger, fear and difficulty as defined in the dictionary. Go back to any page of this narrative and you'll find an example of one or more of these traits. It makes me very proud to be his son.

Love, Ralphy

MY MOTHER, THE ARTIST

a poem by Mollie Bartel

My mother, at the age of sixty-four, lived by herself on Miami Beach.

She was as spry as a lively squirrel and looked for things within her reach.

Nothing to do except to swim or wander up and down the street.

Complaining to me, whenever we met, how bored she was and needed a treat!

She loved music, classics, the best; concert tickets were bought for her.

Though happy she was, for a little while, she soon was ready for another stir.

One day an idea gave her a lift: when she saw a discarded square white tile,

With the help of tubes of various hues, she painted a picture that brought a smile.

"Mom, you can learn from artists of renowned fame; the Bass Museum's not far away.

"Take the City bus right up the street and study their work while you spend the day."

Anxiously waiting for her reply, I called again the very next night.

"To tell the truth," she calmly said, "My visit there was no delight.

"I walked around, and up and down to see what brought these artists fame.

"Not a single picture did I like; They all were worse than their outside frame."

ALEXANDER AND PAULINE HIRSH

Mollie's parents

My mother told me my past long ago (supplemented by Ralph's discussions with my father Alex). My parents' stories remain vividly in my mind. My father, born in Odessa, Russia, was named Elyusha Gershkowitz (Alexander Hirsh, in America). He studied to become an engineer. Only the very bright Jewish boys were accepted in European schools. After completing work at the University of Odessa, he decided to study further at the University of Berlin in Germany, which required five years of study for its best engineering schools. While in Germany, he received word that the Russians were calling up his age group for Army service. He discontinued his studies and his parents arranged for him to be smuggled away to America, never to see any of his family again.

He arrived during the wave of immigration from Europe, in 1905. Immigrants who came through Ellis Island, N.Y. were encouraged to report to Cooper Union. There they were taught English and helped to find housing, locate family and friends, steered to possible jobs, and socialized with other immigrants. A natural scholar, my father became very fluent in English, which he spoke without trace of an accent. He was also at home and could speak, read, and write Russian, German, and Yiddish. While he attended Cooper Union, he met my mother, Pauline Morgan, another native of Odessa. Because of his engineering background, he had no trouble getting work as a tool-and-die maker and was able to support his wife and two children. He had an inventive mind and spent many hours at home and work, thinking of new ideas. At work he made several dies that improved his factory output. He worked on ways to improve people's lives and invented the first home fire alarm system, the first milkshake machine, and the first unbreakable doll, among others. His greatest time was devoted to the perfection of the doll. Not only was it to be unbreakable, but the head, hands, and legs also had to be moveable; the open eyes had to close and stay closed when the doll was put down. Although his health was affected by his constant work indoors and with chemicals, he persisted. After several years, the doll he designed was ready to be manufactured and my father decided to go into business for himself. Uncle Mischa Morgan, Mother's brother, joined him in opening a factory in New York. Costs were high in New York, so family and friends encouraged us to move to Baltimore, Maryland. The family moved there and the Atlas Doll and Toy Factory was established at the end of World War I. It was an immediate success. My younger brother Herman was 5 and I was 7 when we arrived into a pleasant Baltimore apartment, with a school across the street. These were my happiest early years. My fourth grade teacher gave me the keys to open the school doors every morning, since I was "a child always on time and dependable." Every Saturday, Mom dressed both of us in pretty clothes and we shuttled to the factory. It was a real picnic – dolls dressed beautifully and many toys to handle. The workers loved to see us. Business was booming, Father felt better, and life was good. It was too good to last.

Uncle Mischa, the outside man, took Papa's prototype of the first milkshake machine to several manufacturers, who showed no interest. Finally, one of them suggested he leave it with them, to consider. When he returned he was told, they hadn't had time to look into it. The next time, the man in charge was out. Excuses followed each time. The next thing they knew, the Hamilton Beach company was manufacturing a milkshake machine that was exactly like Father's invention. They had gotten a patent for it. It was a tragic and heartbreaking result of all his hard work and ingenuity. It also resulted in a breakup of the relationship with Uncle Mischa and he went back to New York.

After the War, Germany was in terrible financial straits. With its economy ruined, the German mark became almost worthless and the skilled workers were glad to work for low wages. The factories turned out goods at cut rates and soon flooded the world with items that were cheaper than any others. Imitations and copies of Father's productions – at prices he couldn't match – competed for his wares. Orders for his dolls and toys plummeted. He was forced to give up the shop and take what he could, selling out. His dreams failed him and affected him deeply. Father had a complete breakdown and ended in a hospital. He had been a scholar, hard worker and a thinker, but lacked good business skills. We soon found ourselves broke, with no means of making a living.

Mother had a strong drive and determination. She was ready to take over our most unfortunate situation. She jumped right in, knowing this would be difficult. She was a gregarious woman, and easily made friends with her neighbors. Now, in her hour of need, she talked to them. "I'm alone, with two small children, a sick husband, and little money, I need a job!" One lady suggested she try the large men's shirt factory of Aaron Strauss, on Pratt Street. She rushed to the factory and immediately was hired. Across the street from the factory, a decrepit tenement building caught her eye. When she finished the day's work, she walked over to find the owner. Out come Mr. and Mrs. Oitzer, whom she recognized as Jewish, and who used to come to visit ladies on her street. Mother explained her troubles, lack of money and that we needed a place to stay. The couple came to her assistance. "It's not so nice, but it's a roof over your heads, and, no charge, to start." Mother didn't hesitate. "We have to sleep somewhere. Thank you. You're so kind!" (She used to cook and bake and always bring in something to eat.) They remained friends as long as they lived.

Mother had no idea about Pratt Street and the place she'd accepted. Our new "home" was close to the wharf and attracted sailors, derelicts, drunks, anyone looking for a bed to sleep in. Mother followed Mrs. Oitzer into the "apartment." It was a single bedroom, with two beds and a bureau. The kitchen had a rusty sink. No hot water. One bulb hung from the ceiling in each room. The toilet down the hall was dark and filthy, used by all! Mother said, "What shall I do? We must have a place to sleep. It's across from my job. We'll try it!" Herman and I were petrified to use the "facility" in the hall. We had to sleep together in one bed. Dressing for school was shivery. The two of us, young as we were, knew we had no choice and put up with it. Mother never complained. Thinking back to those days, I remember every Friday afternoon carrying a brown paper bag with one clean set of underwear and one pair of stockings for each of us.

The hot water bathhouse was a ten-block walk – each way – rain or shine. Like Mother, we never complained. In school, an unkind teacher asks, "Don't you ever take a bath?" as she passes by. No answer, but my eyes are full of tears, as I silently lower my head. Mother was always very resourceful and thinking of a way to better ourselves. On a leisure walk one day, she spotted an empty store. She decided it was an ideal location – near this big factory – where hundreds walked by daily, to serve breakfast and light lunches. Also, there's a three-room apartment above the store, even though it had no heat or hot water. Still, it was better than what we had now. She would chance it! The move meant more work to set up a clean, pleasant store and living quarters. Again, we were given five cents each, for the bathhouse, a brown bag and one clean piece of underwear and stockings, each, for the ten-block Friday walk. Mother and Father (who was feeling better and could come to the store) made the food and handled the hot things. I – at ten years old – was the waitress and dishwasher.

Herman played with a boy his age next door, a saloon full of drunks whose owners were very kind to us. The "eaters" from the shirt factory came, but brought sandwiches from home, bought only coffee, tea, or milk, or said, "Please, get me a glass of water." Father's health deteriorated again, and he had to go back to the hospital. The year in the store finally ended. Again, Mother decided to look for a new chance to better our lot. No story about Mother would be complete without elaboration about her unique character. In spite of the burden of having to provide for her family and having a sick husband, she had an indomitably positive attitude. Truly, one could say, "She always had a song in her heart." Nothing was going to interfere with her ambition to make things better for her family. She saw nothing wrong with having to get up before daybreak, working hard all day, taking care of her two children, worrying about her poor husband's health, and still find time for a smiling, friendly greeting for everyone she met. Anyone who came in contact with her became a friend and a source of help. Along with that, she somehow found a way of making and saving a dollar – no matter what she did. In spite of the poor results of her efforts to establish an "eating" place on Pratt Street, she somehow scraped together a few dollars and was all set to start on the next project – a solution to her husband's poor health and a better place to live. She heard that people often went to "the mountains" to improve their health. Someone mentioned that there was a weekly excursion to a mountain resort called "PenMar Park," not far from Baltimore. For a few dollars, the whole family could take the train and spend all day in the park. Undaunted, she convinced my father Alex to join us and spend a Sunday at PenMar. The clear fresh air and the lovely surroundings enraptured us all. Before the day was over, Mother had arranged to rent a small cottage for the summer. The return train ride home was filled with enthusiastic plans for our "new summer place."

It didn't take Mother long to realize that there was a chance to make an extra dollar while we were enjoying our mountain vacation. After scrubbing and cleaning the cottage, Mother decided we didn't need all three bedrooms for ourselves. Why not try to rent one room and make up for the cost of our rent? A "Room for Rent" sign brought immediate results. Before the summer ended we had recouped all our costs! Mother was still not satisfied. As told in my other story about PenMar, she found a great desire for a good home-cooked meal and learned there a dearth of Kosher meals available. In spite of her lack of funds she was able to arrange the rent – with an option to buy – a much larger house that was to become the "Glendon Heights Hotel." For the next 18 years – from the age of 12 – through high school, three years of work, Normal School, marriage, mother, teacher, and homemaker, I was to be occupied every summer helping my parents eke out a bare living from this Guest House. This was to be the culminating experience of Mother's struggle on behalf of her family.

After our successful summer experience, Mother was more than ever determined to find a decent place to live. Limited funds dictated a third floor apartment overlooking a stable on East Baltimore Street. With a private bath, bright, larger rooms, hot water on weekends, and a quiet desirable neighborhood, it was an improvement. Mother got a job sewing in a hat factory. Herman and I made new friends and enjoyed the nearby school. A park close by gave both of us a chance to play with our new friends. It was to be our home till we had to go to PenMar for the summer and the new adventure of running the "Glendon Heights Hotel."

The large house Mother had leased needed a lot of work before it could be used as a guesthouse or hotel. Father's health had improved and he was living with us again. As soon as the cold weather disappeared, both of them left me in charge of the apartment while they started the job of getting the hotel ready. In spite of their best efforts, they needed more hands to help. They called and instructed me to try to leave school early so that we could help them. Before I had time to celebrate my 12th birthday, Herman and I were excused and we joined our parents in their new enterprise. Four of us worked for the next several weeks from morning till dark, scrubbing, scraping, painting, and cleaning till the house became a lovely, attractive, white building. Sitting about fifteen feet above the road leading to High Rock, one of the best known lookouts of the area, the house rose three stories high and was an imposing beacon of light to all passersby. A carefully lettered sign proclaimed that this was the "Glendon Heights Hotel." Small letters below promised "running water." Long before we were ready, a number of people came to inquire what we had to offer and when we'd open for business.

To reach the "Hotel" from the steep road, one had to traverse three stone steps (over a ditch, to catch the runoff, after a rain), leading to a ten-foot cement walk, then seven wooden steps until the porch was reached. Flanking both sides of the path were freshly planted flowers to brighten the way. Fourteen newly painted rockers were scattered on the gleaming gray floor. On either end of the porch, a swing waited for friends and lovers. A white screen door invited visitors and guests. Before the end of June we were ready for business! Although Mother and Father were around, it gradually became my job to greet all comers, show rooms, quote rates, explain the meal setup and answer all questions. After a room was rented, I supplied the towels and key, collected the rent and wrote out the receipts. In the mornings, I walked down to the railroad station to greet all arrivals on the 11 o'clock train and invite any that had no reservations to spend their vacation at the "Glendon Heights Hotel," explaining what we had to offer. Then, I picked up the mail.

The entrance of the hotel from the large porch revealed a set of stairs on the left side and a small living room furnished with a little sofa, a couple of overstuffed chairs, a rocking chair, and a Victrola. Before reaching the Victrola, an opening showed a little hall containing a small desk and a bureau that served as the linen closet. At the end of the hall a door led to a bedroom with a private bath – the crown jewel of the "hotel." Past the Victrola another door led to the dining room and the kitchen. The concrete dining room floor had been painted a dark red and was furnished with ten large tables that could accommodate up to six people, each. Large windows on two sides gave a bright appearance. The tables had fresh white linen cloths and were always set to serve the next meal. To the right was a swinging door leading to the kitchen. A small part of the dining room had been enclosed, to serve as a butler's pantry. It held a couple of large bureaus containing the table linens, napkins and cutlery used for service. Since Glendon Heights served Kosher meals, there were two sets of cutlery: one used to serve meat and one for dairy meals. The pantry was the place where I cut the pies and cakes that were served as daily desserts.

The most difficult part of the house to visualize was the kitchen. Here all meals were prepared under the most primitive and challenging conditions imaginable: the storage of perishable goods was in a wooden ice box – about two feet wide by eight feet long and about two feet deep, mounted on four legs, 18 inches above the floor. The iceman delivered two pieces of ice, weighing only 25 pounds each, which were placed into the box. All the meats, chickens, milk and any other perishables were squeezed into the box under the lid. In the best of times, it was barely possible to keep everything from spoiling. A wood stove was used for baking, cooking and boiling water. By 6 a.m., both Mother and Father were busy getting the day's meals cooked and baked in time. For breakfast, eggs were prepared on a four-burner coal oil stove. In spite of these unbelievable obstacles, somehow we managed to fix three very enjoyable meals daily for all our summer occupants, year after year. The bell rang promptly at 8 a.m. for breakfast, Noon, for the main meal (meat or chicken) and then 6 p.m. for supper. The times never varied and all guests were fed as much as they could eat, at every meal. They were served well and were satisfied!

The seven rooms on the second floor, with one bathroom, accommodated all the guests. On the rare occasions when someone could afford the room with the private bath on the first floor – usually a few dollars per week more – our family would move to the third floor. Each of the rooms had two beds and were rented on a share basis. A cot could allow a third person in one of the larger rooms. Four of the rooms had a sink with running water. The others all had a beautiful water pitcher and washbasin. In addition to the beds, covered with white linens and a pretty spread, a bureau and closet served as the storage for personal belongings. A towel rack had two each of face and bath towels, and washcloths. Towels were changed daily and the bed linens lasted a week for the same guest.

At the peak of the summer season, there could be as many as 20 or more paying customers, especially if a family with children were vacationing – almost a full house. The third floor had five rooms, at least one of which was used for storing extra beds and cots. The ceiling slanted towards the small windows, following the shape of the roof. Furnishings consisted of an iron bed with an iron-framed spring made of thick chicken coop-like wiring, covered by the standard lumpy, thin, straw-filled gray and black mattress, that followed the contours of the person getting into bed, always swaying towards the center. A small bureau held one personal things, and the usual pitcher and washbasin. Each room had a single bare electric bulb hanging down from a rafter near the middle. The ceiling consisted of the rafters holding the slanting roof. The center room was the most spacious and saved for my parents. If no other guests needed them, Herman and I had the rooms on either side of our parents. Ralph, our waiter, had one of the tiny end rooms. Since there was no other ventilation, even on a cool night there was little air. During the warm days of summer the heat became unbearable and sleep came only after constant turning, twisting, and total exhaustion.

In spite of everything, our family was able to somehow come out of each summer with enough saved up for the rest of the year. Some years it was barely enough for survival, others, to live frugally. We managed!

The greatest burden was borne by my mother. Father was limited by health and Herman was too young and only reluctantly helped when forced to do so. After the summer in PenMar Park, Mother rented an apartment on East Baltimore Street. It was a cold-water flat on the third floor, overlooking a stable, but had three bedrooms and in a better neighborhood. Again, no hot water. Again, Herman and I took our weekly walk to the public baths, carrying the brown bag with clean underwear and change of stockings. It was close to schools and near a park, where Herman and I found friends and fun. My new friend told me about her weekly piano lessons. I ran to Mother and begged her to let me take some, too. She agreed to give me 50 cents, for my weekly lesson. Luckily, there was a piano in the "parlor," on the first floor. The owner lived in the basement. Mother and I talked with her. She finally gave me a half hour's time to practice every day. "Be sure to close the piano and the door," she called. I had to bundle up when I found the room was never heated and my fingers became livid, almost stiff. Not a day of practice was missed. Much joy had come to me. Mother was sewing at home and teaching me. She received more money and decided to move to a nicer apartment, across the street.

The new apartment was an improvement and we soon made new friends. Among the families were the Levins whose two sons and two daughters were older than I but who welcomed me to their home to listen to their radio. Our friendship was to last for many years even after Ralph and I married. Every Saturday I visited Father in the hospital, carrying a cake he liked, baked by me. For me, a one-cent trolley car ride, then about a half-mile walk. Sometimes a couple, in the hospital, would give me a ride to the trolley. Most of the time I walked.

The next apartment felt like "Heaven." Broadway was a lovely wide street, centered with trees and flowers, no streetcar for blocks. We had a first-floor apartment, roomy, pleasant and furnished with a piano. I promised to take good care of it and did. Father came home to stay in this nice place. He taught me to write Russian, helped us with our homework. His knowledge of mathematics, background and education amazed us and gave us great help when I was in high school and Herman was in junior high. For me at 16, high school graduation became a sad situation – no one to celebrate with me, watching girls receiving bouquets, parents and friends. My Mother worked. A Prom was out of the question. Besides, PenMar needed my help before school ended.

After summer, looking for a job overshadowed everything else. My "youth look" needed a dress-up. As was the custom, dark dress and stockings. These were purchased. A trip to Hutzler's Department Store brought a job for Christmas holidays and weekends. Mother, always eager to provide for better jobs for me, urged me to look for a job in business or in an office. I enrolled at Eaton and Burnett Business School for commercial training – typing, bookkeeping and office work. Three months later our money was depleted and forced me to drop out of classes. An ad in the classified section of the Baltimore Sun required a typist and office clerk. I applied for the job and got it. For the next three months I learned how to file, answer the phone, act as receptionist, take and type letters, using the shorthand and typing skills I had learned at the business school. Each week, after I got paid, the money was given to Mother to help with household expenses. She doled out my carfare and other expenses as needed. I packed my lunch daily, to take to work with me. Then, an older, more experienced worker replaced me. A return to Hutzler's Department store, working in various departments, brought steady pay for Mother to spare 14 cents carfare for me. Lunch came from home, plus I had five cents extra for a candy. Very often I walked the several miles from work, to save the carfare, and came home to soak my feet. The next Christmas, at the jewelry section of the store, several girls from high school came to the counter. The story of their love of Maryland State Normal School excited and saddened me. That evening my sobbing and begging resulted in the fulfillment of my desire to study to become a teacher.

Every summer I was needed at PenMar, so any job I had had to end. I was now qualified to greet prospective vacationers, show and sell rooms, register them, accept payments and give receipts, type letters to inquiries, meet the trains and attract customers, help in the kitchen, be the waitress at mealtime, and help with any other problem that arose. During my "free time," after supper, I could go down to the dance hall and listen to the music of the orchestra. Or, on rare occasions, I could practice bowling duckpins in the park.

I don't know how I did it, but I managed to enroll and graduate two years later from Normal School in June 1932. I was ready to teach! I went back to PenMar for the summer, anxious to learn my teacher ranking and eager to begin. If I came out in the first 20 of the class – as I hoped – a job would be automatically waiting for me. All my dreams would come true. Finally, the news came. I had made it! Out of more than 300 students in my class, I had scored in the top 20! The excitement was unbearable. What school? What grade? In September I would be assigned to my first teaching position! Now, I would really be able to help with our household living expenses, thanks to my teacher's salary. Unfortunately, not all dreams come true as planned. Yes, I did get a job as a teacher the day after Labor Day, 1932. I was one of the 20 lucky ones, assigned to a second grade and was happy to start practicing what I had been taught at Normal School. My enthusiasm was shattered when I learned that – because of the terrible financial situation of the City of Baltimore – the school budget had been cut so much that all newly assigned personnel in the classrooms would be classified as substitutes at $2.50 per day. As such, we would be paid only for the actual days taught, rather than on a monthly basis. All teachers and administrators had their last year's pay cut by ten per cent and no one received the annual pay raise that their contracts called for. It was a sad situation for all teachers. My disappointment was greater since I'd hoped to help my parents more. The Great Depression that featured bank closings, suicides by rich people who suddenly found themselves paupers, and failures of thousands of businesses led to many losses of jobs and incomes. After seeing the plight of others Mother and I decided that any job was better than nothing. At least, now, I was doing the work I loved. Plus, the few dollars earned kept the family together, to await next summer. Maybe business would be better in PenMar. The summer of 1933 proved to be another disappointment. In spite of President Roosevelt's efforts to reopen the banks and propose new national work programs for the needy, the Depression continued. People had little money for pleasures and vacations in the mountains was a luxury that few could afford. We offered the occasional visitor to PenMar the lowest possible rate as an inducement to stay. Mother decided to lower our weekly rate to $12 a week to help get customers. This included three full meals a day, for seven days, plus milk or tea and a snack between meals and before going to bed. A complete full-course Sunday dinner, served from 12 Noon on, to all visitors and family members bringing or collecting a guest, was offered at $1.00. Every extra dinner sold was a triumph. Herman was no longer with us to help out. A guest had taken a liking to him last summer and offered to help him get a job as a manager-in-training for a man's clothing store chain. After training in Johnstown, Pennsylvania, Herman became manager of a Kay Bee men's store in Durham, North Carolina, where he made friends and was very happy. When World War II broke out he was drafted and served as an engineer with the SeaBees in the Pacific. His 1937 Chevy was left with us and awaited him upon his return. Herman's absence put an extra heavier burden on Ralph and me. We couldn't afford to hire anyone else. Ralph had worked with us for the three summers before and our relationship had grown to where he was now considered almost as a member of the family – although no decision about marriage had been made. Ralph's 1931 Chevy was used to carry summer provisions to PenMar Park he brought it with him when school ended and he came up for the summer. We, two, became the waiters, train greeters, shoppers, and general managers of the operation, leaving most of the kitchen work to Mother and ailing Father. Between the four of us we finished the season. Ralph and I returned to our school jobs the day after Labor Day, leaving the folks to rest up for a few weeks and enjoy the beauty of early Fall in the Blue Ridge Mountains. They closed up after the Holidays, draining the pipes and shutting the house till next year. Toward the end of the summer Ralph and I decided that we couldn't go on with our lives like this. Each of us had been the main source of help to our parents during the school year, despite our meager earnings. After more than three years of "going steady" it was time to consider our own future. Ralph agreed to talk to his father, to have him consider our marriage. Ralph had helped his parents by giving them most of his monthly checks since he had started to teach. His brother Mike had married in August of 1932 and had moved into his own apartment. With Ralph teaching, there was no one to deliver orders at his parents' store. Without delivery to the few scattered customers, there was no business and no hope of improvement. The money Ralph gave was used to pay the store's debtors every month. It was like trying to fill a bottomless hole. His parents agreed and the store was closed after the Holidays. Efforts to find a job for his father in Baltimore failed, but a former customer and friend found one for him in Washington. They found a little place to live near his job and sold their house in Baltimore. With Ralph's parents settled and not dependent on him any more, we could now concentrate on our plans to get married. Unfortunately, my parents could not afford to pay for a wedding ceremony. In spite of all our hard work during the summer, they had very little money left. Without my help it was doubtful if they could even survive the winter, let alone plan for a wedding's cost. After many discussions with both our parents, arrangements were made to have a private ceremony in Washington, in a Rabbi's house, with just the parents and no other family members present. Announcements were printed and mailed afterwards to notify family and friends. When we returned from our short honeymoon, Mother would prepare a reception for us at her apartment, We had moved to a place in Park Heights, closer to where I was teaching. Since we were both teaching, the only time we could possibly get married and have time for a short honeymoon was during the Christmas holidays – without losing a day's needed income. Schools would be closed on Friday, December 22 and not reopen until after New Year's. On Sunday morning, December 24, 1933, Ralph picked me and my parents up, drove us to Washington, collected his parents, and drove to Rabbi Silverstone's house. Enough men had been engaged to have a Minyan (religious group) so that the ceremony could proceed. Promptly at noon, the Rabbi had finished and blessed our union with his best wishes. After a dinner with all parents, in our apartment in Baltimore, we took the afternoon train to New York for our honeymoon, with money loaned to us from Ralph's mother. Our meager monthly earnings were paid by the School Board two weeks after the month ended. Since we were paid only for days taught, neither Ralph nor I were able to save anything beyond our bare living expenses for the first few months of the year. When we mentioned that we couldn't afford to go away for a honeymoon, Ralph's mother told him that she had squirreled away $90 and would be glad to lend us the money. We gratefully accepted. When we got to New York, we had no idea where to find a place we could afford. After looking at a couple of hotels in the heart of downtown, we chose one located near restaurants and theaters that looked clean and at a reasonable rate. The next morning, the windowsill had six inches of snow and it had turned bitterly cold. Before we could go anywhere we had to buy rubbers, to protect our shoes and feet. During the five busy days in New York we dined in a different restaurant for each meal and enjoyed the variety. Every day was a challenge and a wonderful experience. Radio City Music Hall was unlike anything we'd ever seen or heard. We attended the old Metropolitan Opera House (on the fifth Balcony) to hear Lily Pons sing her world-famous "Bell Song." (Ralph's first opera). Clifton Webb and Ann Miller starred in the famous show "I DO, I DO!" Their dancing and acting was superb and thrilling. Every afternoon and evening we saw a show or movie or museum. A complete fulfilling vacation in a packed few days. Yet, when we returned home we still had not spent all of the borrowed $90! We moved into my parents' house, using the second floor as our living quarters. Our combined income helped to pay our living expenses. Within a month after we were married, we received a pleasant surprise. The School Board decided to restore teachers who had been demoted to "permanent substitutes" to teacher status again, with credit for the years taught. That meant that Ralph's income for the next five months ($700) would be more than we'd expected for the whole year. I, too, was scheduled to get a teacher's salary of $1,200 next fall. Overjoyed at our good fortune, we soon made plans to find an apartment for ourselves. The small place we shared with my parents deprived them and us of any privacy. Luck was with us. We soon found a very pretty one-bedroom apartment in a quiet section of Forest Park, near a streetcar line, and took it, in spite of the high rent of $35 a month, Mother, always ready to help us, cashed in Father's insurance policy to buy us furniture. The comfortable parlor, oak bedroom, and cherry wood kitchen made our home lovely. By April we had saved enough money to lend Mother so she could get all the supplies for PenMar for the summer. Giving up their apartment, they went to the mountains to open up their house and get it ready for the season. In spite of Father's failing health, they worked hard, mostly by themselves. We joined them on Memorial Day weekend, just in case they needed our help to serve. As soon as school ended we came to the hotel, ready to do our jobs and enjoy the healthy climate before any guests arrived. The economy slowly improved and business at Glendon Heights was better. By the time we were ready to go back to teaching, they had paid us back the money they had borrowed and even lent us some, before we got our first paycheck. This was the pattern we followed each year. We lent them money in the spring and they returned it in the summer. They lent us some before our first paycheck and we paid it back in the fall. With our help, they managed to continue for several years. On Labor Day, Monday, September 2, 1935, our first son was born. Ralph and I had left PenMar after the noon dinner was served, on Sunday, just in time to be ready for our first child's birth. Little did we dream of the changes this event would bring about in our lives. Now, instead of two salaries coming in each month, we would have only one breadwinner. In addition, we'd have another month to feed, diapers to wash, baby clothes, formulas, plus all the other new and added expenses of a baby. Ralph had been taking courses at the University of Maryland, towards his Bachelor's degree. His Diploma from Maryland State Normal School gave him only half the credits needed for a college degree. We couldn't afford to have him continue. Instead, he had to find some way to supplement his teacher's salary to cover our extra costs.

My father's health continued to deteriorate. Mother's burden – although lightened by Ralph and me as her constant summer helpers in PenMar – grew heavier each year. At the end of the summer of 1937, she decided to take Father to Florida for the winter. She rented a one-bedroom apartment on Collins Avenue, hoping that the sea air would help him. Again, her entrepreneurial skills were awakened. In a short time she noticed that there were many inquiries for a place to stay for a week or more. Since her place was fully furnished, with a Bermuda bed in the living room and a lounge on the screen porch, she decided she'd rent the bedroom. Soon she had rented the bedroom to a couple, the porch to a lady, and she and Father were sleeping in the living room. Before the end of February, she had recouped the cost of the apartment's seasonal rent. She became so happy with her success that she wanted to share it with us and bombarded us with letters, urging me to come to Florida. Ralph would stay behind and encouraged me to go with the baby. On March 1, 1938, we took the Silver Meteor train to Miami. It was the most glorious (actually, the first) vacation I had ever had. Every day, we walked the two blocks to the beach and enjoyed the water and cool breezes. On our way back we stopped at the juice stand on Washington Avenue and 14th Street and shared a cool drink. We were tanned a deep brown and looked and felt healthier than ever. Before the end of the month I had fallen in love with Florida and was determined to live here as soon as I could convince Ralph.

My parents remained in Florida until it was time to get ready for PenMar. Father was not getting any better and he ended up in the hospital, never to return. Meanwhile, in early 1939, Ralph and I had bought our first home in Baltimore, a lovely three-story house on Maine Avenue, in Forest Park. It was directly across the street from an elementary school, one block from the junction of two main streetcar lines and a local strip shopping center. It was to be our home until we moved to Florida. Ralph spent several weeks scraping several layers of dark paint and varnish off the beautiful parquet floors and rented out the downstairs four room apartment. We lived in the five-room apartment on the second floor, and kept three spare rooms on the third floor. When Father went to the hospital, Mother came to live with us. Father passed away that year.

Except for the times in PenMar, Mother continued to live with us. Whatever she earned and saved during the summers remained with her, since we never expected nor wanted anything from her. She more than paid her own way by always helping me in the house and insisting on buying some of the food items for our meals. After Alan was born she was on hand to take care of me and help with him. It was a pleasure to have her with us. A live-in baby sitter, cook, dishwasher, and general helper, she acknowledged our right to privacy and never interfered in our lives. For the next 17 years, she was always with us and part of our immediate family. After the summer of 1941, when I was anticipating the birth of our second child, Ralph had a very serious talk with Mother. He pointed out that – although we had always been ready to help her during the summers, in PenMar – it was becoming more and more burdensome to us. To help with the upcoming birth of our second child, we now had Pearl, a young farm girl, with us. It would be very difficult for us to close up our home and drag the two children with us to the mountain; give them the care and attention of a mother, and, take care of the operation of the business. Since, without our help, Mother couldn't possibly run the place, perhaps it was time for her to get out of it. If it couldn't be rented, try to sell it. She agreed. With the war in Europe escalating and conditions in our country unsettled, she found it hard to find a suitable buyer and finally let the farmer, who had supplied her with eggs and vegetables for years, practically steal it from her. It was a sad ending to the 18 continuous summers in PenMar Park. To tell the story of Mother's continuing life and her constant positive outlook can fill several books. Suffice it to say that her enthusiasm for life and her bubbly zest rubbed off on all of us. There was never any hesitation on her part for trying anything new that might eventually better our lives. When Ralph wanted to buy property in Miami Beach she enthusiastically supported him. She lent us her last $200 towards a down payment on our first home. When Ralph and Mollie Glazer (Herman's mother-in-law) considered building income property, she asked to be a partner and invested every dollar she had with them. She proposed to Ralph that we go into the business of selling home made chicken soup, pickles, and borsht in jars long before it became popular by the big companies. (He declined because he knew nothing about such business or marketing and no finances available to consider such enterprises.) Who knows how far we could have gone if we'd had the nerve or wherewithal to follow through? As far as we were concerned, there was no task that we requested that she would refuse. When we sold our house in Miami to help pay for our son's college, we moved to a small apartment and she moved to Miami Beach to be on her own and not to be a burden to us. Yet, each time she took the long bus ride to come visit us, her first question was, "What do you have for me to do?" the minute she stepped into our place. She was always ready, willing, and able to do something, anything, to help. No matter where she lived or where she went she always made friends easily and found something or someone with whom to do. She played cards, practiced painting, even got a job, in her seventies – to keep herself busy. In short, her enthusiasm for life should serve as an inspiration to all of us. We would do well to follow in her footsteps.

by Mollie and Ralph Bartel (written together)

OFFICIAL BIRTHDAYS

Some years ago I tried to clarify the situation about my "Official" Birthdays – all three (3) of them. Apparently my explanation did not work, for there is still some confusion in the family. The only solution is to try again.

The first question is probably, "How authentic is my information?" For a reason I can't explain, I once had photocopied the page in the prayer book which Papa used to record the births of his four children. That copy (the original copy) is among many miscellaneous items that record events in our family's lives, things that I accumulated and kept in a folder labeled "important." Since records kept in bibles are universally accepted as authentic, I accept them as true.

Papa has four entries on that page, each detailing the births of his four children. The entries record the information in Hebrew and Russian in a uniform pattern. To clarify, I'm going to translate his entries as best I can. Bear in mind that my knowledge of both languages is very rusty at this point, since I haven't used either one for decades. So if I make mistakes, you'll know why. Here they are (the punctuation marks are mine).

1- (Hebrew) – Born to me a girl, Chaya Rivke, the 3rd day (of the week, Tuesday), 8 days in the month of Sivan. (In Russian, I can only make a guess at the names of the month.) March 26, 1904??

2 – Born to me a son, Ze'ev, the 4th day, Wednesday, 13th day in the month of Teves. January (I believe) 8, 1906.

3 Born to me a son, the 5th day, Thursday, in the month of Nisan, Y'Rachmiel. April 1, 1910. (Just a few days before Passover, on Thursday.)

4 – Born to me a son, Mayer Chaim, Erev Rosh Hashanah, the 6th day, Friday. September (?) 19, 1911.

If I have interpreted the information correctly, the Biblical entry proclaims that I was born on April 1, 1910, according to the Russian calendar.

I think it was my older sister Chaika who once told me this story. Ten-year-old Chaika was crossing the bridge from the Gymnazia (school) on her way home from the Old Town area of Lyubar to the market place in the New Town when she was congratulated on the birth of a new brother. "Yes, I know!" she answered, "It's April Fool's Day." She was too smart to fall for that. Imagine her surprise when she came home and found out it was not a joke, after all. Or, was it? Is this even a true story? Did they have April Fool's Day in 1910 in a tiny village? I have no idea.

Now let's get back to my "Official" Birthdays. We always commemorated (though I can't remember that we ever celebrated my birthday as a child, like we do here in the U.S.) my birthday according the Hebrew calendar date. As we know, the Hebrew dates don't follow a regular pattern. The dates change every year on the modern calendar, which is why the Jewish Holidays fall on different dates nowadays. It was only after we came to the U.S. that I learned that dates of birth are required quite often – to open a bank account, get a license, get a credit card, join a club or join a team. So, I used April 1st as my birthday.

I was well into my latter teens when I found out that the Russian calendar had never changed from the Julian to the Gregorian dates. I was told that if I had been born in the U. S. – on that same date – my date of birth would have been registered as April 14 instead of the 1st. This was because 13 days had been added to the Julian calendar to make up for the small parts of days that had accumulated in the many years since the Julian calendar was originally adopted. So, I had to add a new "official" date as my day of birth. The trouble was that I had used April 1st for so long, it was too much trouble to try to change it everywhere. It was only when I was in the mood that I pointed out that "officially" my birthday was really the 14th, but . . . and I tried to explain. Without a doubt, it was confusing.

If that's not enough, I have reminded everyone that I still had another birthday – the Hebrew one which my parents used. It would be a long time before I finally decided to omit the Hebrew-dated birthday since it changes yearly.

I bet'cha thought that was the end of the confusion. Boy, have I got news for you! The U. S. bureaucracy decided I needed another birthday! Which leads to another story.

Papa became a citizen in 1928. Mike and I were listed as citizens, also, because we were still minors. It was called "citizenship by derivation." It didn't really affect me, because the only traveling I ever did was to Canada, Mexico, or the Caribbean – where the only requirement of proof of citizenship was satisfied by showing my driver's license. When Mollie and I decided to start to travel abroad I needed to get a Passport. Some countries even required a Visa. (The banks should excuse me – NOT the credit card type, yet, then.) For either the passport or visa, I'd have to show a valid proof of birth.

To prove that I was born, I needed to have a Birth Certificate – impossible. An entry from Papa's Bible or religious record was unacceptable. I couldn't provide a sworn, notarized statement from a person who was present at my birth. I couldn't produce any of those requirements. Finally, someone at the passport agency suggested that, since I'd gone to school in this country, I could write to the first school I'd attended and get my date of birth as recorded there. They would accept that as a legal proof. Easy, huh? Sure! After all, this was 1963 in Hialeah, Florida. Remember, I had registered my birthday in Public School #63 in Baltimore. In 1923 – only 40 years ago! It should be a cinch to drop them a line and get what I wanted. Yeah! Sure! Lotsa Luck!

I wrote. Just in case. We'll see what happens. You know how time drags on, when you're waiting. Each day that passed without any word caused old "worry-wart Ralph" to worry even more. I'd just about given up when I received an envelope that had "Board of Education. Baltimore, Maryland" as the return address. I could hardly wait to see what it contained.

Surprise! Surprise! Date of Birth: March 22, 1910. Crazy, isn't it? After all that waiting, I got an unheard of date like that. I'd completely forgotten that in 1923, when Papa was already getting our life and home ready in Baltimore, I became Bar Mitzvah while still in Montreal. Using the Hebrew calendar that my parents utilized, my birthday – in 1923 – fell on March 22. A couple of weeks later we left for Baltimore. When I registered in P. S. School # 63, we gave them the date of my most recent birthday. I am sure my poor ability to understand English at the time, no doubt, caused confusion. At any rate, here was another authentic "Proof of Birth"!

Well, my dears, I told you I would clarify my "official" Proof of Birth. Here you are. After these three pages of clarification you now know which is my true, authentic, REAL date of birth! BUT, just in case anyone is still confused, I'll summarize the date(s) for you, chronologically:

1 – Is MARCH 22 my "Official" Birthday? Absolutely! See my Citizenship paper. Or, my last Passport.

2 – Is APRIL 1 my "Official" Birthday? Absolutely, too! See copy of Papa's entry.

3 – Is APRIL 14 my "Official" Birthday? Indubitably! See any Hebrew or English Perpetual Calendar: In April, 1910, no THURSDAY fell on the 1st. It DID fall on the 14th!!!!!

So, you see, each and every day above is an authentic, true, Proof of Birth.

Or, to state the obvious, BY THE TIME ONE REACHES MY AGE, ANY DAY – repeat – *ANY DAY* AND EVERY DAY IS PRECIOUS, AND MAY BE SAID TO BE MY BIRTHDAY.

All I can say to each of you is that any time I talk or "hear" from you, in any way, is a GREAT DAY TO CELEBRATE!

Thank you.

Love, Ralphy
April 14, 2007

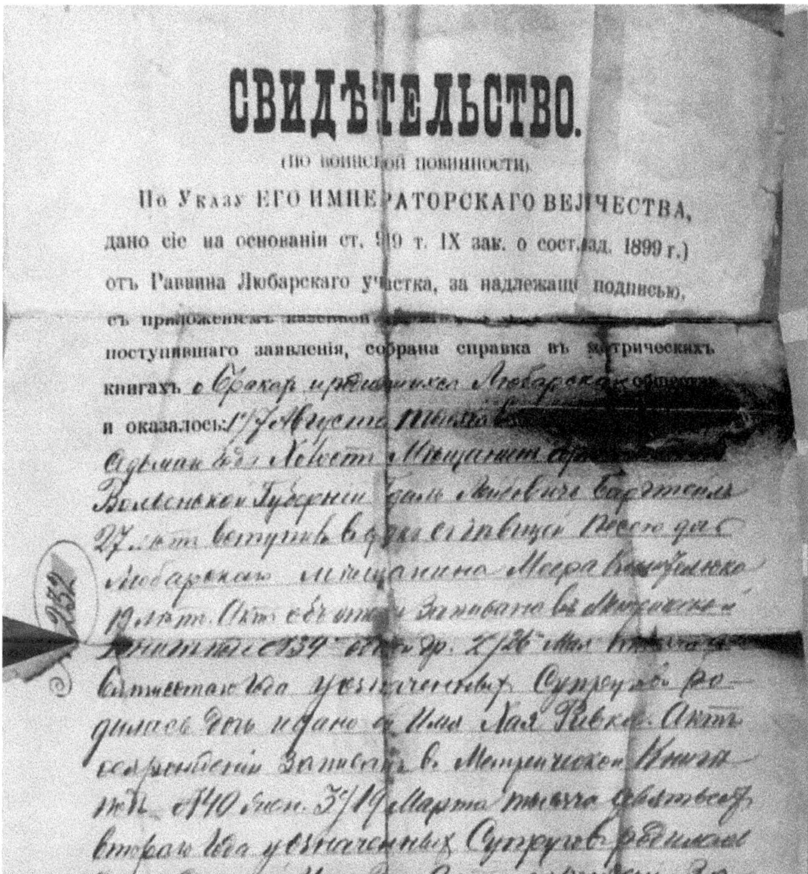

СВИДѢТЕЛЬСТВО.

(ПО ВОИНСКОЙ ПОВИННОСТИ).

По Указу ЕГО ИМПЕРАТОРСКАГО ВЕЛИЧЕСТВА,

дано сіе на основаніи ст. 919 т. IX зак. о сост. изд. 1899 г.)

отъ Раввина Любарскаго участка, за надлежащ подписью,

съ приложеніемъ казенной

поступившаго заявленія, собрана справка въ метрическихъ

книгахъ о *Срокаръ притчавшихся Любарской области*

и оказалось: *17 Августа тысяча*

[handwritten text, largely illegible]

[handwritten text, largely illegible]

[handwritten text, largely illegible]

Волынской губерніи, Новоградволынскаго уѣзда, м. Любарь.

Іюня 19 дня 1905 года.

Раввинъ *[signature]*

Russian birth record of Rachmiel Bargteil (later, Ralph Bartel), 1905.

PAULINE HIRSH

Mollie's mother is Pauline Morganshtern (shortened to Morgan). She came to the United States about 1905, at the time of the great surge of immigrants from Russia. She came from Odessa. Her family, including her mother and two brothers, Mischa and Max, plus two sisters, Katye and Sarah, all settled in New York. There, Pauline met and married Alexander Hirsh, Mollie's father. He, too, was a native of Odessa. I first met Mischa Morgan (who'd joined Alex in their failed enterprise in Baltimore) when he retired – a widower – to Miami Beach, in 1956. His daughter, Phyllis, stayed with us at the Sinclair Hotel for about a month while her husband was finishing his stint in the navy. After visiting Mischa several times, he became quite interested in our endeavor in the apartment buildings in Hialeah. He lent me $2,000 to help us build the second of our three buildings. His sudden passing escalated my repayment of the loan to his daughter, Phyllis, at her insistence. We never heard from her again.

Katye and Mischa Barber (successful in the fur business) raised four daughters, Helen, Edith (about the same age and closest to Mollie), Gertrude, and Lillian. All the girls were single and working when I first met them, during our honeymoon in New York. They were living in a lovely apartment overlooking a park. Helen married a fine man. They had a son, named Edward, who grew up, married, and had a lovely daughter. Helen survived the younger sisters and passed away in a nursing home in Colorado, under the watchful care of Edward. The last we heard from him, upon Helen's passing, he was divorced and still living in Colorado. He was in advertising, I believe.

Max Morgan was a jovial man, a deli salesman who made a nice living and provided for his family. He lost his wife from what was believed to be overeating. They had one son, Herbert, and a daughter, Phoebe, all in New York.

Sarah, Pauline's youngest sister, married Dave – an active union leader in the clothing industry. Except for the Barber sisters, Sarah and Dave visited with us in Baltimore or PenMar most often. He made good wages and lived in a modest apartment in Brooklyn. Whenever we visited them, we always enjoyed the typical delicious New York food. When we left, we carried a box of yummy pastries back with us.

Grandma Pauline Hirsh, as already told by Mollie, was always busy trying to provide for her family when her husband's business enterprises failed and his illness limited his abilities. What I'd like to point out is her indefatigable spirit. In all the years I knew her – Ma Hirsh, as I called her – never complained of her situation. She had one of the most bubbly, positive outlooks on life of anyone in my experience. She could make do, in spite of any unexpected occasion. Many times, in PenMar, she'd suddenly find herself unprepared when strangers came in for dinner – off the road. When one of us would rush into the kitchen and announce the unexpected guests, she'd say, "O. K. I'll take care of it." It didn't faze her at all. In spite of our apprehensions, she always managed to find some means of feeding them. Because of lack of refrigeration, all meals needed to feed the registered guests were planned only one or two day ahead. There were no outlets to provide for Kosher meats or chickens nearby. The Rabbi from Hagerstown, Maryland, who provided for our needs on a weekly basis, left just enough till his next visit. Of course, most times the dinners planned for the family would disappear, as they were needed for the guest. We'd end up eating sardines or such. The paying customer would be happy with the meals and hopefully come back or recommend our place to someone else. Life at PenMar – no matter the difficulties – was always accepted without reservations by Pauline Hirsh. What's more, the Hirsh family survived, thanks to Pauline's unstinting sacrifices. She always managed, and with a song and a smile!

During the worst times of the Depression years, when their meager savings from the summer work in PenMar ran out, she somehow scrounged out something edible for her family. Her spirits were always high. When their closest friends, the Mollies, "dropped in" on almost every Sunday, just before their evening meal, she always found enough food for them, also. After we were married, it was Ma Hirsh who insisted that we move in with them in their apartment. She accepted just enough from us to cover the extra food expenses so we could save our meager incomes. Remember that at first, we were both still paid as daily school substitutes, even though we had full-time jobs.

In February, 1934, when Mollie and I were raised to annual teacher status, and I was transferred to a school in the desirable Forest Park neighborhood, we first started to look for an apartment of our own. We rented our first apartment shortly after on Maine Avenue. When I found a house for sale on Maine Avenue it again was Ma Hirsh who backed me up and lent me part of the down payment I needed to buy it. She immediately offered to provide us with our dining room furniture. It was a lovely house with four rooms on the first floor – which I'd rented to a Mrs. Heideman and her two grown sons – German refugees. With our young son, Mollie and I occupied the five-room apartment on the second floor. The third floor had three spacious rooms, available when my parents or anyone else came to visit. When Ma and Pa Hirsh came back from PenMar in October, we gave them one of our rooms. They stayed with us until Pa Hirsh passed away. From then on, Ma Hirsh remained with us. In spite of our protests, during all the years she stayed with us, Ma Hirsh insisted that she pay something – "at least to cover her food consumption." She also found something, always, that had to be done around the house – cooking, cleaning, mending, taking care of the baby – nothing was too much for her. She was a bundle of energy – always looking for something to do. And, when there was absolutely nothing more to do at home, she'd think nothing of taking the streetcars to go visit with one of her many friends in Baltimore – no matter how many different changes of streetcars that might entail. I can't remember her ever asking me or Mollie to take her anywhere. Her independence was very important to her.

Our move to Florida was at the encouragement and insistence of Ma Hirsh. It was she who assured me that we could make the move without fear. Since I was the only provider for the family, I was reluctant to leave a sure source of income. I was making the maximum teacher's salary, plus a bonus of 10% ($2,420 a year – equivalent to a vice-principal's salary) and was in line for promotion. With the extra income I got from working at Becker's Men's Department Store in my spare time, I was providing fairly well for our family. How does one give up a secure job and move a family to a strange new area without an assured source of revenue? Ma Hirsh pooh-poohed my reluctance. She was certain we could rent a large "guest house" in Miami Beach and derive enough revenue from the rental of the extra rooms during the winter season to live on. In time, she assured me we could even find a small hotel to operate.

She wasn't afraid to take a chance and move. So, we did! It was Ma Hirsh who encouraged me, in 1944, to buy the cottage at 3004 Pacific Avenue in Atlantic City. This was before I left for Florida to look for a larger "guest house" in Miami Beach. She was the one who backed my move to lease the Sinclair Hotel and look for the money needed for its lease and operation – even though it involved a much greater risk and investment than we originally planned. She lent me all her accumulated savings and wrote to her family in New York asking them to help us. With her help, I borrowed sums from all our joint relatives and friends and came up with enough to open for business in October 1944, in Florida. She had complete confidence in my ability to succeed in the Sinclair's operation. Without her encouragement I couldn't possibly have made it – especially with all the problems caused by the War Department to discourage travelers from going to Florida in 1944-45.

While we operated The Sinclair, Morris Margolis, one of its owners who was a constant visitor, offered several times to let me invest – as a partner – in some property he'd located that he felt was a good buy. Ma Hirsh was always in favor of my doing so. Later, after we failed to listen to her, we found that those properties were indeed bargains. Had I listened to her I'd have been much more successful in my Florida ventures. I've tried to portray Pauline Hirsh as a truly remarkable woman, with the instinct and the courage necessary for success. Long before large food companies did it, Pauline Hirsh came to me with the ideas to can her excellent pickles, borscht, chicken soup etc., in jars or cans. I was never convinced and could not go along with the suggestions, mostly because I had no knowledge of the business or the know-how to find out any information. Most of all, I did not know enough about any way to get financing or manufacturing. Even more than her drive and raw business acumen, Pauline Hirsh was the consummate example of a devoted family person. No matter what the problem, she was always ready and willing to help any member of her family. She was always there in times of need – many times before she was asked. Those of us who had the privilege of living with her know only too well that our achievements and success were often influenced by Pauline Hirsh. She taught us that there should never be any doubts about helping family members in need! It was a given!

PREJUDICE

Man is not born prejudiced; it is my belief that it has to be drilled into his conscience, either by education – of teachers or peers – or by parental guidance and influence. If this is true, then any rational person would say that I should have no prejudices. My background includes many lessons dealing with the Judaic Teachings of the equality of man under the law, the sanctity of life, the dignity of the human person, of peace and love as the foundation of justice. My parents not only believed these concepts but practiced them so well that – when our community was subject to the pogroms that followed the Revolution in Russia and the Ukraine – Gentile friends and farmers risked their own lives in order to hide, feed, and shelter us for many days, until the risks subsided. Still, my subconscious seems obsessed with a dislike for a sect of our people that I'm unable to suppress, no matter how hard I try. There are those who say that the best way to eliminate something that bothers you is to talk about it – Face it directly. Perhaps, if I put down the cause, in writing, I can somehow relieve my obsession and get rid of or, at least, lessen my prejudice. It's worth a try.

In the fall of 1920, my father had arranged for our family to escape to Poland, using dangerous and treacherous routes, to prevent detection. Once we arrived in Lemberg to a prearranged safe house, we were greeted warmly and fed. Unfortunately, no one knew what awaited us. Both my sister and my two brothers fell ill with the dreaded Typhus Fever, a disease that I had barely survived as we were escaping. The Fever is a terribly debilitating illness. The victim suffers very high temperatures and perspires profusely, often shivering at the same time, and causes hallucinations. With careful care, the victim overcomes the crisis stage and survives, usually emaciated and undernourished. A person who is inclined to illness or who has been under a severe strain often has a very difficult time and has to be tended and watched constantly. Think about where we were staying, a family of five like ours, four of whom were terribly ill, and the fifth, himself a recent victim and survivor of the illness – a weakened, confused boy of ten. We were in a strange land, in a strange house, hearing a strange dialect and I found it so difficult to understand. I was entirely dependent on a very kind lady with her elderly Polish maid. I didn't know where to turn. My brothers were in one room, quietly but obviously uncomfortable. Cold compresses, provided by the lady or maid, had to be regularly changed. Their sweat had to be wiped off, their covers had to be straightened constantly – and their questions answered. Then, it was time to run into the other bedroom, where Father lay in one bed, Mother in another. The worst time was when Mother became delirious and began to ask questions for which I had no answers. I was young and she was calling for people who weren't there, asking for food that was not available. Finally, in desperation, when Mother kept insisting she wanted "schmaltz herring and potatoes," the lady told me that I'd have to go to a nearby market and buy the herring. She had plenty of potatoes but no herring. She gave me a little *buytel* (change purse), explained the values of the different coins and assured me I'd have no trouble finding the marketplace or the stall of the herring dealer.

Laden with specific instructions and dressed in my warmest coat and scarf, I ventured out into the unknown street in Lemberg and hesitantly but anxiously started towards the marketplace. Without looking right or left, I was bent on my mission when, suddenly, I was surrounded by a motley group of boys, all babbling in a strange dialect and similarly dressed. A couple of them wore caps. The rest all wore *shtriemels* (a round fur-like hat), *kapotas* (long capes or coats that hung to their ankles), and *talit-katans* (a small undergarment that looked like a prayer shawl, with fringes dangling from four corners). Each one had long side curls of hair, called *pay-ess* – which they pronounced "pie-ess" – that waved in the wind as they moved or talked. Completely confused and frightened, I stuttered and stumbled at the barrage of questions. Finally, the leader shushed the others up and took over. I never had the opportunity to tell him who I was, where I'd come from, where I was staying or where I was going. As best I could, I tried to understand his questions and give him answers. When I opened my hand to show him my "beitel," he grabbed it with one hand and pushed me so hard that I fell backwards and landed on the street. Laughing and shrieking, they ran down the street, holding their "shtriemels," with their "kapotas," fringes, and "pie-ess" streaming behind them. Stunned, dismayed, and terrified at this sudden turn of events, I just sat there helplessly, tears gushing from my eyes. Two kindly ladies, witnesses to the entire episode, quickly came to my aid. Still speaking that strange dialect, they tried to calm me down. After eliciting the name of my landlady, they led me to her house and explained what had happened to me. I greeted her with a new burst of tears and ran inside, upset and ashamed of my experience. To this day, whenever I see anyone with a "shtreimel," a "kapota," or – especially – a person with "pie-ess," I get a flashback of my encounter in Lemberg, Poland. My heart starts to beat harder and I relive my fears, dismay, and disappointment. I know that my feeling of repulsion to that individual and what he represents is wrong. Still, somewhere in my mind's tangle of lost memories is one that I cannot forget. I truly wish I could eliminate this lingering prejudice. Or is it anger? Could someone help me?

PREPARING FOR PASSOVER

Talking in the last few weeks about my memories, as a little boy, of Yom Kippur and Sukkot and has tempted me to try to recall the extensive preparations that we used to go through before Passover and all the Holidays. Passover preparations were especially lengthy, colorful, and interesting. The first signs of preparation for the coming holiday appeared shortly after Purim when Papa came home with a new, large tub – for Mom to use in preparing the dough for the matzos for Passover. The household was alerted to refrain from eating anywhere near this tub, since a breadcrumb would contaminate the dough and make it unusable. Mama used a new, clean wooden platform upon which to pour the new flour, which she mixed with water (no yeast) to make the dough. I remember she used to work much harder to beat and roll the dough. After she felt it was properly prepared it was put into the new tub, covered with a clean cloth and moved to a corner of the kitchen, away from our daily uses.

I've often mentioned that Papa was an observant Jew, who whole-heartedly believed in the rituals of the traditional Orthodox practices. At the same time he did not trust everyone he dealt with, so he had to make sure what he ate was strictly Kosher. Thus, I remember that, every year, he brought his own dough to the town baker. The baker was supervised by learned men to make sure that matzos were handled and baked in a Kosher oven and handled properly. He baked our matzos in accordance with Papa's ideas of propriety. Thus, Papa would stay in the bakery until our matzos were finished and bring them home to be stored properly in our house until Passover. Our matzos – unlike the perfectly rounded or square shapes that come in our store-bought packages – were round-like, but with ragged edges since Papa could never roll the dough into perfectly round shapes by hand. Their taste, especially when covered with *schmaltz* (fresh goose fat), was unbelievably delicious. And, when fried with eggs (in schmaltz, of course), for breakfast – what we here call "matzo-brie" – were a heavenly delight I can still taste. Interestingly, I can't recall where or when Papa got the flour – it had to be Kosher for Passover – for the matzos. I distinctly remember our going to the nearby farms in the fall for the threshing of the hay and wheat on the peasant farms. Both men and women peasants handled the long, curving blades of the scythes (a tool to cut wheat) with apparent ease, cutting the hay and stacking it into huge piles. Some of the hay was piled onto our wagon, where Velvel (my, older-by-six-years brother) would pile it up even higher, till the wagon was filled. I can still smell the rich odor of newly cut hay as I rode home with him. The real fun was watching the peasants thresh the wheat fields. After the scythes had cut the wheat from the stalks, another group of peasants, wielding large, thick sticks – about the size of a baseball bat, attached to a long pole – would attack the fallen wheat, hitting it with their big sticks, to separate the chaff (husks) from the seeds. Both the chaff and the seeds were then bagged – the chaff to be used by us as fuel in our large hall oven to heat the house in winter. The seeds went to the mill to be ground into flour. I was always fascinated, watching the wheat seeds being ground into flour. The mules would be chained to large, thick poles which turned horizontally as they moved in a circle. They were attached to an even thicker vertical pole. Large straps whirled around the tall building (the mill), somehow causing two huge stones to rub against each other and grind the seeds, separating the husks from the inner white meal Eventually, after a number of revolutions, the meal became thinner and thinner until a very fine, white flour was milled. This marvelous result was then bagged into white bags, which we took home for Mama to use when she baked bread twice a week, and *challah* (the white twisted special bread) baked Friday mornings for the Sabbath. Since we used this same flour all year long, where did Papa get the Kosher for Passover flour? I don't have the faintest idea. As Passover neared, there were many other rituals that Papa went through to make sure every item used for this holiday was Kosher for Passover. Most of the pots and pans used in daily preparations were changed for the special ones, used only for Passover, which – after use – were put away into a special storage space reserved only for Passover items. On the rare occasions that Mama needed to use an everyday item for the holiday – a big iron kettle, a large, heavy spoon used in cooking – he had a special way to make it Kosher and usable. He would assemble all the kitchen items and take them out to the yard. There he had built a large fire in a pit. After the fire was strong enough, he put all the metal items on the fire, covered them with rocks and left them in the fire to burn away any particle of food which might have still remained on or in it. Long after the fire was out and everything had cooled off, he removed the rocks and retrieved the items. They were now considered Kosher and could be used for Passover. Preparations for removing the Chametz (bread, crumbs, not Kosher for Passover) from the entire house were very elaborate. A couple of days before the first Seder, Papa would invite us to watch as he made the rounds of the house and removed all the Chametz. Even at an early age I always suspected that Papa had "planted" some of the crumbs that he "found" in the most unlikely corners. To do that, he went through an elaborate ceremony. He had prepared a large wooden spoon, carried a rag and a large goose feather, with which he scraped every corner of every room – including such unlikely places as the *pripechick* (the large space above the baking oven, where we lolled, warm and cozy on cold evenings). Of course, he conveniently found some to scrape into the spoon. By the time we finished, he had a quite a lot of crumbs in the spoon, which he wrapped carefully in the rag – so he wouldn't spill any – including the feather, to save that for the next morning, when he burned the spoon, and feather in the pit in the yard. Thus, he declared, our house was now clean of any Chametz and Kosher for Passover. I seem to recall that he sought out the *Shamus* (the man from the Synagogue who handled all the chores and needs of the congregants), whom he paid for "buying" the Chametz from us. Is this confused with something else? I'm not sure. At any rate, all the Chametz items which were forbidden during Passover (rice, beans, etc., including all the pots, dishes, silver, napkins – both those used for milk or meat meals) were removed from their usual places and stored away by the morning before the first Seder, till the holiday was over. A very few essentials, needed for the final breakfast and lunch, were kept available and put away, immediately after lunch. After that, the only snack or food available was matzos – with schmaltz, of course – or fruit. On the last night before Passover, the big job of getting the beautiful dishes, silverware, Holiday table linens and napkins – all selected for their special beauty to use only during the eight days of Passover – were taken out of the large locked China closet in the living room, where they were kept unused all year. Of course, all the everyday, and even the Sabbath and Holiday dishes linens, and silver – both the *Flayshedikeh* and *Milchidikeh* dishes and silver (the meat and dairy dishes and silver) – that were not Kosher for Passover – had to be removed and stored away for the eight days of the holiday. This was no small task and required numerous trips from the China closet to the clean, ready-for-Passover spaces. It required a great deal of physical work, but was especially bitter for little boys – since we were forbidden to touch any of these precious items, for fear we might drop them; and, God forbid, break them. So, I could only watch, wistfully and silently. Oh, my! I forgot! Long before the Holiday, Papa went to the barrel-maker and ordered three or four large new barrels. Papa put them into our dark "cellar" – a large, unfinished hole in the ground, dug out below ground level, back of the kitchen. Here Papa prepared the brine for the pickles, green, unripe, tomatoes, and *borsht* (a pickled beet juice, used for soup, both hot and cold) for Passover. I can't remember our using sauerkraut during Passover. Apparently, cabbage was one of the forbidden foods. These delicacies, a very important part of our daily meals, were strictly for family use. However, Papa's reputation for pickling was well known and we invariably shared his products with friends and neighbors. The smells coming out of the cellar, for days before the big event, were so enticing that Papa kept the door locked, to prevent ravishingly hungry little boys from sampling the goods. Of course, Papa made his own wine – strictly Kosher for Passover – and kept away from any possible contamination, Unless Papa sampled or tasted his own product, to the best of my memory, the wine was virgin until used for the First Seder. But then, it was used by everybody, young and old, at both Sedarim. Papa believed that everyone seated at the Seder should participate in all rituals, including the drinking of four Kosim (goblets or glasses of wine), required during the Seder. His requirement that ALL seated were to participate became a very boring experience to little boys. Mama did all she could to get him to speed the recitations up, before the children fell asleep at the table. Sometimes, he listened. At other times – whether from the imbibing of the wine, or just because we, also, seemed to enjoy it – he insisted we go through all the passages, songs, and rituals prescribed in our fancy *Haggadahs* (special books that are used to conduct and follow rites and order of the Seder). Question: Could four glasses of wine make little boys enjoy a long, drawn-out, dreary, sometimes, uninteresting, evening – even forget their hunger, till the evening meal was served? You'd never know it, at our Seder. The songs that followed unloosed loud and strident participation. Since, among the many restrictions of Passover, a number of daily foods were denied all beans, noodles, many vegetables, ordinary cakes and candies were, also, taboo – we resorted to growing our own vegetables in the big lot, around our house. Instead of shrubberies, tomatoes and cucumbers (mostly for pickles) grew alongside the house, the stems held up and tied by strings. The large, white radishes – grated and served as an appetizer, and served with all meats and fish – were grown, abundantly, in back. Large carrots, used in soups and stews, also a staple, grew alongside. Last, but not least, all dairy products, milk, cream, butter, cheese, as well as all fowl and eggs, came from our own barn. In short, except for meats and fish, everything needed for a joyous celebration of Passover were provided by the hard work and planning before the Holiday. Just writing about it makes me feel good, all over again. May you too, have lasting memories of Holidays and other Joyful Times.

October 19, 2005

A VISIT TO LYUBAR – a Grandson's Journey

by Gary D. Bartel (Ralph's oldest grandson)
September 1995

My grandfather mentioned to me years ago that he had been born in the Ukraine, and had escaped from there at the age of ten during the height of the pogroms. While it has never been a popular or regular topic for discussion in our family, Grandpa Ralph's childhood has always intrigued me, especially since I began traveling to the Soviet Union in the early 1980s. This past summer I mentioned to my grandfather that I was scheduling a business trip to Russia and Ukraine. I was surprised he mentioned that, perhaps if I had time, I would be interested in visiting the village where he was born. He volunteered to supply me with as much of the vital information he could remember about his town. He even went and found a map describing the exact location of this village, Lyubar. Of course, I immediately took advantage of this golden opportunity to discover the roots of a part of my family, and to view – with my own eyes – the place of my grandfather's birth.

My business colleague, Joe Schultz, and I left Kiev for Lyubar at 11 a.m. with our driver Mykhail. It was a bright, sunny day and I was looking forward to the 200 km drive through the Ukrainian countryside. The condition of the roads began to deteriorate once we reached the halfway point at the town of Zhitomir. What began as a two-hour drive to Lyubar would end up being more like three hours. Direction signs were almost non-existent and our driver continually stopped to ask the locals for help. As we continued our journey, the sense of excitement and expectation continued to mount. Finally, at around 2 p.m., I excitedly pointed out the sign announcing the entrance to the town. I made the driver to pull over for a picture.

Upon entering the town limits, we found an old Russian Orthodox Church and decided to stop and ask the clergymen to help us find the Jewish cemetery or the old synagogue. My grandfather had mentioned

Gary Bartel with welcoming Lyubar villagers, 1995.

those as being in the center of the village. Unfortunately, the Church was closed. We stopped a passing party of villagers in a horse and cart and asked them about the old synagogue and the cemetery. I had studied Russian in college and could speak the language, so both Mykhail and I could communicate. The villagers were very friendly and told us that the synagogue had been destroyed in World War II. They had no idea where the synagogue had been, and as far they knew, there were no more Jews in Lyubar, as they had all been killed by the Nazis or emigrated to Israel after the war. One of the older ladies in the group gave us directions to the two Jewish cemeteries in town. As we drove toward the cemeteries, one could not help but have the eerie sensation of being transported back in time. The roads were shared equally by cars and by horses pulling carts filled with villagers in native dress. Cows were commonplace and we were constantly stopping for herds being driven down the road.

After a fruitless search for the cemeteries, we finally stopped and asked a local gentleman if he knew where the Jewish cemeteries were. He replied that there was one in the forest right behind us, but he noted that there was no way we would find it on our own. Dressed in a sports coat and slacks, he insisted on personally showing us the way. I was utterly amazed as he proceeded to lead two strangers (Mykhail and me), without even so much as a hint of a request, on a 30-minute hike through the forest, in what had to be the finest clothes he owned. He led us to two mass graves deep in the forest, on which were etched, under the Star of David, the names of some of the dead who were buried there. This site was apparently one of the mass execution sites used by the Nazis and

Our Lyubar guide with Mykhail at the mass execution site marked with a stone.

Gary Bartel in the overgrown Jewish cemetery in Lyubar.

now was a memorial of sorts. It was emotional. He then walked us back to our car and gave us directions to the other cemetery located about a mile away. Then, as calmly and quickly as he entered this story, he left us.

Mykhail and I found the other location after a few minutes of searching. It was located in a forest next to a gas distribution complex. The gate controller for the gas complex pointed to a hole in the fence and indicated that we could find the old Jewish cemetery through there. We entered the forest and began walking. After a few minutes, I noticed some strangely shaped stones protruding out of the underbrush and trees. Upon closer inspection I saw that these stones contained badly faded Hebrew lettering. We had found the cemetery. As we continued to explore, we found more and more headstones in the cemetery which clearly had not been maintained for at least 50 years. We entered an opening in the forest and suddenly we were surrounded by literally hundreds of headstones and crypts. Some of the newer headstones were legible and I was able to pick out family names such as: Glazer, Rosenburg, Berger, and Kulton. Once again I experienced the

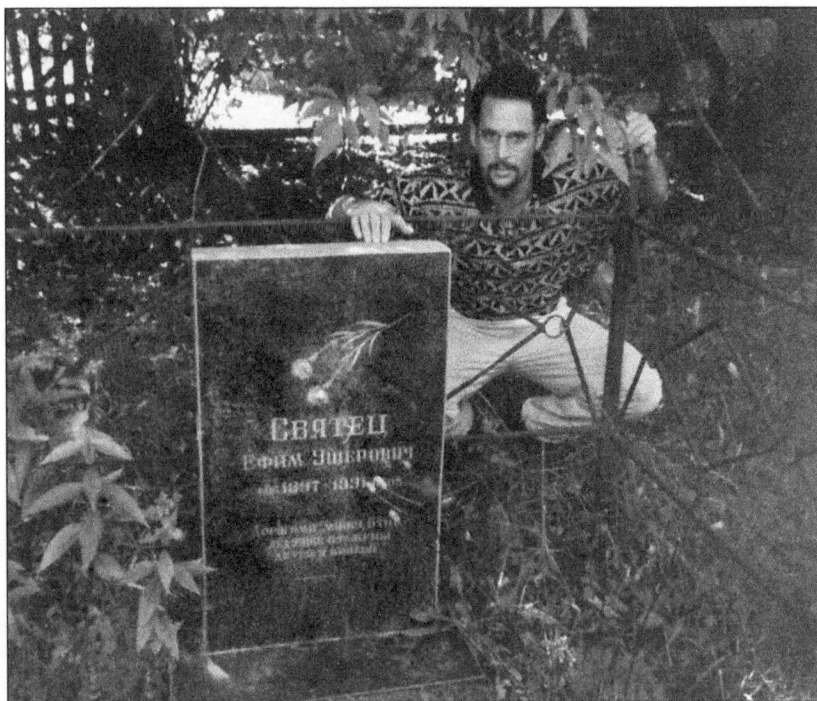

Gary Bartel in the overgrown Jewish cemetery in Lyubar.

overwhelming sensation of being transported back in time to another era. As I continued my unsuccessful search for headstones which may have belonged to my family, I could not help but think that as overgrown and un-maintained as this cemetery was, it still exuded a strong sense of tranquility, stillness and peace. During the course of our search, I began to notice that Mykhail seemed to be very touched by our discovery. Shortly before we returned to our car, he tapped me on the shoulder and showed me his passport. His full name was Mykhail Kreitor, and he too was a Jew!

On the way back to our car, we approached the gas complex attendant and asked if he had any idea where the synagogue may have been. He told us that the only Jew he knew was a 70-year-old lady who lived behind the "Little Café." He said if anyone knew where the synagogue was, she would be the one to speak with. We went to the cafe and asked one of the workers if they knew of this woman. Surprisingly, she did and said she would go get her. Not more than two minutes had passed when an excited old woman dressed in a classic babushka uniform came scurrying around the corner with a look of pure astonishment on her face. She introduced herself as Musuevna Yevginnaya Glazer and told us that she was the last Jew left in Lyubar.

When we inquired as to the location of the old synagogue, she told us that it was destroyed when she was young girl, and that she did not remember where it was actually located. As for the rest of the Jews of Lyubar, she confirmed our earlier conversation with the villagers that most of the Jews were killed by the Nazis and the rest had fled to Israel. She asked us if we were Israelis, and was stunned to learn that I was, in fact, an American. For a person who had lived an incredibly simple life for the past 70 years, our intrusion was almost too emotional for her to bear. Once she regained her composure, she invited us to her house, which could be more appropriately termed a "hovel." What little furniture she had was broken, old and dirty. Her 10-year-old granddaughter who lived with her was scampering about in her bare feet, in spite of the 50-degree weather. She told us that she lived on a $7 (US dollars) a month pension and tearfully described her plight to us. She asked if there was any assistance that we might be able to provide as winter was near and she feared that there might not be enough food to last. I had very little cash on me as I had been unable to find an open bank to exchange my traveler's checks the day before in Kiev.

At that point Mykhail, without any prompting from me, pulled out a $10 bill and gave it to her. With everyone on the verge of tears, our new "babushka" told us that we must be a gift to her from G-d and that all she wanted was to have some joy in the last few years of her life. She indicated that her granddaughter needed some shoes for the winter and that she was worried about the food supply as it had been a very dry summer. I resolved in my mind that I would do whatever I could to help this woman, and indicated to her that we would help her. At this

Musuevna Yevginnaya Glazer (center), the last Jew in Lyubar, with her 10-year-old granddaughter and Gary Bartel.

Mykhail, Gary, Musuevna Yevginnaya Glazer and her neighbor.

point I realized that she was crying freely and that the assistance that we could provide could make the difference between life and death for her. Mykhail and I agreed that since mail delivery was virtually non-existent and extremely unreliable in this rural part of the Ukraine, we would work together to find a way to get her the basic necessities of life that she so badly needed. As I took some pictures of our new friend and her granddaughter, I explained that my grandfather was writing a book about his life, including his memories of Lyubar. I asked if she would mind if we used her photo and story, and she quickly agreed. As we left her, it was hard to believe that this small, hardened woman was the last of our people left in Lyubar.

As it was now approaching dinnertime, we decided to find something to eat before leaving for the long drive back to Kiev. We found a restaurant in the town center, where the workers were astounded to see two very hungry Americans. Never in their wildest dreams, they told us, had they imagined that they would be serving Americans (let alone westerners) in their restaurant. We consumed a feast of tomato and onion salad, Ukrainian bread, sausages, ground pork & meatballs, potatoes, dumplings filled with spicy meat, and dessert pastries. After our coffee and tea, I was shocked when told that the total bill was $8 US dollars.

As I stood in the town square following our meal, gazing at this village that my grandfather had previously attempted to describe to me, I could not help but wonder if Gramps would recognize his birthplace today. Perhaps some things were unchanged, but most of the town's structures had been destroyed by the occupying Nazis during the War and were rebuilt in the typically drab fashion of the Soviet regime. Yet it was still a strange feeling to know that I was now looking at the same landscape in which he was born and began his journey, some 75 years before.

The two images on page 200 and 201 show Gary Bartel standing before Lyubar's church, and on a typical Lyubar street. The third image is a signpost from the days of Lyubar's Soviet past.

SUMMER CAMP

When Gary and Doug (two of my grandsons) expressed their pleasure at their children's summer camp experiences, it brought back memories of the one and only time when I, too, went to camp. Although I've mentioned this before, the story of how this came about is quite unusual.

The story of our family's struggle to adapt to living in a new country, learning to speak a new language, and working hard to earn enough to be able to live in reasonable comfort has been repeatedly told before. Our experiences in the first few years were especially difficult. Since this deals with the summer of 1927, I have to explain our life, then, as I remember it. If I repeat myself, again, please excuse it. I believe it'll make my story more meaningful.

I must remind you of the sad state, generally, of immigrants, in this wonderful country. It was (and, I suspect still is) a constant fight for survival. We did not have the pleasures or conveniences that all of us now take for granted. As I write this the media is full of the awful devastation and chaos now prevailing in New Orleans and surrounding areas, because of Hurricane Katrina. Many of its survivors now face some of the miseries that were an immigrant's way of life, every day. The lack of food, housing, and clothing, and the struggle to obtain them, is reminiscent of what we strove for, daily.

From the moment we arose after settling here, our only thoughts dealt with the work we faced that day, and how best to handle it. There was no time or means to think of fun or entertainment. All our efforts were concentrated on work, work, and work, only. Luxuries were meaningless, since we had none and knew they were beyond our reach until we met our basic minimal needs. Like the rest of my family, I had and wore the same "Union Suit," a one-piece flimsy undergarment, all day. And, I slept in it every night. My vocabulary hardly included words like shorts, pajamas, shower, socks, hot baths, sprays, deodorant, and anything else you and I take for granted. My one pair of knickers, blouse, knee-high black stockings, and high "tennis" shoes ($1.00 a pair) were worn daily till they fell apart or couldn't be mended any more by Mama, and had to be replaced – a special event.

By early 1927 we had accomplished some degree of security. We had bought our first car, that new 1926 Chevy (cash, no credit cards, then). It brought an easement to the daily burdens of business and stress. Now, we could sleep a little longer; we could deliver our orders much faster; we could even begin to think of some pleasures. On Sundays, when we closed the store at 2 p.m., we suddenly found time for a drive – not too far, in case we get a flat tire or get an overheated radiator. When spring was in full force, with its smells of bushes and trees in full bloom permeating the air, we found a new and relatively inexpensive way to enjoy ourselves. It was a wonderful way to forget the daily stresses and enjoy the beauty and quiet of the nearby farmland. In fact, by the middle of summer, we had learned there was a large, free public beach in Southwest Baltimore, with water safe for bathing and swimming. To escape the unbearable, oppressive heat of Baltimore summers, we could go to the beach near the Chesapeake Bay.

A trip to Brager/Eisenberg Bargain Basement provided the cheap, one-piece dark bathing suits then in vogue. Mama's upbringing prevented her from wearing a revealing garment, so she accompanied us, wearing her lightest and most comfortable summer dress. As soon as we found a table for our picnic basket, Papa, Mike, and I – wearing our newly acquired suits – quickly took advantage of the surrounding waters to cool off after our long trip in the hot car. The path to the water from the beach was a long wooden walkway, raised about 18 inches above the surrounding shallow water. At the water end of the walkway, three steps – covered with a thick straw-like material, and with railings on both sides – prevented bathers from slipping, as they stepped into or out of the soothing water.

Naturally, Mike and I ran down the path and into the water. After all, we were or tried to be typical teenagers, and had to do what most guys our age do. Once in the water, it was hard to get us out. Although both of us had been forbidden to learn to swim in the old country, we frolicked, jumped around, splashed water on each other; and, perhaps, used this opportunity to wash off some of our accumulated dirt and sweat. We loved every minute. When Papa finally got us out of the cooling water, we had to run, naturally! In my rush to beat Mike, I accidentally found a nail sticking out of the bottom step and had a nasty gash on the large toe of my left foot! It bled profusely!

Someone noticed the bleeding and led me to the First Aid Station to treat my injury. The white-clad nurse on duty had to sew two stitches before she could stop the bleeding. After carefully bandaging the toe, she instructed me to do as little walking as necessary, to keep my foot as quiet as possible. With a big white bandage on my foot and some continuing pain, it was easy to follow her instructions. We ate our prepared picnic lunches in a somber mood and soon left for home. I can't remember, but probably Mike had to drive us back home.

Regardless of my situation, I still had responsibilities, and – while wearing a slipper on my bandaged foot – I reported for work, as usual, on Monday. I had finished summer school and was pitching in to help in the store, before reporting for my first year in high school. One of the first people to come into the store was Mr. Brightstein, a regular customer, an insurance salesman, who had talked Papa into buying a policy for me, when he'd sold one to Papa. One look at my foot and he asked what'd happened. When I finished my story, he said that my policy covered accidents and gave me a blank to file my claim. By the time my check for ten dollars ($10) came, my toe had healed and I was ready to use it for my first vacation, just two weeks before school started.

During my wait for the check, I'd learned about Camp Airy and had convinced my parents to let me use the proceeds of my claim for a week's stay. After all, it was "found money," and I was entitled to use it as I pleased. Arrangements were made and I reported to the railroad station on Sunday morning, to join all the other eager boys who were lucky enough to get away for a week's change. The Counselors, with their charts on hand, assigned each of us to a Junior Counselor, to take us to a seat in the waiting coaches. My excitement at what was in store for me in the next week, made me anxious for the train to start. Finally, a whistle quieted the raucous group of boys, as we were told what to do when we arrived at the station nearest Camp Airy.

I knew nobody in my coach! Although I was probably the oldest boy (17) on board, I was thrilled at what was happening to me. Imagine! For the first time, in the more than four years since we'd come to Baltimore, I was experiencing a summer camp! A whole week awaited me, to live, play, and sleep, in the cool mountains – away from the overpowering heat and dampness of the Baltimore summer! The shrill voices of several youngsters, who'd apparently been at camp before, reminiscing about their former adventures, helped build a picture of what awaited me. The kids talked about Indian tribes, staged plays on Saturday nights, games and races and contests of bewildering names – "three-legged," "potato," and other strange-sounding races, "breaking the ice," swimming and canoeing. I was excited and confused. Here I was, a gangly, skinny, 17-year-old who had never played or even heard of some of these games and activities, listening to these excited, squeaky voices rave about the fun they'd had and were looking forward to, again. This was the stuff of dreams for a boy – big boy, true, but still a boy – who had always had to work so hard that he had no time for any such foolishness. Well, by golly, I was going to try to do as many new things in the coming week, as I could squeeze in!

Meanwhile, the stuffy, coal-burning engines that spilled so much throat-burning smoke and ashes, together with its many coaches and cars, started to turn and twist as the train gained the "mountains" (high hills?). The scenery changed. Each new curve brought an interesting new vista of wood-filled lands or small, well-tended farms. Before we knew it, the whistle sounded, the noise and babble stopped, and the conductor announced that we were approaching Thurmont, Maryland, which was the closest train stop to camp. Instructions followed, to organize our descent from the train – to form into lines, listen to our Counselors, and board the waiting buses. The cacophony of sounds that followed made it difficult for anyone to try to communicate. But, who cared? This was what we were all waiting for – the camp! At last!

In the hustle and bustle of gathering our belongings and suitcases before the train stopped, I once again began to visualize the many scenarios of what I was facing in my forthcoming experiences. Glancing about me at the eager young boys I could picture myself excelling at the many activities they'd described. Hah! I'd show these kids! The many hours I'd spent working in my father's store had built my skinny frame with invisible muscles that enabled me to lift and carry 100-pound bags of sugar or flour and even heavier sacks of potatoes. All I needed was a chance and I'd surprise a lot of people. Yes, even the counselors, too, might be surprised. I was going to have a week full of fun and excitement and I planned to enjoy every minute! No matter what faced me, I was going to make the most of it. Although I wasn't too sure exactly what was facing me, I was prepared to have an exciting week.

As I dragged my beat-up old cloth-covered suitcase down from the baggage rack above my seat, I was thrilled at the number of new things I had packed, in line with the list of suggested items Camp Airy had recommended.

I can't recall everything on that list. I remember that we were to bring three of each item – socks, underwear, handkerchiefs, shorts, and so on. This number was something new in my experience. I had never owned more than two items of anything before. A quick visit to an Army and Navy store, armed with my hard-earned savings, provided the fill-ins. Another novelty required having my name written on a tag and sewn on each item. Mama had scrunched up a long piece of 3/8-inch hemming liner in her sewing basket and spent hours cutting strips and sewing each on everything I was to take with me. I was still wearing the familiar one-piece "union-suit" regularly, but had acquired boxer shorts and undershirts when I "dressed up" and wore my one (1) pair of "long pants" purchased for my brother Willie's wedding. I had worked hard, to write my name in black ink with a newly sharpened quill pen. So, now I was prepared.

Soon I became very self-conscious at the appearance of my hands and arms, blackened from the smoke and soot spouted by the coal-burning locomotive of the chugging train huffing and puffing through the curves in the woods. As I glanced around at some of the other boys, who were also sitting at the open windows of our coach, I saw that their faces and blouses, too, were smeared with black. We looked at each other and burst out in laughter.

Lined up in rows of two, the descending group of campers stood on the loading platform of the station, waiting for further instruction. A busy-looking older counselor soon came by. As we called out our names, he consulted his charts, checked it off and assigned us to one of the three buses standing near the platform, with a counselor standing by each door. Each bus was named after a local wild animal. The counselor at the door checked off our names on his list, told us to stack our suitcases at the back of the bus, and take the first empty seat, starting with the back rows. The seats consisted of plain unpainted or unvarnished planks of wood, on either side. Another young counselor directed us to each plank, with room for two or three boys.

When all the boys assigned to our bus had been checked off, and a count confirmed that everybody was there, we started the winding drive through the woods. I noticed that our bus, with the older boys, was not full. We soon divided ourselves into two boys to a row seat. The cool air coming from the open windows was a welcome change from the stuffy, smelly heat of the train.

Riding on a bus in 1927, was an experience. Unlike the present day buses, with all the gadgets – automatic starter, windshield wipers, large tires, springs, air-conditioning, safety features, piped music, and so on – a bus was a metal shell with wooden seats, windows only brute strength could open, motors that just stopped if you went over a bad bump, a hand-controlled windshield wiper, a starter that had to be started by a crank stuck under the radiator (that required a strong hand and quick reactions when it caught on or you could end up with a broken arm), solid, air-less tires that could stand the tough roads. The list is endless. It was strictly a convenience; certainly not a luxury. But, it served its purpose. It took you somewhere and brought you back. You hoped.

The grinding sound made when the counselor-driver changed gears – done by using the clutch on the left and hand-changing the gear, and required by the poor road conditions and the climb up the mountains – were hard on my ears. I was probably the only camper who was an experienced driver. Eventually we reached Camp Airy and were welcomed by a sign above the entrance.

The cabin to which I was assigned, the "Navajo," was set back among a group scattered through a wooded area. It was built from about six-inch wide logs, that covered the lower half of the building, with the rest covered by screening. I don't recall any windows. The building was set on posts that kept it about 18 inches off the ground and away from any snakes. It had an overhang, to prevent the rain from soaking us. Inside there were bunks for about 14 to 16 boys, spaced apart to accommodate our satchels or trunks, which stored our belongings. It also had room for our Counselor. Each bunk had a tight-fitting blanket which served as its bedspread. No sooner had we plopped on our assigned bunks than the counselor started to explain that for the rest of our stay we were "Navajos," how we were expected to behave, the rules of the bunk, the cabin, schedules for each day, dining, bugle calls, "breaking the ice," and so many other things it became impossible to remember half of them. Fortunately, he ended by referring any questions to the campers already there.

If you are still with me, I thank you for your endurance and courage to stay the course. I know that the only reason you've read this far is because you're interested in the good part – how I really spent this great week of camping. In what areas did I succeed and/or excel? Right? You're certainly entitled!

Unfortunately, your flattering praise for my retentive memory is about to be shocked into reality. I am compelled to resort to the famous answer that my son Alan purportedly gave to a professor during his anatomy class – "YOU ARE DOOMED TO A GREAT DISAPPOINTMENT!"

The "honest truth," as one of my fellow immigrant friends used to say, is that my mind appears to have drawn a blank. For the life of me, I can't remember any game or physical exercise in which I excelled. I couldn't keep up with the pace set in the basketball game between our team of Navajo Indians and that of another tribe. My best recollection of my participation in the softball game is that the umpire called "strike three! You're out!" every time I went to bat. In trying to learn how to use a bow and arrow, I was very consistent. My arrow always fell short of the target! This remarkable trait was also true in all my tries at racing, even in the "three-legged" and "Potato-sack" races. In short, I didn't "show them" anything I could be proud of during my week in camp, as I'd envisioned during my train trip. There was absolutely nothing I could boast of upon my return home. All I could say was, "I had a wonderful time." And, yet, in spite of all my failures, I still felt I really had a fine time during that week – as long as I didn't have to go into details.

Oh, yes! There were two things that are still very vivid in my memories. First, I soon learned what "Breaking the Ice" meant. As soon as we got dressed, on Monday morning, we were taken to a lagoon into which water flowed steadily down from a rock near the entrance. Each one of us was encouraged (meaning, forced) to walk or jump into the shallow water. The water was shockingly cold! Hence the name. If you weren't totally awake when you got there, you sure woke up quickly, once you hit the water. I hated it.

Next, we changed clothes and went to eat breakfast. That's where I got the moniker, "The Guy with the Big Appetite," after my first breakfast. Our table was set with paper napkins, bowls and large spoons. We were ready to eat.

There were several large pitchers full of milk and a couple of small bowls with brown sugar. Soon a server came by and put down three large platters of hot cereal. I watched as my tablemates filled their bowls with heaping servings of cereal, sprinkled some brown sugar on, and poured milk from the pitchers. I suddenly realized I was starved and followed suit. It was scrumptious, as my niece Rosie would have said. I wolfed it down and emptied my bowl before anyone else was finished. Seeing some cereal left in the serving dish, I quickly refilled my bowl and soon finished that, too. Several of the boys glanced at me curiously, but I was enjoying it too much to care.

After I'd finished my second bowl, I looked around the table and noticed there was some food sill left further down the table. Without thinking I asked if anyone else wanted that, pointing to the platter. All eyes seemed to be on me. But, I still felt hungry and hated to see food going to waste. I ate and enjoyed my third bowl of cereal, ignoring my companions, eyeing me. That's when someone called out, "Boy, that guy's got a big appetite, doesn't he?"

From that meal on, I was known and pointed out as "The Guy with the Big Appetite." The name stuck with me, because I truly lived up to it for the rest of the week. I don't know whether it was the novelty of being in camp, the cool air of my surroundings, or because I was used to consuming large portions of food at home – perhaps caused by my working hard at the store and needing the extra intake to keep up my strength – or because I participated so strenuously, albeit unsuccessfully, in all camp activities, but I was always hungry! Whatever the reason, the nickname was well deserved. I earned it.

And that, my loves, is the end of my story. I sincerely apologize if you expected more and I left you unfulfilled. That's all there is! There ain't no more! And, that's the "honest truth!"

Love, Ralphy

TENDING THE COW

A poem by Ralph

I was wide-awake as soon as I felt his gentle yet firm touch. The light breeze wafting into the dark bedroom brought promise of another glorious spring day. Silently but swiftly, I donned the clothes, prepared before going to bed last night. Just as quietly, the door was closed, so no one would be disturbed, meanwhile carefully tiptoeing my way towards the kitchen, where the light from the fireplace lit the way. The milk and cookies are almost swallowed, in my haste to go outside and into the barn. At last, the long-awaited day had finally arrived! What an adventure for a five-year-old boy. Today, I'd get my first chance to take our cow into the fields, to pasture, all by myself!!

THE CHALUTZ

M y brother Willie's wife, Pauline (yes, the same name as Mollie's mother), was an active member of a Women's Zionist organization. Her younger brother, Nathan Marder, had become friends with Mike and me on one of our visits to their home and store. Nathan encouraged us to join him in a Gordonia Club that was being formed. The Club, named for A. D. Gordon, an early *Chalutz* (pioneer) who had bravely fought and died in Palestine, while establishing a *Kibbutz* (a co-operative farm). The story of his bravery and struggles was an inspiration to all young people and re-aroused our interest and belief in Zionism.

Mike and I became very enthusiastic members of the Club and started out immediately collecting funds for the Jewish National Fund from all of the people in our neighborhood. In my stamp album, marked "Palestine," are examples of the J.N.F. stamps we gave to each contributor when a few pennies or a rare nickel or better was donated. Today, some of the Jewish stamps have value. The Club, made up of a very varied and multi-talented group of young men and women, met monthly at the Young Men's Hebrew Association (Y.M.H.A., the "Jewish Y"), in downtown Baltimore. Our advisor, Dr. Stuart H. Ginsburgh, originally from Germany, had earned a PhD from Johns Hopkins, spoke several languages, including Hebrew, and gave excellent inspirational lectures and guidance about Palestine and its Pioneers. Our meetings led to many enthusiastic drives to raise funds for Palestine, including our getting the local War Memorial Arena, for a benefit drive, plays at the "Y," and dances, all done to make money for a cause, by willing volunteers. Although I was a very dedicated member, my enthusiasm waned when I started Normal School (teachers' college).

The demands on my time and interests as I strove to become a teacher became my priorities and I gradually distanced myself from the Club and its mission. But, not my brother Mike. If anything, his devotion to the Zionist movement grew larger month by month. He always came back from a meeting with an interesting story or item to talk about. One night, in the spring of 1930, he was so excited about a new project discussed at the Club Meeting, he insisted all of us stop everything and let him explain. Pop, Mom, and I listened. He overwhelmed us with his enthusiasm. It seemed that a member of the *Zeire Zion* (Labor Zionist Party) Movement, our Senior Party Sponsor, had offered the Gordonia Club the free use of a ten-acre parcel of land on Old York Road, on the outskirts of Baltimore, for the purpose of training Club members to become farmer Chalutzim! Mike of course, had been the first one to volunteer! Several other members had tentatively offered to join him. But, he was going to be the first one to train to became a farmer and then emigrate to Palestine and become a Chalutz! He had it all figured out. Since my first year at Normal School was almost over and I had no job for the summer, I could take over for him at the store. The plot had an old farmhouse on it. He'd live there and work the land, just like the Chalutzim had done in Palestine. When he had learned how to raise things and felt fully trained, he'd emigrate! We were completely dumbstruck. I, of course, could not argue against him. After all, he had volunteered to let me go to High School and on to Normal School while he worked full time at the store. For almost three years, he'd given me the opportunities I'd craved. How could I deny him the chance to do what was in his heart? It would only be for the summer, he said. He was sure that by the time I was ready to go back for my last year, before I became a teacher, he felt certain he'd be fully trained.

Knowing Mike and his strong will and determination, I had no doubt that he could do it – if anyone could. No matter what argument Mom or Pop had against the idea, he had an answer, showing it was possible for him to overcome the objection. In any case, he concluded, all he asked from us was to give him the chance to train – for the summer months. If it didn't work, he'd be back, so I could finish my last year. It was settled. Gleefully, he trudged up to his room, singing a Palestinian song. From that day on, Mike used every spare minute to plan and prepare for his new endeavor. A fund had been established for use in getting the place habitable and usable.

Egged on by Mike's enthusiasm and careful planning, several Club members helped him clean up and whitewash the old frame farmhouse. A rickety kitchen table and several very old chairs became the first floor furniture. The ancient wood-burning stove became usable again and an old icebox (not a refrigerator, but a box that held ice in a top compartment, to cool everything below) was cleaned up and installed in the kitchen. A rusty metal bed with a bent spring supported a clean gray striped mattress in an upstairs bedroom. Water and electricity were connected, and Mike moved in before I came home on the last day of Normal School. The transition from my dressed-up days at school to work clothes went smoothly and I became so busy with the store that I could only make my first visit to the "farm" more than a week after he left. When I got there the stark whiteness of the old house in the middle of a flat, large, empty lot was startling, even though Mike had prepared me for it, beforehand. No one answered my call, so I tried the door and found it unlocked. Inside, the bare furnishings were almost spooky in their isolation. They brought back many unpleasant memories of our first "apartment," above the store. It actually felt scary to stay in this barren, empty place and I quickly went out the kitchen door, to look for Mike or anyone else who might be there. It was only then that I noticed the newly plowed furrows and rows of dirt and pieces of stone that marked the signs of recent farming attempts. A yet aroused me to see Mike far down at the back of the lot, beckoning for me to join him. Carefully making my way through the uneven footing, I finally reached him, watching him as he knelt and carefully put a piece of what looked like dirty garbage into the ground, covering it with newly rowed dirt, and patting it in place with dirty, bare hands. He was completely at home – as if he had been doing this kind of work all his life. Amazing! "Hi!" he said, "I'm almost through this row. How are you?" And continued working. When he came to the end of the row, he stood up, brushed his hands on his overalls and turned to shake hands. "I've been planting potatoes" he explained, as he pointed to his 'garbage'. "Where are the others?" I asked. "Oh," he answered, "there aren't any others. I'm all alone now. A couple of people came out at first, Sylvia, Ben, but they didn't want to get dirty or spare the time, so they left. I don't care. I can do it myself. I only have this one row left to do," he continued. "Let me finish it and we'll go back to the house." As he worked he filled me in with the details of all he'd read and what he intended to do before the summer was over. Nothing seemed to faze him. He'd made definite plans and, so far, everything was going well. No matter the problem, he either already knew the solution or would find someone to help him solve it.

Although Mike and I had been as close as any two brothers could possibly be – we'd slept in the same bed, in the same bedroom, since coming to America, and shared our thoughts on many topics – I learned more about him in the next couple of hours than ever before or since. The extent of his commitment to the Chalutz movement was unshakable and unwavering. He'd put his heart and soul into becoming a knowledgeable and successful farmer and fully intended to utilize those skills when he made *Aliya* (moving to Palestine) as soon as he felt he was ready! When Mike made up his mind about something, as I well knew, he'd never stop until he reached his goal. During our talk that afternoon, he told me – confidentially – that he and Hannah Stone, a girl we had met at one of the Gordonia meetings, had dated several times. They had seriously discussed his going to Palestine and she approved it very much. In fact she'd said at their last meeting, she intended to broach the subject of her going, also, with her parents. He hadn't heard from her yet. Since he had no phone on the farm and he'd been too busy working the field to call her, he had no idea what became of that idea. Anyway, it was too early to worry about it, now. His chief concern and priority was to plant different vegetables on every spot on the big lot and see how successful he was by the end of the summer. He planned to work all day, from daybreak to dark.

Meanwhile Mike had scoured his hands with a hand cleaner and invited me to share his lunch. Not surprisingly, he had a full larder of canned goods bought from our store but paid for from the "Farm Fund." There was a choice of sardines, tuna, pink salmon, fruit, and vegetables, and about a dozen loaves of white bread. "Why so much bread?" I asked. "Isn't it going to get stale?" "No way" he laughed, "I'll use them all up by tomorrow, probably." Amazed, I could only watch as he proceeded to finish an entire loaf of bread with his opened can of sardines. Both of us had always been prodigious eaters when we worked in the store, but never to that extent. Since he began working such long hours, he told me, he was always hungry and consumed several loaves of white bread – the only kind delivered by his milkman – together with at least two quarts of milk, every day. By the middle of that summer, Mike had a bronzed like Charles Atlas (the well-known bodybuilder of those days) and filled out. In short, Mike succeeded in raising a field of potatoes, carrots, cucumbers, and large, white radishes during that summer – to no one's surprise. What was amazing was that he did it all by himself! The one time I volunteered to help him dig up potatoes, one Saturday, I worked until both my hands swelled with blisters and I had to quit. Mike continued while I watched, till I left early in July.

I received a telephone call from a very angry woman. Her name was Mrs. Stone, the mother of Hannah Stone. She had called before and was upset because she tried to speak to my parents but couldn't make them understand. Mr. and Mrs. Stone had a very serious problem to discuss with them that involved their daughter and Mike. It had to be discussed face to face. When could they meet? Since they couldn't speak Yiddish and our parents apparently had trouble with English, I offered to act as interpreter. We arranged to meet at our house next Sunday night. Neither our parents nor I had any idea what this was all about and couldn't understand why Mike, who was working on the "farm," could develop a "serious problem" with a girl we had met at a Gordonia Club. I told them that I had met Hannah at the Club and had danced with her once. As far as I know she seemed to be a nice girl. She told me she attended Goucher College – a very exclusive women's college in Baltimore. In fact, I wondered aloud, I was surprised they even allowed a Jewish girl into the school. In those days, every college had tight restrictions on the number of Jews, if any, accepted. I'd have to wait till Sunday.

The sober-faced couple that faced me when I opened the door on Sunday evening looked like they were attending a loved one's funeral. In answer to my greeting's question whether they were Mr. and Mrs. Stone, she grumbled a grumpy "Yes!" They walked in without another word and acknowledged our parents' welcome with a curt nod. The two of them sat down, "stone-faced," (no pun intended) without saying a word. Finally, to break the silence, I asked them to explain their problem. Mrs. Stone showed who was "wearing the pants" in that family, with a tirade that lasted for several minutes. The gist of her ire went something like this: "How DARE Mike poison their one and only superior-educated daughter with his proposal to marry her? How could he, an uneducated immigrant nobody who hadn't even finished High School, compare himself to their Hannah, who was already enrolled at the prestigious world-famous Goucher College and had graduated from high school on the Honor Roll at the age of 16? Worst of all, he had the audacity to brainwash her with his idiotic plans to take her away to Palestine, to work along with all the crazies from Europe on a farm and endangering her very life, surrounded by those fanatic Arabs! Besides, Mr. Stone was seriously ill with diabetes and would surely die if "our Hannah were to leave like that." And so on and so on.

The more she spoke, the angrier I became. Although neither Mom nor Pop could express themselves in English as eloquently as Mrs. Stone, they had no problem in understanding her. As I glanced at them, I could tell that they, too, were getting very upset at her tirade and, especially, at her tone of voice. But, Pop motioned to me not to say anything. Pop somehow suppressed his anger at the insulting speech, which he obviously understood perfectly. Pop asked me to stay calm and explain, in English, how well Mike did in Cheder and in school when he attended. Pop insisted that I not use any language that demeans us in our guests' eyes.

Forcing myself – against my sincere wishes – I told them that everything about Mike's and Hannah's plans were a total surprise to all of us. But, like all teenagers, which they and I still were, we all have and express ideas and ideals and dreams when we talk. In most cases, they end up only as dreams. Since the Stones hadn't met Mike yet, they ought to at least give him the opportunity to talk to them, before they pass judgment on his intellect. I then proceeded in enumerating Mike's accomplishments, from being a prodigy at Cheder before age five, and going on to show that he didn't finish high school only because he'd sacrificed his own education to help me achieve mine. How he'd been bored in junior high with the mediocre teachers who couldn't keep his interest in the subjects they were teaching. I described how he'd shown up his Geometry teacher in night school by writing the correct theorem on the board, how the embarrassed teacher had started to argue with Mike, leading to an exchange of blows and Mike's ultimate "expulsion." I invited them to visit Mike at the "'Farm" on Old York Road and see what he'd accomplished in so short a time at a task he'd never attempted before, and without any help. All his success resulted from his own initiatives. And from his reading of publications he'd never heard of or seen before! If that wasn't education, what would they call it? As for their marriage plans, let's wait and see. Maryland was a notorious haven for allowing eloping couples to get married. Any hurried or angry action might do more harm than good.

Mr. Stone, in a rather subdued tone, finally suggested that perhaps it would be better if they met Mike and had a face-to-face talk with him and Hannah. Especially since both were too young and required parental permission for marriage, we had time. Apparently, it worked. Mike came back to work in the store, when I returned to Normal School for my last year. Hannah completed two years successfully at Goucher. They were married in a very quiet ceremony on August 28, 1932. Mike was a couple of weeks away from his 21st birthday and Hannah (born on April 1st) was a year younger, I believe. They kept their pledge not to leave for Palestine while Mr. Stone was alive. Despite the Stones' fears for Hannah's fate, Mike proved to be a devoted husband and father, who always found the means for providing for them, without any help from parents or family. Even Mrs. Stone gloried in their many endeavors as they overcame numerous tragedies and, finally, took their first trip to the State of Israel in 1970. Their dreams were realized that year as they bought their first apartment in Israel while it was being built. Their enthusiastic involvement in their new unit – Israel – and their achievements, culminating in Mike's receiving Jerusalem's most coveted "Citizenship Award" – where he kept the audience enchanted in Hebrew with his acceptance speech – are legendary and require telling in a separate story. Suffice it to say that the "uneducated immigrant" young man who'd dared to ask Hannah to marry him proved beyond any doubt that there are many ways to get an education, outside of and beyond the structured school buildings. No one who knew Mike in his adult years ever questioned his intelligence or education.

Interestingly enough, none of the Gordonia Club members ever became Chalutzim. Only one other member – except for Mike and Hannah – moved permanently to Israel. Rose Kramer, one of the founding members, married Stuart Ginsburgh (changed her first name to Shoshana) and moved into our neighborhood when Stuart Ginsburgh became the Educational Director of our Synagogue. Their daughter, Aviva, was our son's friend and playmate. When Stuart died of a sudden heart attack, Shoshana and Aviva emigrated to Israel and worked – I believe – in the Education Department. I'm not aware of Mike ever contacting her. In any case, our Chalutzim made it to Israel and made us all very proud, even I didn't make it to a Kibbutz.

April 5, 2000

THE YARRID

Next to observing the Sabbath, the most interesting day of the week for our family was Sunday. Our town had the *Yarrid* (an open market day when vendors came to barter or sell of all goodies and goods, including animals), and it opened twice a week. The one on Wednesday was mainly a local and smaller affair – thus not very exciting to small boys. The Sunday *Yarrid* offered many different people from different farms and villages, often with many surprising items or skills. "Tradesmen," peddlers, pickpockets, and even entertainers came to offer their wares or trick the unwary. Mama always cautioned us to beware of strangers and had to know exactly where we were going when we left the safety of the store.

Our older (by nearly six years than me) brother, Velvel, was small but wise for his age. He had a lot of experience with Yarrids and watched over us. He was a fine student at the *Gymnasia*. The Gymnasia was a school that prepared one for possible admittance to University, and could only be attended after passing a stiff entrance and annual examinations. One Sunday, Velvel took us for a surprise program at the building that served as a theater.

This was our first visit to this mysterious place. The dimly lit large room was divided into two sections of rows of large benches, already occupied by many excited loud-speaking people, mostly children. Velvel led us down the center aisle to a row that held some boys he knew and squeezed us onto the bench. In our excitement of being in such strange company and surroundings we pummeled Velvel with questions. He slyly smiled, put a finger to his lips to quiet us, and told us to wait. Finally, two boys went down each outside aisle and took up the coal-oil lanterns, one by one, to the rear.

As the room grew darker the noise lessened until the silence added to the mystery. When only one lantern remained in each side, someone began to stamp their shoes/boots on the floor. Naturally, we did, too, without a clue why. At last a great glaring light lit the wall facing us at the front of the large room, showing hundreds of dust particles floating among us. As we craned our necks to discover the source of this light it suddenly flickered from light to shadows. Everyone now turned back to the front wall. To our amazement the flickering lights looked like people moving around in a field.

The surprising mystery of what we were seeing quieted the crowd and we just sat there, squirming on our uncomfortable benches and watching the strange sights. In a few minutes the flickering stopped and the glaring light remained. Again, feet began stamping the floor. Somebody shouted something, glaring at the source of the light at the back. We did, too – again, without knowing why. This kept happening and we couldn't remember a single thing about what we were supposed to be seeing.

The best part of that day is the part I remember most clearly. Once outside, we saw a large group of children surrounding a man, with several people standing nearby and licking something on spoons. The lickers were enjoying *morozhineh* (ice cream). For a *groschen* (half a kopek, 1/100 of a ruble) we could wait our turn till one of the lickers finished. The spoon was "cleaned" by inserting it in a glass half-filled with creamy water, then dipped into a milk can with the creamy mound on the spoon was given to the next customer to enjoy. To this day I can still taste the wonderful vanilla flavor of my first – ever – ice cream. I licked and licked that heavenly creation on my "sanitary" teaspoon. How did we avoid an epidemic?

August 27, 2001

WHAT JUDAISM HAS MEANT TO ME

Until Doug (the third of my four grandson) made a "request" that I explain what Judaism has meant to me, I never gave that much thought. It dawns on me that this requires a philosophic approach, one into which I've never knowingly ventured. I have no idea where this will lead or how this will come out. If I digress or roam into unrelated fields, understand that this is a new experience. Of course, I'll try. Where to start?

The Beginning – Source

Jewish life in Lyubar, were I was born and lived to age 10.5, was synonymous with Orthodox Religious teachings. We were never exposed to anything but orthodoxy. Everything related to life, good or bad, was the result of following the precepts, customs, practices, and teachings of the Orthodox form of the Jewish religion.

The word "sin" was a dominant word of daily life. No matter which way you turned or what you did, as a child, you were warned, constantly, of the dangers of committing a "sin." A few typical examples:

✓ To break any of the many forbidden rules of the Sabbath – smoking, putting a light on, riding, swimming, carrying money or any objects on your person, writing, working, the list continues.

✓ Disobeying your parents or elders.

✓ Looking at a church or a statue of a Christian Saint, in passing.

✓ Eating: non-Kosher food.

✓ Eating a dairy product less than six hours after eating a meat dish.

✓ Not finishing everything on the plate.

Prayers had to be said before or after practically every action – upon arising, going to bed, coming or going, eating, kissing the *Mezuzah* upon entering or leaving a house.

There were so many restrictions that one wonders how any child could possibly live a sinful life, without fear of the dreadful consequences. According to Jewish tradition and law, a boy's sins fall upon his father till the boy became a Bar Mitzvah. As I grew older and became aware of the burden I could put on my father, I made every conscious effort to conform to all the rules and regulations. I loved to listen to the men – mostly old scholars who spent their days either at home or in the synagogues, studying the Torah. They remained after Services on Saturdays and discussed the teachings of that week's portion or some other question of ethical or moral behavior. I was an attentive listener.

Many years would pass before I concluded that many of these observances were based on customs and superstitions. I was well into my teens before I dared to break with any of these daily habitual practices. Many of these ethical teachings – of the Bible – remained with me. I never knowingly did any forbidden acts, certainly not in the sight of my parents. Respect for them was ingrained in me.

In my last years in Lyubar I loved being at home and listening to the many discussions of my sister Chaika's friends. It was then I began to wonder why some of her friends – including Muni, whom she eventually married – were apparently not observant of all the rules and regulations of our daily lives. Plus, their talk of going to Palestine or favoring the Revolutionary Movement, fomenting in Russia, was very confusing to me.

The Revolution – Discoveries and Adjustments

The subsequent changes in our lives caused by the Revolution in our country, plus the pogroms that followed in our town, had our family less concerned with traditions – survival became our uppermost concern. Suddenly, many of the usual observances were ignored as we strove to meet the new stresses that faced us. Our plans to escape and find a new life and adjust to the strange new world were more important. The revolution of the new discoveries and challenges of adjustments to life in a large city, with new people, languages, and living styles, forced us to adapt. While we remained as observant Jews as possible, the many changes we faced in our temporary abodes (from 1920 to 1923) forced the abandonment of a number of our practices. I can't recall any visits to a synagogue while were in Poland, our first stop on the voyage to America. When we got to Montreal, there was an Orthodox Shul in a converted house right near our first home. That synagogue is where my brother-in-law Muni took me to become Bar Mitzvah. It was a Thursday morning, in March, 1923. Muni took me as my father had already left for Baltimore to set up the store he'd operate for the next ten years.

It wasn't until we settled in Baltimore, while adjusting to life in America, that we returned to some of our former practices. The following few years saw many changes in my way of life – both acceptance and rejection of some of my earlier teachings and beliefs.

Judaism in America – Revelations and Acceptances

Life in Baltimore required a large number of adjustments for us "Greenhorns," as we were dubbed. Most of our neighbors were *Gentiles* (non-Jews), except for Tante Bilich, Uncle, and Fannie, with whom we lived; in addition to a few other Jewish families in our block. Being a Jew in a Gentile neighborhood caused many problems.

Fallbrook, the section of Northwest Baltimore into which we'd come, was a mixed area. While not restricted, the Jewish residents were scattered over several miles and in every direction. However, Uncle felt there were enough of them to justify opening a kosher butcher store. With a promise of free delivery, the business was established. Since he and Papa were not expected to do the delivery, Mike and I came in.

My older brother, Willie, had found work in a grocery store. So, suddenly, we were appointed to work in a strange place, with strange people who were speaking English. Although I'd been exposed to the differences in Yiddish spoken in both Galicia and Poland, and while I had learned the nuances of Romanian Yiddish, I found that many Jews in our neighborhood in Baltimore spoke Yiddish with a Lithuanian accent. That which posed even more problems for me. The limited broken English I'd acquired, in our short stay in Canada, was more of a handicap than an asset. Speaking broken English often led to laughter and ridicule for me from my classmates and neighbors, even beatings by the Irish and physically stronger kids. That meant I had to rely on my Yiddish. Much to my surprise, most Jews in America spoke English, only, and did not even understand Yiddish.

When he arrived in Baltimore, Papa had found a beautiful Orthodox Synagogue about a mile from the store with a Hebrew school. He in enrolled Mike and me soon after our arrival. Within a short time the school and we, too, realized there was nothing we could learn there.

Both of us – even with our limited, interrupted schooling in Lyubar – were far more advanced in Hebrew.

A synagogue supervisor came to visit Papa and offered to procure scholarships for us at a *Yeshiva* in New York, the school devoted to the study of the Bible. She explained that the only drawback was that we had to furnish a New York address in order to get free tuition. Papa explained that he had a sister who lived in New York and would have no difficulty using her address. In any case he'd like to take a few days to discuss it with us and would get back to her. This was in mid-1923.

You must understand that – where we came from – the greatest honor for Jews was to have a son attend a Yeshiva. To be offered the opportunity to have not only one son but also two enroll in a Yeshiva, and for free, made my parents very proud. Still, Papa was a wise man and realized that life in America was different and had other standards.

Picture this: two ever-hungry, scrawny little boys – who'd just been exposed to the rigors of adapting to a new community, schools, language, and relatives, being sent away to live with a widowed sister in New York, who was herself burdened with providing for herself and four grown children. This required very serious consideration. When Papa asked us how we liked the idea, both of us protested very strongly. In America, we protested, English was more important than being a Yeshiva scholar. If we enrolled in Baltimore's public schools in the fall, we had a chance to learn the language and adapt to American life. Baltimore was a very large city and we'd not even gotten used to living here. New York was ten times as big and had more than ten times as many people – all strangers. If we remained home, we could enroll in a night class at the Baltimore Hebrew College. That way we could learn English in public school and continue our Hebrew studies, too. Besides, Papa needed us to help deliver meats and groceries. And, we have to pay our Aunt in New York something for our care and board. We couldn't afford that. Our parents agreed and we ended up, happily, remaining at home.

So, "what's all the above have to do with the question of the effect of Judaism on my life?"

It reverts back to my assertion that my early life made it hard to differentiate Judaism from my exposure to the Orthodox teachings. Although I'd been told that many *Chalutzim* (Pioneers) in Palestine did not observe the tenets of Judaism I'd been taught, it was only after we came to America that I consciously realized that being Jewish did not necessarily mean Orthodox Judaism. Still, my parents lived and practiced according to the customs of Orthodox Judaism and I did the same – without question – well into my late teens. Revelations came to me as I became proficient in English. Exposure to the writings of scholars and philosophers, Jews and non-Jews, caused me to reexamine my beliefs and practices. I discovered that Jews in Baltimore could still be Jews, even if they went to services in a Synagogue where men and women sat together. I had never seen such a thing, or that many men did not even cover their heads when they prayed! And, men and women came dressed to temple in fancy clothes and jewels! It was also said that some of them ate *treiffe* (non-Kosher) food and drove to their Synagogues and Temples on Saturdays and Holidays. In fact, many of them worked or kept their businesses open on the Sabbath.

They not only survived, they were among the richest and most respected Jews in the city!

How could this be? Subconsciously, I began to question myself, "Could Jews still be Jews and not observe all the teachings and customs on which we'd been raised?" However, I continued to live and practice the mores I'd been raised on since nothing had caused me to stop living any differently.

Now, it's time to try to fulfill the request and to answer my grandson's request…

How Judaism Has Affected My Life

I've tried to show the sources of Jewish influence on my family and me. I could probably have saved time and paper by simply saying that early teachings of Biblical commands and admonitions – as practiced and taught especially by my parents, were the root of all my eventual behavior. Although I gave up many of the Orthodox customs and practices, all my moral and ethical beliefs stem from historical Jewish teachings.

Here are a few typical examples:

CHARITY – Of all Jewish influences in my life I believe that Charity is probably the most important. From my earliest recollections of practices my parents taught me, this stands out as the bulwark of Jewish life. Our greatest responsibility is to help those in need and less fortunate. I could fill many pages with details of my involvement in Jewish charities and causes, and I have written about some. My contributions pale in comparison with those of my son, Alan, and my daughter-in-law Dolores. I swell with pride each time I hear of their continuing to work for the betterment of people with disabilities, or how they support their Jewish community in Virginia. Each of my grandsons has worked for, volunteered for or contributed to a host of charities and continues to do so.

FAMILY – Perhaps an even more important Jewish influence in my life has been the emphasis on a strong belief of Family. My greatest joy is to see the members of our family getting together as much a possible. Even more important, in my opinion, is the belief that each of us should always be available to help each other out in every possible way. Regardless of the need, whether it's to help one who needs financial or simply sympathetic aid, we should always be ready to give each other a hand. I believe that my family's help was a very great contribution to what little success I achieved in my lifetime. By the same token I hope that I, too, helped my family members in their time of need. Curiously, I don't regret or miss a single dollar of the thousands I've "lost", in helping the various members of my family. I'd do it again, without a moment's hesitation. That's what Family is all about. A very important aspect of family life is the acceptance of each and every member, regardless of his or her strengths or weaknesses. Even if one of us does not meet our own standards, it's our obligation to accept that member as he or she is.

RELIGION – Of all things related to Judaism the subject of Religion is the most controversial. My father believed and practiced Orthodox customs and traditions in every phase of his daily life. He taught me – early in my life – to tolerate others' beliefs and practices. As I grew older and read and learned more about Judaism and other religions, customs, and practices, I gave up many of my early thoughts (prejudices) about non-Jews. My conclusion is that Religion is strictly a private matter and that each one of us has the absolute right to believe or nor believe in whatever he or she chooses. More important to me, is that each one of us has the obligation to never question another person's rights or beliefs. Each one of us should respect others. The obligation of parents, I now believe, is to expose or teach their children their family's customs and practices, and to acquaint children with the beliefs of others. This allows their children – when they're mature enough – to choose for themselves. Yes, I take great pride in our Jewish heritage and tradition and it makes me proud to see that continue on. But, far more important is the legacy of tolerance towards everyone's rights and beliefs.

MUSIC – My exposure to Jewish music came at home from my mother's and sister's singing, in Yiddish. It also came from the beautiful Hebrew melodies in the Synagogue. Both left me with a love that endured till my hearing started to worsen in my old age. Even now, when I lead in the commemoration of our various Holidays at our retirement community, I still hear those sounds in my mind, although I don't dare try to sing them out loud. The rhythm and beat lives on. Thanks to my beloved wife Mollie, I was exposed to opera and classical music and found much joy in those, too. Music, Jewish and in general, has enriched my life tremendously, I think it's an important duty of all parents to expose their children to music in its many forms, both vocal and instrumental. It's a source of great pleasure to all of us, young and old.

ISRAEL – Our bond to the land of Israel and to Jews everywhere is strong and this has been instilled in me from earliest childhood. It started with Biblical teachings, followed by the constant referral in our prayers to "Next year in Jerusalem" and then in songs. The tendency to associate ourselves with the achievements of Jews in all fields of endeavor – ranging from all the way from Nobel prizes to politics and sports – is inbred in me. I swell with pride to hear or read that a Jew has made the headlines. Vicariously, that achievement by a member of our extended "family" is a cause of celebration. If a Jew is hurt or wronged, anywhere, I, too, feel the pain – to this day.

MORALS AND HONESTY – Without a doubt, all of my behavior throughout my life has been guided and molded by my parents, and by the Jewish Biblical teachings that they believed and practiced. I've tried, both by word and example, to leave this as my legacy.

Judaism, my faith, has been my rock and my foundation.

Ralph, December 17, 2004

MY TWO SONS

Some of the family has urged me to continue writing. While these stories keep me busy and I enjoy it, I enjoy more seeing your pleasure. I think some of my writings have given you some insights, things you might be surprised at. I've tried to write about my sister and brothers, especially about my younger brother Mike. I've written much about Mollie's brother Herman. And, I've shared many stories about both of our parents. I've included details about my sister, Chaika, but not an entire story about her. In all truth, she was ten years older and lived away from me for so long that I don't know as much about her ups and downs in her life. We remained close and her children and grandchildren are dear to us. My brother, Willie, six years older lived closer to us, though I was so much younger that I don't know or recall as much about him, either. Anything I'd tell would be second-hand information. The most important thing is that family has always been so important to me and to Mollie.

It occurs to me that I've neglected to record some things about our two sons, and their lives, the many doings that led to our being so proud of them and their accomplishments. Before I continue, let me make something perfectly clear. Parents, in general, and grandparents, in particular, are notoriously prejudiced in their evaluations of their own offspring. Invariably, they tend to see only the good in them and can't or won't ever accept the fact that their own flesh and blood could ever be guilty of anything undesirable or wrong. In spite of my father's admonition not to prejudge others' doings or behavior, I claim that right and privilege as a parent. I definitely want to tell everything I can think of. Just as definitely, I am sure there are things I am not including but should have. This is one parent's attempt, and perhaps I am guilty of tunnel vision! Sounds pedantic? My privilege!

Before I can start to describe the details of the lives of our two sons, I believe I need to include the places where they were born and raised.

(Skip this, if you've heard it heard before.) After Mollie and I were married in 1934, we moved into a room in her parents' small apartment in the Pimlico section of Baltimore. My parents had sold their Baltimore house and moved to Washington. We had no choice but to live with the Hirshes, since our combined substitute teacher salaries were so small. When the School Board restored our full-time status, our income increased and we looked around for a place for ourselves. We found a small, beautifully furnished three-room converted apartment in a picture-book setting, on the second floor of a cottage on Maine Avenue in Forest Park. This is the same street where we later bought our first home. Our first son was born in this tiny but lovely apartment. We kept him in a playpen/bed in our small bedroom; a crib was a luxury we couldn't afford. He thrived and we decided it was time for all of us to have some privacy and more space. Somewhat reluctantly, we moved to a larger (also furnished) apartment a few blocks further north on Belle Avenue, also in Forest Park. This would be home until we bought our own house on Maine Avenue in 1939.

I remember we would take the baby with us to Washington, to visit my parents. We'd put him in a hammock, bundled in a warm outfit. The hammock was stretched between the two clothes hooks in the back of the Chevy, and he'd sleep or just coo as we drove. After he woke up, day or night, he'd just lie in his playpen/bed, cooing or making sounds only he understood, as he played with his teddy bear. When he was old enough to crawl out of his playpen/bed, he would wake up in the mornings, drag a pillow with him and sit down, outside our bedroom door (never on the bare floor), waiting till one of us got up so he could greet us with a smile. I can't remember his ever trying to wake us or open our bedroom door.

After the school year ended in those early years, we all went to PenMar Park to help run the Glendon Heights "Hotel." Amazingly, this little boy could stay in a playpen for hours, sleeping or playing cheerfully with his toys. When guests started to come, we moved the playpen outdoors, near the dining room window, where we could watch him. The guests and our country girl/maids were crazy about him.

As he got a little older, when we'd go anywhere together, he'd stand between us on the front car seat and call out the names of the cars we'd be passing. Most of them were either Chevys or Fords. In those years, all carmakers had only a limited number of models – a touring car, couple or roadster. We had the "touring" car. It had four doors, with open sides in lieu of windows, and canvas weather-resistant covers that clipped on in the winter or if it rained. The "coupe" model back then was a two-door with closed metal sides and closed windows. Or, one could have a "roadster", also a two-door, but with a canvas top. Regardless, all cars had the same individual overall frame or body shape. Each make of car was distinguishable with their individual caps mounted on the top front of the hood. The only time our bright boy had trouble distinguishing one was when an occasional Cadillac, Packard, or Buick came along. Then, if he didn't recognize it, he'd call it a "half-Chevy, half-Ford." We had fun!

We moved to that larger, roomier apartment on Belle Avenue because it also had a big back yard where a child could enjoy outdoor living – a luxury denied in our first cramped, tiny apartment. Mollie made friends with several Jewish neighbors, who had children about the same age as we did. This would be our home for several years, until we bought our first house on Maine Avenue. It was in this apartment where our then 5-year-old son got scarlet fever. We were quarantined for three weeks and I had to move out during that period if I wanted to keep my job as a teacher.

If my memory is correct, the only immunization for children back then was for smallpox. Otherwise, all children were expected to actually contract the usual children's diseases – measles, mumps, chicken pox, whooping cough, and scarlet fever. All had to be dealt with.

Some explanation of the effect of quarantines bears clarification. The Baltimore City Health Department was very strict about observing quarantines. It decreed that when someone had a severely contagious disease, the residence had to be marked with a colored tag that warned everyone that this place was out of bounds. No one was allowed to go in-or-out except for doctors or the health department people. If you had to go to work or business, like me, you had to leave and could not return until the quarantine sign came down – usually for about three weeks. Needless to say, it caused many hardships for everybody. A teacher whose home was quarantined could come to teach only under these school board rules: 1) find another place to stay for the entire period; 2) report the new address; 3) stay away from school and old home for the first week; 4) report for duty for the balance of the quarantined period, while residing away from the old home. If you complied with these rules, you would not lose any pay. Naturally, I complied.

Can you imagine what it was like for Mollie to be cooped up in a second floor apartment with a sick boy – with a very contagious disease – and to nurse him, all alone? Scarlet Fever was especially dangerous, because it could cause permanent ear trouble if not cared for properly. All deliveries to the apartment had to be left outside the door. Mollie could not go out to shop or for anything. As for me, Tante (Aunt) Bilich had plenty of room in her home and was willing to accommodate me. But I was frustrated from the start with my situation, as I did not feel comfortable imposing on my old Aunt.

After my first meal and a pleasant chat with her, I felt that I'd exhausted all my topics of conversation. And, after several phone calls to Mollie, what else was there for me to do? So, after a boring day, looking at the four walls of my bedroom, I decided I'd be better off with my parents in Washington till I could go back to teaching. Early the next morning I drove the 40 miles to their apartment. Mom and Pop had a three-room upstairs of a single-family row house on Park Avenue, around the corner from the underground market where Pop was then working on 14th street as a Kosher butcher for Mr. Abe Posin. The couch in their living room would be my bed as long as I needed it. Mr. Posin, who was very fond of Pop and our whole family, knew that I worked as a shoe salesman on Saturdays. He came up with the idea of my getting a part-time job while I was in Washington, working at Hahn's Shoe store, also on 14th Street. I saw Mr. Gottlieb, the manager, who invited me to come in the next day and demonstrate my abilities. I would go on to work at Hahn's for several years, driving to Washington to earn a 7% commission (or a $10 week-end guarantee).

Back to our first son and his growing up. Mollie's good care pulled him through with no after-effects. He continued to thrive while we lived on Belle Avenue until we bought our home on Maine Avenue, with the back yard. It gave him much more room to play in, inside and out, and a new friend. A friend from the Gordonia Club, Rose Kramer, had married our Club Advisor, Dr. Stanley H. Ginsburgh. Dr. Ginsburgh was now the Educational Director of our neighborhood Synagogue. Their daughter was Aviva and a perfect neighborhood playmate.

When it was time for him to start school, there was no problem. He loved it and always did well. At "Open House" – when we had a chance to meet his teachers – they were profuse in their praise. The only time we were ever called to school was before he finished primary grades. The principal explained that the teachers had discussed things thoroughly, and all felt that our bright boy was not being challenged enough.

Much against our will, she urged us to let him skip a grade. Reluctantly, we agreed. He had no trouble adjusting and continued to get top grades. By the time we left for Florida – just after his ninth birthday – he was ready for fifth grade. When we left Miami Beach, in 1946, he'd finished sixth grade with excellent grades, academically ready for Junior High.

Shenandoah Junior High was one of the better schools in Miami. With an excellent faculty, an active parent-teachers association and caring parents, the students had many opportunities to get a good education, make lasting friends and to participate in a variety of activities. He joined the local Boy Scouts and soon met and passed the many challenges the Scouts offered. I'm not sure if he made "Eagle Scout" but I do know he came home very often and showed the patches he'd gotten for passing a goodly number of tests required, to achieve a higher rank. He attended Boy Scout summer camp and enjoyed it. I'm not sure whether he made some of his lifelong friends here, at the Junior High level or at Miami High.

When a boy approaches Bar Mitzvah age, it is the obligation of his Jewish parents to get him prepared. This requires instruction in reading and singing certain prayers, including ones he reads/sings upon being called up – for the first time – before the Torah. I'd never had the chance to learn the musical accompaniment for Bar Mitzvahs, so I looked around for a Hebrew School or Synagogue to help us. While Miami Beach boasted of a number of Orthodox, Conservative, and Reformed Houses of worship, the City of Miami offered them only in the downtown area which was much too far from where we lived at the time. When I heard they were building a synagogue at SW 12th Avenue and 11th Street, a little over a mile from our home, I quickly went to investigate. I found a shell of a building, empty, with unfinished concrete-block walls. A peek inside showed a bare wooden floor, with pieces of lumber strewn all around.

On one end, two toilet bowls sat between temporary bath partitions. A sheet of paper on the door listed a telephone number for information. Upon inquiry, I spoke to the president of the planned Synagogue, who informed me that construction had been halted, temporarily, for lack of funds. However, since he himself was the builder, he hoped to make it usable for the upcoming High Holidays. "It is going to be the best Orthodox Synagogue in Florida!" he said. Although they did not yet have a Hebrew School, Rabbi Simon April, who'd already been hired, would be happy to prepare our boy for his Bar Mitzvah. After the Holidays the board had already planned to call a general meeting of the congregation, to discuss starting a Hebrew School. He urged me to join and take part – sight unseen. I guess they needed all the help they could get, and the money.

Since I had no choice and wanted the family to attend services during the approaching Holidays, I joined. Rabbi April agreed to help with the Bar Mitzvah preparations. On the day of his Bar Mitzvah, our son was so prepared and talented. Yes, I may be biased but I have had the opportunity to watch and listen to hundreds of Bar Mitzvahs, attending services for many years, and especially during my later years as a Bar Mitzvah photographer. On that special day in 1948, we watched with surprise and pride as our son put on his new *Tallit* (Prayer Shawl) and proceeded to do the entire Saturday Service, from the *Shachrit* (beginning or morning) to the *Mussaf* (afternoon or ending).

In most Orthodox Congregations, Shachrit is done by a learned layman or Rabbi. When this ends, the Torah Reading is done by a specially trained person, who reads the week's portion for the several honored family member and others. The Bar Mitzvah boy is thought to be well-trained if he is able to read even a small section of the week's portion. Our son proceeded to read the entire week's Torah portion – for all the people called up! He was so good at reading the Torah that he and the Rabbi had concocted the idea to have our son do all the Rabbi's normal Saturday service jobs. When he made his prepared "Today I Am a Man" Bar Mitzvah speech, there were a lot of people who needed a tissue or handkerchief. After finishing the service, it seemed like every person in attendance came by to shake my hand to congratulate us both.

As if he did not have enough on his plate, he attended Hebrew High School for a year or so, with no difficulty. 1950 brought a new challenge. Because of Alan's bout with polio, I left the Bancroft Hotel to take over the Atlantis Hotel (for six months from May 1st to November 1st), so Alan could use its swimming pool to strengthen his weakened legs. My contract as resident manager called for the use of two oceanfront rooms for my family. Every morning Mollie made breakfast for the boys in their room. My breakfast was served to me by the coffee shop on the pool-deck when I came down each morning – one of the perks of being the Manager. The boys would come down to the beautiful pool-deck, where Alan would get help from Wally Spence, one of our two pool-deck managers, to strengthen Alan's broomstick-size legs. Big brother, meanwhile, an accomplished swimmer, would swim laps. This tall, good-looking, thin but strong youth, taking the smooth strokes that propelled him from one end of the pool to the other so quickly, soon attracted the attention of guests as well as of Wally Baker, the main pool manager.

The entire pool-deck of the Atlantis covered a large area, about the size of a football field. The eastern side of the concrete "boardwalk" ran from the famous Roney Plaza Hotel (on 23rd Street) all the way to 31st Street. All of the oceanfront decks belonging to the different hotels were private at the time – for the exclusive use of the adjoining hotels or apartment buildings that fronted on Collins Avenue. Our guests at the Atlantis, and any cabana renters, had the use of our deck surrounding the area of the large clean swimming pool. Directly in front of the cabanas, which bordered the entire north and south sides, were lines of wooden-slat lounge chairs for guests. This was the center of all activities and the source of all the income of the two pool managers and their helpers (except for the cabana rentals, which were handled by the hotel, by me).

Wally Baker was the cheerful, friendly official "greeter" of the guests as they came down to the pool. The wooden lounge chairs – free to hotel guests – were not very comfortable. To ease that, Wally offered to rent comparatively soft waterproof pads to cover the wooden slats.

For a dollar per day, or five dollars per week, a lounge could be rented for the exclusive use of the guest. Beach boys – Wally's helpers – supplied the mats, gave free beach towels, adjusted umbrellas as long as they were available – and saw to the comfort and convenience of each guest. Wally apparently made enough to support his wife and children. It was such a lucrative business that some hotels actually sold the service, as a concession, to dependable family men for a considerable fee. The beach boy helpers were allowed to rent lounges, too, when traffic was heavy or Wally had other duties or swimming lessons. They made tips, too.

Back to our "swimming son." It didn't take him long to realize that he, too, could be a beach boy. In a few days he asked me to talk to Wally Baker, to let him become a beach boy. I pointed out that, in addition to handling the mats, umbrellas, and towels, beach boys were responsible for cleaning up at the end of the day. After gathering all the dirty towels and taking them down to the laundry room, the beach boys had to remove, wipe off and store all mats and umbrellas. Then, the entire deck area was cleaned, hosed down, and readied by the boys for the next day. This task usually lasted a good few hours. I made Wally promise there would be no special treatment, so we agreed on a trial basis. That became permanent when Wally discovered how pleased the guests were with our son's polished manners and service. His tips grew, too.

Before the summer ended, he was given the job of being the emcee for Wally Spence's special shows of visiting teams of divers and swimmers. Plus tips for renting lounge-chair mats. After we left the Atlantis, he was able – all on his own, using the references of Wally Spence – to get jobs in oceanfront hotels in succeeding summers, to get spending money while at college.

Like many parents, Mollie and I didn't take our son seriously, at first, when he said he was planning to go to Harvard. We knew only that Harvard was a very select school for the very gifted and the very rich. But he never forgot about his dream to go there – it was "Harvard or Bust, and Watch my Dust." Our son, then 15 or 16 years old, proceeded to apply for admission to Harvard all on his own. When he showed me the costs, I sat down with him, explained what my monthly income was at the Bancroft Hotel and what our expenses were. I then pointed out how impossible it would be for us – with me as the sole breadwinner of the family – to meet our current obligations and have enough left over to pay for his costs, too, even for a year. No matter how we tried, the figures just would not work. Reluctantly, we both agreed that it was an impossible situation. Too bad!

One day I received a phone call while at work. "Dad," he said, almost yelling, "Could I go to Harvard if I got a partial scholarship?" "What are you talking about?" I asked. "I just got a partial tuition scholarship to Harvard!" he yelled. "I can't talk about this while at work – over the phone. Wait till I get home and we'll discuss it tonight." I think I was just as excited as he was and could hardly wait till my shift ended. That night he explained how he'd gone for an interview with the president of the Harvard Club of Miami and inveigled the man to grant a half-year tuition scholarship – renewable as long as GPA requirements were met.

A quick side story (or rather another quick side story). I have always admired – and envied – youngsters who've made lasting, lifelong friends as they've gone through life and schools. It is something I'd been denied in my youth, because of circumstances over which I had no control. Growing up in a normal, typical American household, both our sons made those lifelong friends. Of those I recall, all became successful professionals – each in his own preference: Bobby Blank, the dentist whom I used to take care of my teeth, went on to be an orthodontist; Phil Catalano, a brilliant student, would be a dermatologist in southwest Florida; Clay Choate, the son of a renowned and respected federal judge, became an aeronautical engineer, involved in NASA. And their childhood friend, our son, would go on to Harvard for both college and law school, without any help from us.

When we learned, in 1952, about the half-tuition scholarship of $400, I was forced to point out, once more, that even with that, we were still short of having enough income to meet all the school needs for freshman year. The cost of room and board, books, clothing, travel, the other half of tuition, plus miscellaneous expenses, added up to more than we could realistically afford. Sadly, we had no savings or other source of income and just couldn't see how we could make this work. Heartbroken and disappointed, we all agreed that this proposed scholarship was amazing, but not enough. It didn't take long for us to find out how determined our big son was, for he went back and somehow received promise of a full-tuition scholarship for his first year at Harvard! No matter how hard it would be for us to find a way to help pay, we could not deny him the opportunity. Our first decision was to sell our house, to take the equity remaining and insure his first year's expenses. Because of our rush to raise the funds we needed, we were forced to sell our home at a considerable loss – a perfect example of what happens when someone is forced to sell real estate quickly. (In all my many dealings in real estate, this was – by far – my worst loss in any sale.)

At Harvard, his struggles were many – adjusting to a new school and new roommates, all several years older and all with different backgrounds. Yet, in spite of his social, financial, and scholastic adjustments, this young man overcame all obstacles. To sum it up, he made the Dean's list regularly; won several honorary prizes; became a member of Phi Beta Kappa (much to our joyful and proud surprise); and even found ways to earn extra spending money by becoming a "soda jerk" – as his Grandma Hirsh called it – at a local soda fountain shop. He would graduate Harvard with tuition-free scholarship to Harvard Law School, again to our complete joyful and very proud surprise.

I remember his coming home that first year of college with two packages, in addition to all his dirty clothes. One was a copy of the yearbook, containing a picture of him participating in one of the school's activities. Very proudly he turned to the page in which he's pictured – shooting pool! When I started to express my disappointment at his "shooting pool," he quickly corrected me to say that he was shooting billiards, not pool, which was considered quite an art by learned gentlemen! Then, to our continued surprise, he unwrapped his second package, to show us his very own prized billiard cue! He'd become so expert, he explained, that he needed his own cue, to ensure his continued success. He was so proud of his achievement that we found it difficult to criticize his choice of activity in his first year at Harvard. To assuage our disappointment, he nonchalantly mentioned that he'd made the Harvard swimming team during that freshman year.

When we came to his graduation in 1956, we climbed up to his 5th floor room to inspect the living quarters he'd shared with his several roommates. I was shocked to see a very large collection of records that he'd accumulated. At first I was quite upset to think he'd squandered so much of his and our hard-earned money on records. Then it dawned on me that his love for opera was so great, he probably was better off spending his spare dollars on his records than on some less-desirable self-indulgences. In fact, to this day – as he approaches his 70th birthday – opera is still a great part of his life.

With many accomplishments during his career as a lawyer, he also blessed Mollie and me with two of our four wonderful and successful grandsons. Jeff and Doug are now busy raising their own families and in their own careers.

Now to our second son, of whom I am beyond proud. The circumstances that prevailed before the birth of each of the boys were so different that they now need some explanation or clarification. Our oldest was not a planned baby, as you've no doubt assumed from my stories. At the time, Mollie and I were newlywed and facing many struggles at the end of a prevailing Depression. It certainly did not help to have Mollie, as a new mother, forced to stay home for three years by the dictates of a cruel school board policy.

During the six years between the boys' births, our personal lives as well as national and international events changed drastically. Some of the changes affected us directly. The strains of the Depression were displaced by new concerns as Europe exploded into what would be called World War II. Although the U.S. was not supposed to be involved directly, the Lend-Lease program initiated by President Roosevelt, which led to the shipping of goods and material to England to help them fight the Germans, affected the industries of our country. Many industries became involved in producing goods and services for military use. The demand for people to work in war-related industries caused many men to change to those jobs because of the higher pay offered. Now, for the first time, women found high-paying jobs in industries that had always used men. Men who'd been drafted or volunteered for military training were replaced by women. The merchant marine shipping industry expanded and needed new recruits. In short, the life patterns of many people changed.

Our own financial situation had improved, even with me as the sole breadwinner. There was an annual $100 increase in school pay, plus the extra income from my weekend stints as a shoe salesman. I earned $100 for each of the two demonstration lessons I gave to teachers, as well as the money I earned as the Youth Activities Director at the local Synagogue four nights a week. In June 1938, I received my B.S. in Industrial Education at the University of Maryland, and started graduate level courses toward a Master's Degree in Guidance and Counseling at both University of Maryland and Johns Hopkins University. And we had our summers working in PenMar.

Pa Hirsh's health had deteriorated at that time (as I've detailed) to the extent that Mollie had to replace him in the kitchen as well as take care of the front when guests came and went. At the end of the 1938 season in PenMar Park, Ma Hirsh decided to go to Florida for the winter, in hopes of improving Pa Hirsh's health. Innovative Ma Hirsh also found a way to retrieve some of her expenses of living in Florida. She had rented a ground-floor one-bedroom apartment one block from the beach. Soon she found out that other tenants were sub-leasing parts of their one-bedroom apartments. Within a month she'd rented out their bedroom, in cash, for the price she'd paid for the entire apartment. She and Pa slept in the kitchen and front porch. In fact, she did so well that she wrote and invited Mollie to bring her grandson and spend the month of March with them. When she came back to Baltimore, Ma Hirsh had most of the money they'd left with, and – for the first time – did not need to borrow money from us to equip and start her annual business in PenMar. Unfortunately, Pa's health did not improve and he finally succumbed to what we'd now probably call emphysema.

I've mentioned before our hurried race back from PenMar to Baltimore on Labor Day weekend in 1935, just in time for the birth of our oldest son and the start of that school year. That was not the case with our second son, born on November 1, 1941. Alan was attended to by Ma Hirsh – who'd been living with us in our new home since Pa Hirsh died. We also had help from Pearl, a lovely young Army widow whom we brought back with us from PenMar to help with the boys. I should mention that unlike today, with either baby, we had no sonar or other way of knowing whether we'd have another boy or a new little girl.

Pearl was everything her name implied. One of 18 children from a poor family who somehow survived the Depression and supplied us with good summer help at PenMar, Pearl was a wonderful worker with a lovely disposition. She bubbled with enthusiasm and was ready, willing, and able to do any domestic task. She worshipped Mollie, worked in the kitchen and helped with the boys, and showed Mollie how to care for the flowers. She proved to be a devoted blessing, for the way she took care of Alan.

From the minute mother and baby came home from the hospital, Pearl stepped in. Mollie did not nurse either boy, so the baby bottles were routinely prepared and ready, usually by Pearl. In the middle of the nights, at the first peep from Alan, Pearl immediately ran from her third-floor bedroom to quiet and take care of him. Neither Mollie nor I lost much sleep while Alan gradually learned to sleep through the night. By the time Pearl decided to go back home, in late spring of 1942, Alan was a happy, healthy baby. He was sitting up and getting ready to stand and walk. I should mention this was after having overcome a problem with his feet when he was young, which required Alan to wearing casts for a short time. His exuberant personality, and, often, surprising wit, gave us many moments of pure joy, as he grew up to be a fine, healthy and enthusiastic youngster. From the time he was a baby, Alan was always determined and hard working – even if he was working at playing. It was a trait he was to exhibit for years.

As I reflect on the growth and development of Alan (actually, both boys), I marvel at the lack of advantages he had – as compared to our grandchildren and so many other children nowadays. We struggled to simply exist, let alone buy toys for him. Unfortunately, the grandparents were never able to buy many toys or presents, either. There were no TV programs or games to play or books to learn from. There were private pre-school programs, but we could not afford them. All the credit for their proper growth and development must go to their mother. Mollie certainly did a fantastic job, especially given the financial constraints, didn't she?

Alan was only 2 years old in June of 1944, when we sold our home in Baltimore and left for Atlantic City. It didn't bother him that we'd moved to a strange city, into a new and different house, away from familiar surroundings. Nor did it faze him to have perfect strangers at the guest house there that would come and go, week after week. He adapted quickly and – as usual – enthusiastically, to our and different way of life. It thrilled us the easy way he accepted the people and the wonderfully friendly way he dealt with them. In their short stay, perfect strangers fell in love with him.

While both boys were scared of the very cold water on the Atlantic City Beach and the strong "icy" waves, it didn't take long for them to get used to it, even if I first had to carry them and hold their hands very tightly, as we entered the water. We learned to gradually dip our bodies into the small waves near the shore, and slowly walk out to the bigger waves. (Estelle Gomborov, whom we knew from Baltimore, had rented an apartment for the summer near us. She had two children also, was an excellent swimmer, and became our instructor when we all went to the beach. She was a big help to all of us, and to the boys, especially.) Before the summer was over, we had learned to dip into the cold water as soon as we went out; then, gradually go out further and further. As for Alan, as long as an adult held his hand, he was ready. Every day, all of us went to the beach. Thanks to Ma Hirsh, even Mollie would join us most days.

After the 1944 summer in Atlantic City we moved again, this time to the Sinclair Hotel in Miami Beach. Again, a little boy had to learn a new way to live, in a new place. For the next two winters, Alan adjusted to living in a hotel with constantly changing faces and people. Time and again, he surprised us and guests at the hotel with his wisdom and ability to accept changes and new or different circumstances. I can't recall his ever complaining over what we did when we had to move.

Note (June 5, 2005) – This morning I must interrupt my reminiscences to point out, once more, how different life and opportunity is now for infants and children, as compared to our boys and their early childhood. The Sun-Sentinel had a headline this morning that intrigued me. It proclaimed that nursery school children – aged 2 to 5 – are now using the Internet to learn words, colors, and numbers. Just yesterday, I was privileged to see a demonstration by my great-granddaughter Lauren – at the ripe old age of 15½ months – of her amazing skill at naming colors, words, and numbers. Just recently, my grandson Doug showed me how he'd converted my old computer for his son Brett's personal use (Brett is not even 5). Doug told me that on a recent car trip to Atlanta, he'd rigged up a system in the back of the car for the three children to watch videos on the drive. Gary has done similar with his children in Virginia. So now let me tell you – as an example – of how we made the trip with our boys from Atlantic City to Miami Beach, back in late September of 1944.

Our difficult trip from Atlantic City to Florida has been described in detail before. However, it bears doing a refresher, a reminder, if only because it adds a little humor – even if it wasn't so funny to us at the time. We left Atlantic City at the end of the 1944 summer, in Herman's patched-up 1937 two-door Chevy. It was packed and heavily loaded with all our worldly possessions. The running board on the driver's side of the car was filled with Alan's playpen and other items, blocking the driver's door. We therefore had to use the passenger's door both to enter and leave the car. For all of us to get in, we it was necessary to do so in a certain order. These exercises in and out, while eliciting laughter and fun at first, soon became a nuisance as we were forced to stop often to deal with a bad water pump.

Anyhow, how do you keep two boys entertained on a long, treacherous, 1,300-plus-mile trip in a bumpy car that can make even an adult so exhausted he/she can easily get crabby? Be innovative!

Remember, this was long before dual (divided) highways, air conditioning, automatic steering or anything else like that. There was no cruise control or safe, quality tires that we take for granted nowadays. A day that did not have a flat tire was a day to celebrate. The two-lane roads – the best ones like U.S. 1 – had a macadam (broken stone) finish as opposed to the gravel or dirt roads that were narrow or dangerous, especially in rain or darkness. For us, just to cover 300 miles a day was an accomplishment, riding in a car that had two springs to relieve the shock of going over the many bumps. Even the best and strongest driver was completely exhausted at the end of a day's drive, no matter how lucky you were. The motels available, if any, were miserable accommodations. The first thing Mollie did, when we finally found one a motel, was to look at the mattress – to make sure there were no bed bugs!

So, given those conditions, how did we keep our two boys amused and busy? It wasn't easy. We sang songs they knew, including nursery rhymes. We told stories and played games. With Alan only a toddler, we had to keep his interest by keeping the games simple, yet interesting and challenging. A typical game I remember was to try to finish the popular Burma Shave ads. I can't remember them, but it went something like this: As you rode along you'd come across a narrow sign (a smaller billboard) that would say "IF YOU'D LIKE." After a minute or so, you'd see the second sign, "TO STAY ALIVE." After another short distance, you'd see the third sign, "JUST DON'T DRINK." Now you'd try to tell what the fourth sign says.

In another short distance would be "WHEN YOU DRIVE." The fifth and last sign would always just say "BURMA SHAVE." The sayings were much more clever and different. The fun part was to try to imagine what the next sign might say. Each of us would take turns, trying to see if we could fill in the blanks and compare our version with theirs. Alan would still show an interest, even if he couldn't help.

The "Alphabet" game was a popular one that even Alan could take part in. As we drove along, Alan would be asked to find a word that had an "L" in it. It could be in a billboard sign, a road name, a storefront or even a barn on the side of the road. After he found it, one boy would have to find a "B", then, each of us, in turn, would look for the next letter of the alphabet until we'd found the "Z." This game kept everyone on the alert, looking for letters. It was not fair to point out a letter when it was not your turn, but we did help Alan if he had difficulty and we'd see the letter he was looking for, by showing where to look.

The "geography" game was another that kept everyone alert and interested. This game had a couple of versions. The simplest started by naming a place that began with "a," the next person had to think of a place that began with a "b," and so on, till every latter of the alphabet was covered. Another, more difficult version – which could be used by adults – (and was, by us, at parties) required a person to name a place that began with an "a." The next participant would then have to name a place that began with the last letter of the first named place. For instance: I start with the word Alaska; next person must also start with an "a" because Alaska ends with "a." It becomes much more complicated if someone starts with Egypt, which requires a "t" or Essex, which requires an "x." As mentioned, this can be a very challenging game.

The trip continue, with each day a challenge for us to come up with something to do to keep everyone amused, alert, and interested. For songs, we sang everything from "I've Been Working on the Railroad" to "99 Bottles of Beer on the Wall" to "Mary Had a Little Lamb" to many other popular songs we may have heard on the radio. All of us sang together with gusto. We had fun!

In spite of all the hardships we mastered all obstacles and arrived safely in Miami Beach, four days later in October 1944.

We spent two seasons at the Sinclair Hotel. When we realized that living at a hotel in Miami Beach, like our time at the guest house in Atlantic City, was not the best way to raise our fine boys, we sold our interests in both and decided to move into a regular house. It was time to give up our gypsy lifestyle, find good schools for both boys, a good neighborhood with playgrounds and more normal life for all of us. I joined the Winchell Real Estate Co. as a salesman while Mollie got us settled in the new home on S.W. 16th Street in Miami, which had a variety of different native fruit trees in our backyard. Mollie truly made our house into a home for all of us. Ma Hirsh and her brother Herman came to live with us, and we soon became a happy family.

It was therefore a terrible shock to all of us when Alan suddenly contracted polio while in the second grade. The courage and strength it took for him to survive still amaze me. He had to endure the pain of wearing those thick heavy steel braces and heavy shoes, day and night until his legs were strengthened. In spite of the misery he endured, he was a happy and cheerful little boy, always ready to go and do whatever the rest of us wanted to do. I still marvel at the strength and willpower it took for him just to walk, braces and all, from our home on 24th Avenue and 16th Street, all the way to 11th Street and 12th Avenue, to go to High Holiday Services. It was a distance of over two miles. Though we did not use the car on High Holidays, I had offered to drive him and drop him on a street close to the Synagogue, yet he refused. If we could walk, so could he, he said!

With the help of Drs. Adler and Kaiser in nearby Coral Gables – the ones who prescribed the braces and told us how to strengthen Alan's skinny legs – he eventually overcame the condition. Alan developed habits of exercise that have lasted to this day. Anyone looking at Alan today, seeing his strong and muscled frame, would never know that he'd once had polio and been such a weakling. You bet I'm proud! He grew to become a healthy boy, always eager and anxious to play and do what every other boy did. When his big brother went to the playground to play, Alan went too. The only problem was that when Alan played any kind of game, he always played so enthusiastically that he picked-up all the dirt on the playground and bought it home on his clothes. Yes, one boy returned from the playground neat and clean, the younger one covered in dust, dirt and sweat. One wonders who had the most fun?

Like his older brother, Alan formed friendships with boys and girls at Shenandoah Junior High and at Miami High. Decades later, he still keeps in touch with a number of them. Among his friends was Ronny Shapo, his college roommate and a successful attorney for many years in Miami, who later moved to Sarasota. It's interesting to note that Ronny's father, a real estate broker, is actually the one who eventually bought our home on 16th Street. Another of Alan's boyhood friends was Ronny Friedman, an attorney who followed in his father's footsteps and is now also a judge. By coincidence, Ronny's father, Milton Friedman, was the presiding judge many years later when I was involved in a lawsuit at El Conquistador condominiums in West Kendall. That's an entirely other long story about a group of residents (condo owners) taking on the developer.

Some of Alan's other friends included Eli Feinberg, involved in running political campaigns; Hardy Katz, involved in organizing and running large sports conventions; and Steve Morris (whom I can still picture with that big "oompah, oompah" horn in his stout arms) who's now an optometrist.

Unlike his older brother, Alan did not show much interest in being a Boy Scout. However, Alan was very popular with girls, so much so that he was chosen as the heartthrob of a very well-known girls' Jewish youth group while in high school. At the University of Florida, he was popular among peers as well, and sought after by several fraternity houses. When he finally chose one, he was assigned to be the recruiter of the incoming freshman class. A few months later, he later resigned from pledging to concentrate on his studies.

Among his friends at U.F. he renewed his friendship with Dolores Norris, a girl whom he'd known from the one year he'd spent at Miami Beach Junior High. The friendship became more, with Alan and Dolores deciding to get married while they were both still in school in Gainesville. Like all mothers, Mollie wanted her sons to choose a profession. While his older brother chose law, Alan was not sure, at first, what he wanted to study in college. In spite of his mother's urging to take up dentistry (which, she told him, was a lucrative profession that'd still enable him to work decent hours), Alan chose to just take courses in liberal arts and science that first year, without choosing a major. It was during his sophomore year that Alan told us he'd decided to apply for admission to the U.F. Medical School after completing three years of pre-med courses. He proceeded to apply and was accepted while still an undergraduate. Can you believe that this successful and highly regarded doctor (both by his patients and peers) technically never got his bachelor's degree? Shouldn't we all be ashamed of this "black sheep" in our family?

Despite the concerns of Dolores' mother, Alice Norris, Alan and Dolores were quietly married in Miami on June 12, 1962, with a promise that it would not interfere with Alan's completion of his studies. They certainly kept their promise.

Their son Gary, our first of four grandsons, was born in January of 1964 with Alan still in school in Gainesville. He and Dolores moved to an apartment for married students, while he continued with his studies. Two years later, in 1966, Alan graduated with distinction from the University of Florida with his M.D. degree. Needless to say, we were thrilled to know that both of our sons had succeeded in graduating in a profession they'd chosen. Unlike his brother and the practice of law, Alan's choice of medicine required many more years of hard work before he'd actually be able to start practicing.

For his first year of internship, Alan selected Jackson Memorial Hospital back in Miami, the main public hospital. His choice, he said, was because was a hospital that catered to many poor and indigent people, with so many different ailments, would offer him a variety of experiences. It would help him choose which kind of medicine he wanted to practice. Another plus for that choice was that Jackson was crowded and handled many accident victims and emergencies. He wanted to get a lot of different experiences. Boy, did he get that wish! After a few 48-hour shifts he probably wondered whether he'd made the right choice. At any rate, before Alan finished that year, he decided he wanted to become a cardiologist. During that year, Alan and Dolores rented an inexpensive apartment. With a young child, and the little pay he earned from the hospital, they couldn't even afford the rent, but somehow managed.

During this time, Uncle Sam required all prospective doctors to serve two years in the Armed Forces, sometimes even before they could complete requirements for private practice. Alan applied for an alternative program. It required that the two years be spent working on an approved project sponsored by a government health agency. At the end of his internship, Alan was accepted by a doctor in Claxton, Georgia doing research on the habits and life expectancies of black men in that small town. Claxton was known as the "Fruitcake Capital of the U.S." A typical small southern town an hour from Savannah, Claxton had no Jewish families. In addition, as I've mentioned, Gary was born with hearing challenges and Claxton had nobody qualified to help with speech therapy. Alan and Dolores decided to find a place to live in Savannah and Alan drove 63 miles in an old Plymouth back and forth, every day (the car he had acquired at a government auction, I believe). They loved Savannah, a beautiful yet quaint old historic Southern city. Gary thrived, thanks to an excellent, caring speech therapist who helped prepare him for school. When they moved there, I had given them a small portable double-reel tape recorder so we could send audible tapes of communication to each other. I still recall how much pleasure we got from hearing Gary read his first words, on tape, with his distinct Southern drawl. To help with their expenses, Dolores became the manager of an apartment complex. Mollie and I enjoyed our visits to Savannah.

Alan's work on the project in Claxton made quite an impression on the doctors from Duke University, who actually supervised the research. Before his stint at Claxton ended, Alan was offered the opportunity for a fellowship at Duke where he could do his Medical Residency and Cardiology training.

Of course, we were all thrilled at this offer from the world-renowned Duke Medical School. It was there that Alan got his fine training at the then-comparatively new practice of diagnostic catheterization. He became so expert at this new area of medicine that Duke invited Alan to join its faculty and teach this art to prospective doctors. To have the prestige of Duke University on your resumé is quite an honor, but to be part of its Medical Staff was an even bigger feather in one's cap. Alan became an Assistant Professor there, until he realized that it was difficult to live on the pay he got from Duke – even with all the prestige it brought. After all the many years of hard work and study, he and his young family deserved to enjoy the fruits of all his efforts. Even after Duke offered him an Associate Professorship, which paid about $31,000.00 a year, Alan found it insufficient for his family's needs and decided to look for other opportunities.

He was offered good position to join cardiology practices in Texas, at guaranteed minimums of at least $50,000. However, Alan had enjoyed the teaching experiences at Duke and was looking for a place where he could earn more while still being involved in teaching. We would have liked for them to come back to Florida, but neither Alan nor Dolores was interested in "joining the rat race" of the competitive medical practice in our state. After a considerable national search, Alan found that a new program at Eastern Virginia Medical School in Norfolk offered everything he wanted. He and Dolores fell in love with Virginia Beach. Life there was at a slower pace than the hectic rush of Florida living. They found a house in a modest neighborhood, a tight Jewish community, and soon formed friendships with people their own age and interests. After all these years, their love for life in the Virginia Beach area has not diminished.

It didn't take long for Alan to become recognized as one of the foremost Cardiologists in the Tidewater area around Norfolk-Virginia Beach. In just a few years at the medical school there, it became apparent that Alan was not being fully compensated for his share of work. The number of catheterizations he himself performed exceeded the combined efforts of all the other doctors. Alan and another physician, Carl Hartman (how's that for a cardiologist's name), decided to form a partnership and open a private practice. In spite of established competition and attempted obstruction to the use of Norfolk General Hospital facilities, they opened the best-equipped catheterization lab in the area, Cardiovascular Associates. It became a renowned and successful practice. That two-man office started by Alan and Carl still would function (and grow into) the foremost cardiologist group in the area, although it now takes about eight times as many doctors to service multiple offices.

Soon after they settled in Virginia Beach, Alan and Dolores became affiliated with a Reform Temple in nearby Norfolk. Friendships were formed and they began to feel at home, living there. At about the same time, Mollie and I retired from teaching and were able to visit them frequently, especially for holidays. From our first visit, we were impressed with the esteem in which Alan was held by their new friends and neighbors. Their life seemed to have none of the pressures of city living that we seemed to have in Florida. They'd blended into the new community as if they'd always lived there. Their new friends welcomed us as very graciously. It gave us much pleasure to see them so happy and accepted.

Parents always strive to see their offspring achieve success and offer advice on ways to reach such goals. We were no exception. Our two sons saw things quite differently from one another. Almost from his first paycheck, I urged my older son to take a small percentage off each paycheck so that he'd have some money to invest if the opportunity came along. In those early days of his practicing law, he said that it was more important for him to invest in a home, car and a lifestyle to impress his Miami clients. His philosophy then, he told me, was to live more for the present than for the future. I'd had some success with my real estate investments and tried to get him interested in that field. At first, he resisted, then he grudgingly joined me in taking a 15% share in an 80-acre partnership I'd formed. When I decided to build a mini-warehouse project in Boynton Beach, I finally convinced him to invest. That 80-acre partnership did not turn out so well, but the mini-warehouse certainly did. Both of my sons had invested and each earned a return of almost ten times as much as they'd invested. The only other real estate venture he took was an industrial development with a friend and partner – an investment that would help pay for his son's college.

Alan had an entirely different attitude. From the time they lived in North Carolina and I pointed out vacant property on roads – properties I believe, that later became part of what is now the world-famous Research Triangle—Alan paid close attention and expressed interest. At the time, though, he was far from being in a position to invest in anything. It apparently sank in, because soon after he became established in his new cardiology practice in the Tidewater area, Alan ventured into a partnership in a real estate acquisition. He'd found an old acquaintance from his grade school years, Irwin Hurwitz, a dentist, living in the area. Irwin had offered him a one-third interest in a partnership to buy a small office building on the corner of an up-and-coming neighborhood. He accepted. During our next visit Alan proudly offered to show me his new venture. I loved it. It was located on a corner of a divided four-lane, very busy highway, directly across from a fully-developed residential neighborhood. Alan and Irwin paid off the mortgage and made a very good return on their investment. They then acquired several vacant lots in the same block for future development. Alan's small investment in that little office building further aroused an interest in real estate as a means of investment. That interest eventually led to him acquiring a large variety of parcels in and around the Tidewater area (the name given to the many different towns and cities that abut the Norfolk/Virginia Beach communities). Practically every time we visited Alan and Dolores, Alan told us or asked our advice about an investment property. During the many, many years they've lived in Virginia Beach, Alan has bought and sold practically every kind of real estate imaginable. Much of the time, this included the help of a knowledgeable partner who found, managed, rented, and took care of all details of owning and operating each acquisition until they had a chance to sell it at a good profit. At one time or another, Alan has had – or still has – an interest in apartment buildings, vacant lots, warehouses, a multi-story office building, homes near the beach and so on. Sometimes it's just a small percent interest in the property (with others); other times, it has been outright owner-ship. In practically every instance, the property showed a good return on the investment and was sold at a considerable profit. Alan continues to invest wisely and I am beyond proud of his success in real estate, cardiology, charity and his community. It's worth noting that thanks to their investments and hard work, he and Dolores established a trust many years ago for their son, Craig – our third grandson who has special needs. In addition to ensuring Craig's future is secure, Alan and his wife have established an incredible legacy in the Virginia Beach area by supporting and leading so many causes that help children and families.

So here we are. This story of My Two Sons was started more than three months ago. I wanted to finish by today, June 10th, because Alan and Dolores celebrate their 43rd Wedding Anniversary today, and I want to wish them Many, Many Happy Returns. I know that I've left out many details about my two sons and their lives, but there is a limit as to how much I can write. I'm sure the family will understand and forgive me.

Love, Ralphy
June 10, 2005

CHANGES IN MY LIFE

L ife, today, is so much different from the way it was in my youth and early adulthood. Sometimes I'm troubled and ask myself whether – in spite of all the wonderful inventions and advantages we have today – have we lost something in our rush to change, are things better now? There are many, many topics that come to mind. Obviously, I can't even attempt to cover them all, but permit me to list several and explain them – not in any specific order of importance. If I wander off, please overlook it. I'll eventually explain.

Let's skip my life when I was a little boy, living in a little *shtetl* (town) in Europe. I'll start with the time when I came to live in America. In March 1923, as I've written about, I observed my Bar Mitzvah in Montreal on a Thursday morning, called up to say the blessings of the Torah Service, in an Orthodox Synagogue. Muni, my sister Chaika's husband, represented the family in the absence of Papa. Papa had left a month before for Baltimore, to open a Kosher butcher shop and to prepare for our family's arrival. A few days after my Bar Mitzvah, Mama, Yelvel (Willie), Mayer (Mike) and I left for Baltimore. I should mention that Chaika and Muni never left Canada and raised their children there. Their grandchildren, our nieces and nephews with whom we're all still close, continue to live in Montreal and Toronto.

From the very first days of our arrival in Baltimore that day in March 1923, life was so different – more slow, calm and deliberate. My brothers and I slept in the bedroom above the store. As I've already explained in an earlier story, our quarters were the second floor "apartment" above the store. It was built in the former garage. If you can picture it, the space was divided into a sparsely-furnished bedroom for us boys, and an even narrower room that served as the kitchen and dining area – all in a space of about 9' x 19'. But, after living the past year-and-a-half in Montreal, in a third-floor walkup with only cold water flat, we accepted any accommodations available. Mama and Papa slept in a bedroom in my Aunt and Uncle Bilich's main house. Papa drew $8.00 a week's wages and could take as much meat and other food as needed for our family's use.

Within a few days of arriving, Mayer and I were helping in the store and delivering orders. Deliveries were limited to the areas within walking distance – less than a mile away. We each had to carry our orders in large straw baskets. I was barely 132 pounds and because we were both so young and not very strong, we could not carry heavy deliveries and often made several trips before we were finished the daily deliveries. By the time we were through each day, it was almost time to close the store and have supper.

During the week, we ate in the above-the-store apartment. Our meals were usually simple and limited to what Mama could prepare in the small space that served as the kitchen. For lunch, P. S. #63 let the children walk home from school from 12 noon until 1, to eat. So Mayer and I walked the four blocks home to have our cold lunches. Friday nights we were guests at a typical Sabbath meal in the beautiful Bilich main house. The sumptuous and delicious meal never seemed enough to satisfy my scrawny, half-starved body.

We were learning to adjust to the new neighborhood, language, and customs. Our stay and schooling in Montreal had not properly prepared us for life in the Fallbrook section of Baltimore. (Please forgive me for repeating any parts of previous stories, but I feel a need to explain how things were, and in case anyone missed it.) My ability to read and speak English, coming most recently from a predominately French and immigrant society in Montreal, did little to help me learn and adjust to Baltimore. In Canada, the school I had attended emphasized French lessons. My classmates there were French or immigrants from many European countries, each one with peculiar individual pronunciations. Even the Yiddish of my immediate neighbors in Montreal was different from what I knew. My Chinese schoolmates had their own peculiar language. The result was, I had to unlearn the little English I'd acquired in Canada and start all over once in Baltimore. It would be years before I overcame my terrible accent and the resulting embarrassment when I tried speaking to an American.

Even with all the drawbacks, school in Baltimore was a pleasure to attend. They didn't know what to do with me – a *langer locksh* (a long noodle) as Mama called me. Here was this skinny, gawky kid, with little ability to speak but proficiency in arithmetic beyond the other students. I was placed into a second grade for two weeks, then to a fourth grade. The following year, in fifth grade, I was a well-behaved, serious boy, attentive and eager to learn. My teachers were very tolerant and helpful and I made quick progress. Eventually that year, I was promoted to the lower half of the 6th grade. In a few weeks I was skipped into Grade 6A. I had to learn about decimals and percent on my own, as I adjusted to the new class. My teacher helped. Mrs. Chambers was no doubt my most influential guide. When I completed 6A, I was again skipped into 7A. The second half of the 7th grade, I went to the new Forest Park Junior/Senior High School that had opened in 1924.

Mrs. Chambers helped me overcome my reading difficulties by sending me to the local public library, about a half mile away. The librarian suggested introduced me to "Uncle Wiggily" and "Br'er Rabbit" series of books – books that were meant to be read by beginning readers. I devoured them. Beginning with those simple, funny, little books I became fascinated with reading. I got a library card and regularly drew the five-book limit home with me to read. Gradually my reading level grew until I was reading at or above grade. Somebody introduced me to little soft-covered series of books (a smaller and very much cheaper version of our current paperbacks) which changed my life.

The discovery of the "pocket" books, as we called them, truly developed my love of reading.

During every waking moment of every day – no matter where I was or what I was doing (except in the synagogue) – I had a book handy to read. While I ate, in the store, on the street car, in bed before I fell asleep – I read and read and read some more. My reading appetite was insatiable. The Hardy Boys, Frank Merriwell, Horatio Alger – you name the series, I read them all. No matter the subject: mystery, adventure, westerns, school, morals, I consumed them all. Interestingly, none of them had to rely on curses or favorite four-letter "dirty" words that are so common nowadays in books. On the contrary, in the majority of these books, the good guys or the orphans were the heroes of the story, and almost always succeeded. Some books even ended with: "and, the moral of this story is –."

Whatever success I attained in later years stemmed from my exposure to and love of reading. For the benefit of those of you who've never read details of my education or who may have forgotten, let me clarify it. I was fortunate to have been born with an insatiable curiosity. Everything was of interest to me growing up and always has been. Moreover, I easily remembered everything I read or heard. The family and others say that I recall facts and details like few others, or call this a "photographic memory." To me, it is just natural. In any event, school was always fun and easy for me. I loved it.

When I came to Forest Park Junior/Senior High, recall that I had been skipped to 7A, the last half of 7th grade. No problem! I adjusted easily to the six-period day, with six different teachers, and I made good grades in all. I was successful in 8th grade and anxiously awaited the next year, because 9th grade meant the beginning of High School. From there, I dreamed of college – the dream of many students, and, even more, of every immigrant boy!

Unfortunately as I've detailed, fate dictated otherwise. Papa needed my help! When he decided to buy out Uncle Bilich's partnership interest in the store, Papa didn't realize the added burden he was assuming. It became physically impossible for him and Mama to operate the store by themselves. The success of the business depended entirely on deliveries – since our Jewish customers were scattered throughout the Fallbrook section of Baltimore. He could not afford to hire anyone and was on the verge of failure unless he could quickly find someone to help – at little or no cost. Willie (the three of us boys had now Americanized our names) was working and saving up for his forthcoming marriage. The only solution was me! I'd helped a lot, delivering orders before and on the way to school. But that wasn't enough. Both Papa and Mama were needed full time tending store and making up the orders that came in during the day. Neither of them had the strength or means to carry and deliver orders for miles in every direction.

When Papa told me that I'd have to leave school and work in the store full time, I was heartbroken. But, as a dutiful son, I realized he had no other choice. Children under 16 could only work full time by getting a work permit if the family's needs required it. I got my permit and left school at the end of January, 1925, after I'd successfully finished 8th grade and a few months before my 16th birthday. Full time work wasn't my only problem. I had other things to worry about. We were living in a new environment and I had to adjust to life in the Baltimore. Unlike the slums we'd come from in Montreal, the people around us in Fallbrook were a mixed, unrestricted, middle class working community. Quite a number of areas in Baltimore were very restricted – which meant that only Caucasian Christian families were allowed. To a boy like me, who had been forbidden to ever even talk to a non-Jew, it was a difficult situation. Life as a practicing Orthodox family had meant observing Jewish traditions, beliefs, superstitions and practices. Moving into this strange neighborhood, without the ability to communicate, led to many awkward situations. To suddenly be confronted by these strangers on all sides – at home, at school and in the street – often resulted in confrontations and even beatings. It was, as I've said, a frightening and miserable experience.

I did my best to deliberately avoid these strange, sometime hostile, encounters. What bothered me the most was that many of our neighbors and their parents were also immigrants. They were from places like Italy and Ireland, and also had trouble speaking English. Yet, either through ignorance or their home teachings, they had a dislike or distrust for us, the strange people called Jews, who had suddenly invaded their territory. It took a while for most of them to learn that we had no "horns" – that we were not there to take anything away from them. In time, most) would accept us as neighbors – some willingly, others grudgingly and a few, never.

There were no other Jewish children in our neighborhood. Plus, since I was put to work, helping in the store and delivering orders, I had neither the time nor opportunity to make friends. As hard as it may be to believe, I have never had a childhood friend like so many of my peers – someone to treasure, trust and love. I'm thankful to see that my children and grandchildren have developed these special kinds of relationships with family and with friends– it one of the greatest gifts.

Something else that may be hard to understand (and that has certainly changed for me and in common culture) has to do with personal hygiene. For reasons I can't explain, hygiene was not a priority for many people (or for me) back then. When I woke up as a small child, I immediately put on my one-and-only everyday blouse, a pair of knickers and my knee-high black stockings. I laced my $1.00 pair of flat, thin, high-top tennis shoes, used the bathroom, rinsed my face and hands in the cold water, swallowed my milk and bread, added a sweater or jacket (if it was cold), and I was ready for work or school. I can't remember the age at when we began to brush our teeth or when I first visited a dentist.

When I smiled or laughed I displayed a mouthful of yellow-coated, obviously neglected, teeth. No one in my family or colleagues ever said anything or encouraged me to do something about it. The only time I washed all the parts of my body was when I took a bath on Fridays, or, just before a Holiday! Those were the only times when the water heater was lit. And, those were the times when I really had to scrub the tub because of the black ring that formed all around it from the accumulated dirt that came off my body! To the best of my knowledge, everybody else did the same thing back then. Living within a few blocks of the Western Maryland Railroad line didn't help, with the thick black soot coating everybody and everything within several block. I guess that the old saying, "ignorance is bliss" applies here. How could anyone tolerate the body odors? I can't explain it, and sorry for bringing it up – but it's true.

Let me interrupt myself. If you think I'm clarifying the way I lived to make you believe how bad things were for me, to arouse your sympathies, you are very wrong! All I'm trying to do is paint a picture of history as it affected my way of life. I honestly never complained or felt sorry for myself – then or now. This is just how life was, and most of us accepted it. It's only now – after all the improvements and innovations that all of us take for granted – that we can make comparisons and realize the differences. Hindsight can show the bad of yesterday as well as the good of today. Should we decry or give thanks? Truthfully, I much prefer to say I've been blessed. I am thankful to have survived and lived to enjoy so many advantages.

I must return to education. Although disappointed at having to quit high school, I was determined to continue my education in the hope that someday, in some way, I'd be able to finish and go onto college. Forest Park also had a Night School, where students could take the same subjects as in the day school. My English teacher, Miss Mageer, was also disappointed when I was compelled to quit. So she sent me to Dr. Otto K. Schmitt, the head of the night school department, to enroll in the 9th grade night classes part time. Thanks to his guidance and her encouragement, I completed the entire 9th grade requirements by taking classes at night and in the summer. As all of you know, I went back to school and concentrated on enlarging my vocabulary and academic goals. In the process I got rid of my accent. Eventually, after my many college courses and continued devotion to reading on a wide variety of subjects, I felt at ease in talking to people – no matter the topic.

I've barely touched on transportation, though it certainly as it affected me. My original means of delivering orders was by foot. North Avenue, the main avenue nearest our family store, was a wide, macadam-paved, street. It was serviced by two streetcar lines that went or connected to many other lines, so that one could reach most any part of the large City of Baltimore. In addition, the street also had room for all auto, truck, or wagon traffic – on both sides of the double tracks of streetcar lines. Wide, paved sidewalks covered both sides of North Avenue, going east and west. For many years, the streetcar lines became our means of delivering our orders to the farthest customers.

Early on, Papa used the streetcar twice a week to go to the wholesale markets. I had no idea the struggles he endured to accomplish that task, till one time I went with him.

On that morning, I was awakened from a deep sleep – in total darkness – by his gentle touch on my shoulder. Papa whispered for me to get dressed quickly and join him in the kitchen. I slipped on my weekly clothes (my union-suit) and stumbled into the kitchen, confused and still half asleep. The clock said it was not quite 3 o'clock! In the middle of the night! He handed me a glass of milk and a piece of bread and told me to hurry. We were going to the (wholesale) market. He handed me one of the large straw baskets. Grabbing the other basket he led me outside. Going to market, even in the cold of the night, was an exciting adventure.

We boarded the #31 Streetcar Line, which ran eastward for a couple miles, then turned south towards downtown – through the heavily-populated and restricted "colored town." When we reached Baltimore Street, we transferred to an eastward-bound line till we reached the busy, raucous mob at the market. It was a scene of bedlam unlike anything I'd ever encountered. Wherever you looked, there were people screaming. Farmers and wholesale merchants yelled to onlookers, describing the value and price of their products. The prospective buyers, in turn, yelled just as loudly, bargaining for the goods. At least, that's how it seemed to me. Without Papa, I would have been completely lost.

Smiling, Papa signed for me to follow him. We moved through the din and mob till we reached a large building. Through the open doors, I saw people milling about the stands and the counters, each laden with goods. As we entered the building the noise level gradually diminished and the smells increased. We immediately went to a counter that held several coops of live chickens. Papa and the merchant conducted their business. Papa then selected several chickens. The seller quickly bound the chicken's feet with string, threw then on a hanging scale, and we walked away, carrying the bound and squawking chickens.

Our next stop was to the cubicle belonging to the *Shochet* – the bearded old man qualified to kill the chickens in the Kosher manner prescribed under Jewish laws. After an exchange of a few words, we dropped our chickens in a special bin. I watched, fascinated, as the Shochet picked one hen, held her under his left elbow while he grabbed her head and turned it upward so that its neck was exposed. He plucked a few small feathers from the neck.

And in a smooth move, he slit its neck with a sharp razor-like instrument. Then he bent its neck back as the blood poured from the open cut, and he threw it thrashing and bleeding on to the already bloody cement floor. After a few moments, a middle aged woman picked up the now-dead fowl and de-feathered it. I remember feeling like I was going to throw up. Papa may have noticed my reaction because we walked away and Papa said we'd come back for the plucked chickens later Papa led me to the produce market. This section consisted of a group of stores where all the fresh fruit and vegetables were sold. A new and different phase of my education was about to begin.

Papa told me to watch and listen carefully as he handled the people and the goods we were about to buy. Buying the wide variety of goods in the produce department required its own "language," peculiar to the trade. Since we were dealing in small lots as well as small amounts of money, the difference between making a profit or loss depended not only on one's skill in judging the freshness and quality of the goods but also on one's ability to haggle and bargain. I watched and listened and questioned every move he made before I understood why and what he did. It would take several visits with Papa before I could venture to try on my own. Remember, we were dealing in very perishable merchandise and there was little means of refrigeration. Whatever food we bought had to be of such quality and value that we could sell it easily and quickly. So, a penny saved really meant something.

I have neither the patience nor the strength to describe all the many details. Suffice it to say, going to the market was an arduous and acquired task. The biggest problem was to figure out how much we could pack into the two large baskets we carried with us – what else we could drag along and, finally, how to get our purchases to the store. Papa's ability to handle large and cumbersome weights always amazed me. Fortunately, by the time I'd started to work full time for Papa, I'd developed enough muscle to carry fairly heavy weights, too – in spite of my skinny appearance. Somehow that morning, we managed to schlep one basket, each, over one shoulder to the corner where the streetcar stopped. The motorman usually was very lenient and allowed us to place our baskets in the space behind his seat. When we reached the junction of Line #31 we transferred our load to the home destination. By the time we came to our stop it would be around six o'clock.

Unloading and arranging our purchases was another daunting exercise. I have to remind you, again, that the capacity of the store was very limited. The permanent fixtures took up half the space of the store, such as the large walk-in ice box that kept all the meats, chickens, and dairy products reasonably protected from spoiling. Then, there were the shelves on the walls, where we displayed the canned Kosher-only goods and breads. That all left little space for anyone or anything else. Still, we managed to display what we'd bought that day and every time, and we usually ended up with a small profit.

On Thursday mornings, we repeated the visit to the market, and added a visit to the fish market to purchase live (or fresh) fish for the Sabbath meals. Then, we had to make room for that. Before Passover or other Holidays, we had to find room for displays of special goods. We also had to find room to display a bag or basket of vegetable and fruit.

Add Mama, Papa and me, and you can imagine how much room was available for walk-in customers. Two at a time was truly a crowd!

Both Mama and Papa were attending night school themselves, preparing to learn enough English and American History to pass their citizenship exams. Even after getting their papers, they still found it hard to understand and speak with customers on the phone. Answering the phone became a priority, on top of delivering the orders correctly and on time. As the business grew, because of our dedication to please the customers, depending upon the large straw baskets for deliveries became too heavy a burden for me—literally too heavy. One of us soon found a larger sized bright "little red wagon" that was popular with youngsters then. For a short time this helped, though barely.

Papa, as mentioned, was dedicated to operating our Kosher butcher and grocery store in the strictest observance of Biblical Laws. Every item had to be strictly Kosher – all meats, fish, and fowl had to be stored, wrapped and kept separate from the dairy products. Yes, everything was even separated in the cramped space of our walk-in ice box, which was cooled by 300-pound cakes of ice. Under no circumstances would a meat item be stored on a shelf or space next to the butter, cheese, or any other milk product. We used a different color, shape or size to wrap, weigh, or bag each meat or dairy item. One order could consist of several different bags of items that each had to be kept apart from the others – thus calling for extra space. Papa abided by all the rules and rituals, and was highly respected for doing so. Making sure it was carried and delivered properly was my responsibility.

By the end of the summer of 1926 it was obvious that the only solution to our transportation problems was to buy a car. This was a big decision. Our choices were limited to a Ford or Chevy, the two lowest-priced brands available. Neither Papa nor I had ever displayed any mechanical skills or interest in driving one of these dangerous contraptions. To tell the truth, the very idea of trying to manipulate such a strange and dangerous vehicle was very scary. It was not like modern cars, where you simply get in, start the car and go. And the idea of deriving pleasure from driving never entered our minds. Since we had no other solution, Papa decided we'd buy a car. Deciding which car to buy was easy. Henry Ford was known to be Anti-Semite, who sponsored the printing and distribution of the spurious lies contained in the published "Protocols of Zion." We could never buy a product manufactured by anyone who expressed a hatred of Jews, so we went to the nearest Chevy dealer.

To buy a car required cash – at least $600 – a very large sum to come up with so suddenly. There was no such thing as a credit card in those days. To buy something on credit was almost impossible. The store bought its wares on monthly credit. Papa paid his bills, by check, from an account he maintained at the Chesapeake Bank.

Again, Papa surprised us. During the entire three years since the store opened, he somehow had regularly and systematically saved and deposited some small amounts of money into a savings account. Back then, there were two kinds of institutions that encouraged people to open an account and save. There were banks. There were Buildings & Loans (as they called them in Baltimore). Papa's tiny regular savings had earned interest and by the time we were ready to buy the Chevy, he somehow was able to come up with enough cash – an unbelievable feat, to me. To be able to save tiny, tiny amounts measured in nickels and dimes – was amazing!

Choosing the car was comparatively easy. The cheapest model Chevy was the four-door "Tourist Sedan" which I've described in detail before. Naturally, that was Papa's choice. There was no bargaining. The dealer, through the salesman, was obligated to teach the buyer how to drive and to help get a driver's license. Papa tried and tried but failed to grasp the skills necessary to drive. After two weeks of futile attempts the salesman told me that – if we insisted (and gave him $15.00) – he'd get Papa a Driver's License. But, he not be responsible for any accidents that Papa's driving might cause. None of us was willing to take that risk so it was decided that I'd be the one to learn how to drive and get a license.

None of you can possibly believe the pressure that I was under. None of you can conceive how difficult it was to learn how to drive at the time – you didn't slide easily into your comfortable and fully automated car, turn a key, press a button or two, and head off. I'll try to describe my experience and hope you'll understand.

Before I start, let's clarify one point. There were practically no female drivers back then. The daring exceptions were very brave individuals, but were not held in high esteem by society. Most people considered it unladylike for a girl or woman to drive. Social customs, the long dresses they wore, plus the physical strength needed to operate an ordinary car, served as deterrents for women to drive. So, we brave males shouldered the burden. Like me. I wish it was possible for me to tell that I learned easily. Nothing could be further than the truth. My brain could not grasp the intricacies and skills necessary to drive a 1926 model car. Let me explain. Elementary Schools were designed to teach the basic elementary skills of reading, writing, and arithmetic. The vast majority of parents aimed to send their children to school long enough to acquire these basic skills. The greatest effort was to educate the boys, since few girls were expected to go to work after completing their education. To finish High School was a great achievement and honor – especially in Jewish families. Immigrants had even more ambition, for to have a son become a professional was the ultimate source of pride. So, the usual aim was for a boy to attend a school that taught the academic skills that led to a profession. My parents were no different in their ambition for me.

I should mention that if a girl had ambitions to not only finish High School but learn business skills, so she could become a secretary, clerk, or bookkeeper, classes were available for her to do so. As for the boy who showed an interest in mechanical work, there were schools that taught technical or mechanical skills. By the time we finished Junior High our career ambitions had determined which high school we'd attend. Since my parents' goal was for me to become a doctor, if possible, I had attended Baltimore City College – the oldest and most respected Academic High School in the area. (I mention "if possible" because there was never a guarantee that a Jewish student would be accepted by a Medical School – no matter how good his grades might be. All Medical Schools had a strict quota limiting admission – usually about 50 – of Jewish applicants.

Mollie's brother, Herman, son of an engineer – who showed an interest in anything mechanical – graduated from Baltimore Polytechnic High. He could always improvise or repair any mechanical problem. Me? No! I could spend pages explaining how hard it was for an average person, especially one whose whole life had been centered on learning and books, plus, unused or untrained in handling anything mechanical, to learn to coordinate and execute the skills necessary to drive. Simply put – the early cars were complicated and poorly built, apt to fail or break down at any time. Truthfully, you took your life in your hands from the moment you tried to start the car. The physical and mental strain needed to drive a car frightened most people! But, I had no other choice. Too much and too many people depended on me. So I learned. And I taught many others how to drive, including Mollie (years later) and our sons. Tired of this subject? Me, too! Let's move on.

How about sports and recreation? I never did do well in sports. But, I was always very dependable. You could always depend on me to be the last one chosen on any team, on the rare occasions when I did participate in a game. Still, I loved sports. Actually, I did manage to learn how to bowl, thanks to Mollie, while in PenMar Park. Eventually, I became an average bowler (and Mollie and both played on leagues in our retirement). While in High School I found out I could enjoy sports, vicariously, simply by watching others play. After watching the City College football team beat Poly – its biggest and longest rival – I was sold. From then on I tried to learn all the rules of every sport and managed to watch so many games that I became an enthusiastic follower/spectator of many games and teams. I can't even describe, when it comes to sports, the difference between then and now!

During my last year in High School the hallowed City College was moved from its crowded dowdy building in downtown Baltimore to a beautiful, bright, brand new campus thirty-some blocks north. Alongside the spacious new building was a stadium that accommodated thousands of spectators to its games. Local colleges started playing intra-college games, and my interest in sports became even greater. The epitome of football fever was achieved when the Army-Navy and the Navy-Notre Dame games were scheduled to be played at "our" new stadium that year. The Naval Academy, at Annapolis, Maryland, and the Army, at West Point, were bitter rivals, always trying to outdo each other for the glory of their service. Their annual football game was a national event. The entire cadres of plebes and cadets were enthusiastic spectators, occupied assigned sections, and boisterously participated in cheering for their teams. Nationally, each branch had its large group of loyal followers of families and friends, who steadfastly attended the annual games. Although West Point had a large stadium to accommodate the huge crowds of rooters and students, Navy's facilities were too small. When Navy's turn to host the game came it was scheduled in the nearest large city. The City College's new stadium became Navy's home base. I, and many other Baltimore residents, became Navy's loyal followers.

I became such an enthusiastic football fan that I taught my (then) girlfriend, Mollie, the basic points and rules of the game and invited her to join me when I attended a college game. The height of my enthusiastic support of Navy's football team was achieved in 1933, when Mollie and I witnessed Navy's first ever defeat of Notre Dame – the best-known and strongest team in the nation – in a football game. This was the beginning of our many years of attending and enjoying football games, culminating in our becoming regular attendees at the University of Miami and Miami Dolphins games, before television viewing became popular.

Even before football I enjoyed sports. The City of Baltimore supported and invited its citizens to watch several sporting events in Druid Hill Park, a public facility located about three miles east of Fallbrook. Most games were free and scheduled for Saturdays (Baltimore had Blue Laws, which prohibited all businesses and even sports activities – except Jewish stores that were closed on Saturdays – from being operated on Sundays). Since I was a practicing Orthodox Jew I didn't ride on Saturdays. So, after Services and mid-day dinner, I used to walk to the park to watch the various games. There were always several games being played – tennis, softball, and baseball were the most popular – and we were able to watch whatever interested us. My favorite games were the baseball games played by the Negro teams, who played with so much enthusiasm and skill that it was a joy to watch them. Unfortunately, they were not allowed to join the white professional ball clubs, then.

When we first came to Baltimore, *Tante* (Aunt) Bilich gave Mike and me a dime apiece, to go to the movies on Saturday. Admission was only 5 cents. The rest was used for penny, broken-pieces of hard or chewy grab-bags of candy (at one cent, each) or other delicacies sold during intermissions of the comedy, main picture, and the weekly chapter of a never-ending serial picture. We usually sat thru at least two viewings of the movies. In spite of our parents' strict adherence to the Orthodox regulations to abstain from carrying money and seeing entertainment on Saturdays, Tante assured them that – since we were so young and anxious to learn American ways of life – we should be allowed to go. She'd take our sins on her conscience. As we grew older, the Tarzan and Westerns grew less and less appealing and we substituted sports for our dimes and movies.

Back to our Chevy, we used the new car for business, only, till I became comfortable and used to its tendencies. On Tuesday and Thursday mornings I drove Papa down to the markets. Now we could carry larger and more varied loads and could do it in less time than before. By the time Spring of 1927 came, I ventured to take the family out to the country. The quiet and serenity of the empty roads, mingled with the smells of the honeysuckle bushes and lilac trees, made our Sunday excursions wonderful, happy experiences. My first date with a girl was at age 18 – a late Sunday night movie, followed by a chocolate-nut sundae at a drugstore soda fountain counter. I had no time, money, interest, or inclination for any other recreation. It wasn't until I was in high school, in 1929, and was asked whom I was planning to take to the Prom, that I realized I had no answer. I didn't even know what "prom" meant. Worse yet, when I did find out, I knew no girl I could invite. Somehow I did find a classmate who explained and took me in his car to the Prom. His girlfriend brought a friend for me and I did have a good time but have no idea who she was. This experience led to my serious platonic interest in girls. I never dated more than one girl at a time. I had a succession of relationships. All of these ended abruptly when I met my future wife, whom I helped register at Maryland State Normal School in the Fall of 1930. Mollie and I became "an item" which lasted till she passed away on November 11, 2003.

I would be remiss if I didn't mention Mollie's experiences with fun and recreation. To do so I must explain Maryland school practices in those early days. When I got my first job of teaching Pre-Vocational boys, I was told my class would be limited to a maximum of 20 students. Within the first few days of confusion I suddenly became aware that there were only 13 boys in daily attendance. Because I was very nervous and fearful of my lack of knowledge of teaching such a challenging group, I was glad there were no more. But after a couple of weeks I felt more at ease and asked one of my new colleagues where my missing boys were. He told me that they were still working on the farms and would be in by the middle of October. Though still confused I was too embarrassed to show my ignorance by asking any more questions and soon forgot about them.

Sure enough, during the middle of October six more boys were added to my class. Then I found out that – in the Curtis Bay section of Baltimore where I was teaching – a number of the boys from poorer families were excused from school, early in May, to work on tobacco and cotton farms. They remained on their jobs throughout the summer and were allowed to stay till the harvest ended. Their jobs were more important to their families than their schooling and the local school board agreed. Interesting, eh?

Now, back to Mollie. When her folks started to operate their summer business at PenMar Park, Mollie was 12 years old. The frame building had been closed during the winter; the water pipes opened and drained to prevent freezing and bursting. The whole building had to be cleaned, painted, and prepared to accommodate the hoped-for summer guests. As I've related in my earlier stories, Alexander Hirsh, Mollie's father, and Pauline, his wife, took possession of their new home and business at the end of April. Until that school year ended, they left 12-year-old Mollie back in Baltimore with family, together with her 10-year-old brother, Herman. When the parents started the tedious and hard job of getting the large building ready for business, they found that – no matter how hard they tried – the work was just too hard for Alex. He was too weak and tired too easily. As we know the family couldn't afford outside help. The only solution was to get the two children out of school, early, to help. Mollie had heard of the early release of children, to work on farms. She went to see her principal and pleaded her case. In short, both were given homework to cover the absent days' work and left in mid-May. Both passed their grade requirements. Mollie was just 16 when she graduated Western High School. Herman finished Polytechnic High School. Unfortunately, while they both graduated with their respective classes, neither had the opportunity to attend their Senior Bowl celebrations.

Many years would pass before I learned that even the simple things that people found pleasurable – taking rides in the country, going to the beach, watching ball games, a school excursion to celebrate the Baltimore and Ohio Railroad's 100th Anniversary, or the excursion to honor Lindbergh on his solo airplane-crossing of the Atlantic – all were denied to Mollie. When we went on a weekend cruise excursion on the Chesapeake, to visit the Bilich family in Cape Charles, it was Mollie's first trip on a ship. She'd never gone to an amusement park; rarely ridden in an automobile, never went to a beach – on and on. The couple of times she took the train to New York were to visit her mother's sisters and brother and their families. Thanks to Mollie's friend Jean Tellem, she did attend a few concerts and operas – though mostly as standing room only. She never complained, though it is clear Mollie had less of a fun childhood than many others, and certainly nothing compare to how children are growing up now.

There are many other drastic changes that have taken place during my lifetime – most of which have enriched and prolonged my life. Probably the most obvious and greatest are in the fields of health and medicine – areas I couldn't possibly attempt to cover. The field of technology scares me out of my wits! There was a time when I felt I had an adequate English vocabulary. But the introduction of new words or the use of known words with an entirely new, different meaning makes me feel like an idiot. I'm typing this in a "notebook computer" that has so many other functions – graphics, files, windows, (and these are the easy ones) and on and on. There are endless other words and technologies that I'm afraid to even mention.

When we arrived in this country, we soon learned that a telephone was one of the most desirable instruments to have in our home. We waited for more than nine months before our first four-party phone was installed. Can you picture our joy at being able to communicate with family and friends – in spite of the inconvenience of all the static that pervaded each call. And, because it was a four-party line, many times someone was already using the line. Just imagine what fun it was trying to get them off and let you make your call – no matter how urgent your need. Or, the number of times your call could not be completed because the line was busy. Talk about frustration, you can't possibly imagine. One of our finest achievements? We finally got our first private line – about two years later! Believe me, it's true. I can't blame you if you find impossible to grasp such a situation. How can I, when you have not only multiple-line home phones, but a wireless little gadget – that's called a "cell." And, here I always thought a cell was a tiny space, often in a jail. No, it's a phone that not only lets you talk to someone thousands of miles away, it almost instantaneously can receive or send messages, music, photos or codes. Plus, according to the latest item in the paper, a phone can be used to take your pulse, check your body fat and to time your jogs. What's next? Will it soon be able to answer my questions? No doubt! Nothing would surprise me, now!

To reiterate, the introduction of so many new words in our vocabulary – as a consequence of the many new innovations and developments in the technology fields – is just too much for an old codger like me to grasp. So, I'll just leave them to you, young ones. Have fun! Enjoy! Enjoy!

I realize that I've been rambling too much, on too many fronts. If you're now bored, I don't blame you a bit. That's just me – once I get started I don't know when or where to stop. I thank you for your patience, and beg you to please bear with me just a bit longer. Before I end this long tirade, I feel I must tell you a couple of other things that lead to more questions.

A huge headline in this Sunday's local paper had the following news: NAVY FINALLY ENDS LONG IRISH STRING. Can you believe it? After 43 – yes, that's true – after 43 successive losses to the Notre Dame football team, Navy beat them on Saturday, November 3, 2007. Why am I so excited over such a triviality? Well, I didn't finish my explanation of my interest in sports.

When we came to Florida, in 1944, to operate the Sinclair Hotel, I had no time to interest myself in local sports. It was only after we moved into our first home, in 1946, that any of us had free time. Our first quest was to find a bowling alley. Much to our great disappointment, we learned that the local bowling alleys were completely different from the ones we'd seen in Baltimore and at PenMar. There, we used three hard balls, about the size of a softball, to knock down ten small pins called "duck" pins. Here, in Miami and Coral Gables, they used two huge hard balls to knock down ten large "ten" pins. In the entire county there was only one alley that had duck pin bowling – on Miami Avenue, in downtown Miami – way too far for us to go to. So, Mollie and I had to learn how to bowl all over again. It would be three years before we ventured to join the Coral Gables chapter of B'Nai B'rith bowling league.

It didn't take us long to discover that the only "game in town" was the University of Miami football team, which had its home games on about six Friday nights during the year. Neither of our sons was in high school yet, so we didn't go to watch the high school games. And this was long before football games were televised. We lived not far from the Orange Bowl in Miami so when possible, we went to see the UM Hurricanes play. All these years later, it is hard for me to watch anything but sports on TV, because of my hearing loss. Even with closed-captioned service, the words move so quickly and I'm easily lost. I get my news from the newspaper and when it comes to television, I spend my time watching sports. Of all the many sports shows, both professional and college, I enjoy basketball and football (American style) most. Of course, I favor the Miami Heat and Miami Dolphins – again, when available. If not, I cope!

Something else has changed over the years, and I find it a very troublesome topic – the financial crises that face the future of this country and my family. Hardly a day passes by without my reading about something bad or wrong. Our country's debt is in the trillions, burdening every man, woman and child. If we add on the personal debts that most people have – mortgages, car payments, credit card balances and all other personal obligations, it is hard to fathom the average person's plight and burden. The big banks and other lenders of mortgages have suffered billions in losses and thousands of people have lost their homes because they'd been enticed a few years ago by lenders with low initial interest rates. Imagine what happens when someone loses their job, and have little savings?

I could go on and on about big companies, Wall Street, the economy, people living paycheck to paycheck. It worries me that the majority of people feel they must acquire the latest and most expensive gadgets, just because it's the "in" thing to do! The constant craving for material items is unbelievable. When a new cell phone called an iPhone – whatever that's supposed to mean – went on the market recently, it cost $600 and they sold out in days – selling more than five million of them in the initial offering! According to a recent article I read in a magazine, "more than half of all U.S. workers said they didn't feel they had enough time for themselves, their partner or their children"! Yet, these same workers also planned to buy a new flat-screen HDTV when they did their Christmas shopping this year! We're talking about a TV that costs more than a thousand dollars!

So much has changed in my lifetime, and we could debate and discuss what is now better and what is now worse. It dawns on me that I may be seeing only deep, dark holes right now. It's time I quit and offer you a chance to challenge me.

Love, Ralphy
November 9, 2007

EPILOGUE

by the grandchildren of Ralph and Mollie Bartel

The legacy of our grandparents certainly does not end with the last story featured in this book, written in November 2007. As our father/uncle said in the Prologue, what is included in this book is just a sample of the stories and poems which both Ralph and Mollie wrote over the course of fifteen years, while in their 80s and 90s. For this book, we deliberately chose to include the stories that best captured their struggles and their history. The truth is, we are lucky to have hundreds of pages of writings by them both.

As we organized and re-read the many pages, we were each reminded of Grandpa Ralph's incredible memory. He could always recall names, dates, people, streets, stores and historical facts with such tremendous precision. Ralph often posed questions in his sentences, so allow us to use one, too. How does this story end? There is so much we could say about Ralph and Mollie Bartel. We respected, admired and adored each and both of them. We may not recall details like Ralph did, but we have such fond memories of growing up with them as a huge force in our lives.

Although neither was a "mushy" kind of person – largely because of their upbringing described in this book – Mollie and Ralph were beyond kind, funny, supportive and loving. And, theirs was a true love story. Grandma Mollie (called GiGi by the great-grandchildren) passed away at age 92 in November 2003, just a month before they would have celebrated their 70th anniversary. The last ten or so years, every birthday and anniversary was a "simcha" our family celebrated together. Honestly, she was healthy up until that last year and lived to see five of her seven great-grandchildren. Grandpa Ralph (called Gramps by the great-grand-children) did surprisingly well after her passing. He continued to write and lead holiday services at their retirement community, and we all saw him frequently. He passed away peacefully in October 2008, at the age of

98. His greatest joy were visits by his great grandchildren.

These writings, organized as best we could in chronological order, weave together quite a story – of struggle and success. Mollie and Ralph raised one son, a distinguished attorney in Florida and another son, a prominent physician in Virginia. The four grandsons Mollie and Ralph adored are now raising their eight great-grandchildren. Education, hard work, faith and family are an integral part of us, because of them.

The struggles our grandparents endured are almost unimaginable to us, the younger generation. But it is abundantly clear that their stories, their immigrant journey and their memory are a blessing to us and to so many others. As our own children grow up and have children of their own, we are thankful that they too will have the opportunity to explore and share a part of their roots, as described by Gram and Gramps.

September 2018

Ralph Bartel at age 95, rooting for his favorite basketball team, the Miami "Heat."

www.ingramcontent.com/pod-product-compliance
Lightning Source LLC
Chambersburg PA
CBHW021355090426
42742CB00009B/858